T0305464

The Dynamics of Innovation and Interfirm Networks

The Dynamics of Innovation and Interfirm Networks

Exploration, Exploitation and Co-Evolution

Victor Gilsing

Senior Researcher, ECIS, Eindhoven University of Technology, The Netherlands

Edward Elgar
Cheltenham, UK • Northampton, MA, USA

Published by
Edward Elgar Publishing Limited
Glensanda House
Montpellier Parade
Cheltenham
Glos GL50 1UA
UK

Edward Elgar Publishing, Inc.
136 West Street
Suite 202
Northampton
Massachusetts 01060
USA

A catalogue record for this book
is available from the British Library

Library of Congress Cataloguing in Publication Data
Gilsing, Victor, 1969-
    The dynamics of innovation and interfirm networks : exploration, exploitation, and co-evolution / Victor Gilsing.
        p. cm.
    Presented to Erasmus University as his Ph.D. thesis in December 2003.
    Includes bibliographical references and index.
    ISBN 1-84542-273-2
    1. Technological innovations–Economic aspects. 2. Strategic alliances (Business) 3. Organizational learning. 4. Communities of practice. 5. Business networks. 6. Organizational change. I. Title.

    HC79.T4G55 2005
    658.4'062–dc22   2005049828

ISBN 1 84542 273 2

Printed and bound in Great Britain by MPG Books Ltd, Bodmin, Cornwall

To Marianne,
David and Charlotte

Contents

Figures

Tables

About the author

Victor Gilsing was born in Amstelveen on 18 September 1969. After completing the Gemeentelijk Gymnasium in Hilversum he studied Technology and Business Administration at Twente University from 1987–93. After graduation he started working for Unilever where he held different positions in the field of innovation and business-to-business marketing in the speciality oleochemicals business. From 1998 he worked as a senior policy advisor in the field of innovation policy at the Ministry of Economic Affairs in the Hague. Alongside his duties as a policy advisor, he started his PhD thesis in December 1999 at ERIM (Erasmus University), which he completed in December 2003. Since October 2003 he has been (full-time) employed at ECIS, Eindhoven University of Technology.

Foreword

There is a large literature on the effects of interfirm networks on performance of participating firms, or of the network as a whole. Focusing on networks for innovation, this book makes three original contributions.

First, there has been a long debate on whether the purpose of access to new knowledge ties in the network should be sparse (non-dense) and weak, or, on the contrary, dense and strong. Recent literature indicates that there are arguments for both, and that it depends on the industry and other contingencies. This book follows that up in studying the differential effects of network structure and strength of ties on networks of exploration (radical innovation) and networks of exploitation (incremental innovation), in two different industries: multi-media and biotechnology.

Second, while networks have generally been accepted as given, this book also looks at them as dependent variables: how do they emerge? Here, the book makes use of a theory on a 'cycle of discovery' concerning the way in which exploration and exploitation build on each other, in the development of radically new technologies and products and novel structures for their production and distribution.

Third, while arguments for sparse/weak ties tend to be oriented at the competence side of relations, which in the present context means dynamic capabilities of generating innovation, arguments for dense/strong ties tend to be oriented at the governance side of relations, i.e. the management of relational risks of dependence and loss of appropriability due to spillover. Sparse/weak ties yield variety, flexibility and low costs of searching for new information. Dense/weak ties yield social capital, in reputation, shared values and norms, and personal trust building, and coalition formation to constrain deviant behaviour. This book looks at both sides of interfirm relations, which is needed to arrive at an adequate assessment. It yields new arguments for density and strength of ties not only for governance but also for dynamic competence.

The book uses a method of comparative, qualitative case studies, in histories of the emergence of networks for exploration and exploitation in the two industries, pieced together from a variety of sources, including articles, industry reports and interviews with industry specialists. Variables are measured not in ratio scales but in nominal or ordinal scales. The case histories are rich in description, and by themselves give interesting insights in the two industries studied, but they also yield analyses that enable an assessment of causal hypotheses. Such methodology yields obvious limits in the rigour and the generalizability of results, but it does allow for tests of causal hypotheses in the form of refutation, with insight as to why hypothesized effects do not obtain, either due to new, unexpected effects, or due to contingencies that modify causal logic.

The book offers a valuable contribution, with interesting hypotheses, case histories, and a revision and extension of theoretical insights.

Bart Nooteboom, Tilburg University
The Hague, 15 July 2005

Acknowledgements

This book originates from the research that I carried out as a researcher at ERIM, Rotterdam School of Management, Erasmus University. Although writing a book like this is a mostly stand-alone activity, it would have been impossible without the help of many people.

First of all, and most of all, I would like to thank my supervisor Bart Nooteboom at ERIM (currently with Tilburg University). He is someone who combines a profound knowledge on a wide spectrum of literature with an excellent feel of how to keep me motivated. Secondly, I would like to thank John Groenewegen at Erasmus University and Delft University of Technology, who played a great role as the 'devil's advocate' and in this way helped me to substantially improve the work-in-progress.

I am particularly also indebted to Geert Duysters at ECIS for his useful comments on earlier versions, and also because he has been a very stimulating person to me. Moreover, I would like to thank Bo Carlsson (Case Western Reserve University, Cleveland, Ohio), Patrick Cohendet (BETA, University of Strassbourg), Felix Janszen (Erasmus University) and Niels Noorderhaven (Tilburg University) for their useful comments on earlier draft versions of this book.

Discussions with numerous people at various seminars have also been helpful, notably seminars and annual conferences at DRUID, MERIT, ETIC, EGOS, CHIMES 2002, Conference 'Empirical Research on Routines' 2002 (Odensee) and ERIM.

I also would like to thank Pim den Hertog and Sven Maltha of Dialogic for reading and commenting upon an earlier version of the chapter on multimedia, as well as Christien Enzing at TNO and Sander Kern at Dialogic (formerly TNO) for their useful comments on an earlier version of the chapter on biotechnology. Moreover, I would to thank Nienke Rave who has done a great job in dealing with Edward Elgar's (tough!) quality standards.

My greatest debt is to Marianne who has constantly supported and encouraged me throughout this research endeavour.

Victor A. Gilsing
ECIS, Eindhoven 2005

1. Introduction

LEARNING AND INNOVATION IN INDUSTRIES

The topic of this book is processes of innovation among firms in an industry. When we study innovation processes in an industry it becomes clear that firms do not innovate in isolation (Jarillo, 1988; Porter, 1990, 1998; Lundvall, 1992, 1993; Hakansson and Johansson, 1993; Grabher, 1993; Duysters, 1995; Uzzi, 1997). To innovate successfully, firms need to search for new sources of knowledge and technology in order to be able to continuously develop new products and processes. As a consequence, the competitiveness of firms is becoming more dependent on complementary knowledge from other firms as well as from knowledge providers or carriers such as universities, research institutes, consultants, and so on (Baden-Fuller and Lorenzoni, 1995; Chen, 1997; Porter, 1998; Nooteboom, 1999a; Rindova and Fombrun, 1999). This increasing dependency poses new challenges for firms as the environment in which firms operate becomes more and more important for strengthening their innovation performance and competitive advantage. The increased dependency on other firms is also reflected in a growing number of studies on alliances (Hamel and Prahalad, 1990; Smith Ring and van de Ven, 1994; Hagedoorn, 1993; Hagedoorn and Schakenraad, 1994; Spekman et al., 1995; Uzzi, 1997; Nooteboom, 1999a; Rowley et al., 2000). Still, most of these studies adopt a firm-level perspective and do not take the increasing interwovenness of firms and their industry-environment into account. Some studies take a more specific interest in the relation between (inter-)firm behaviour and industry-characteristics by making the generic differentiation between high-tech, medium-tech and low-tech industries (for example Hagedoorn and Duysters, 1999; Hagedoorn, 2002), as also used in OECD studies.

Overall, these studies neglect the specific circumstances and conditions in which technical change and innovation are operating. This is rather striking as these circumstances and conditions can differ considerably among industries as well as among nations and can significantly affect the behaviour of firms (Lundvall, 1992; Nelson, 1993; Edquist, 1997; Malerba and Breschi, 1997; Mowery and Nelson, 1999; Nooteboom, 2000). As argued by these innovation scholars, firm behaviour is shaped by the conditions in which it is embedded and is path-dependent (Arthur, 1989). This path-dependency manifests itself at the network-level and at the firm level. Firms' capabilities have been defined and refined by the types of problems tackled in the past, the nature of which has been shaped by the characteristics of the value networks in which firms have historically competed and collaborated. As a consequence, firm capabilities are highly specialized and context-specific (Nelson and Winter, 1982; Dosi et al., 1988; Mowery and Nelson, 1999; McEvily and Zaheer, 1999; Rowley et al., 2000). This embeddedness manifests itself in strategies, structures, policies and procedures that are based on the specific network structure. This may lead to the development of cohesive and integrated structures within networks and as such lead to the build-up of a competitive position. However, in this is a potential danger such as a 'robust system' that is not very inclined to adapt when circumstances change (Whitley, 1994; Porter, 1998; Nooteboom, 2000). A (sudden) need for change may run counter to behavioural and professional norms in networks (Coleman, 1988). Proven approaches have institutionalized into habits and routines (Nelson and Winter, 1982) and powerful forces may work against modifying strategies. Firms can lose competitive advantage because of emerging weaknesses in their environment (Porter, 1990). When a network in which a firm operates is not able to respond to new (technological) developments, the consequences for the networks as well as for (some of) its firms can be severe (Nahapiet and Ghoshal, 1998).

Such dynamic aspects of learning and innovation within networks still remain relatively unexplored in the literature (McEvily and Zaheer, 1999; Pavitt, 2002). Therefore, in this study we make an effort to identify how the evolution of knowledge, learning and innovation takes place within networks of firms. We will make use of Grandori's definition of networks as 'a set of firms, generally characterized by different preferences and resources, coordinated through a mix of mechanisms not limited to price, exit and background regulation' (Grandori, 1999: 2).

ONTOLOGY AND RESEARCH AIM

In this section we describe and explain the object of study. In doing so, we start by discussing some ontological issues. Based on that we discuss the relevance of the (national) systems of innovation (NSI) approach for our study. Next we formulate our research aim.

Some Ontological Issues

Ontology entails the set of basic assumptions on the nature of actors and how we see the relationship between actors and their environment.

Our research starts from the assumption that knowledge is the most important resource for innovation and learning its key-process (Lundvall, 1992) and we adopt an endogenous view on them. In addition, we assume that actors who engage in learning are boundedly rational. So, their information processing capabilities are limited and costly and hence information will be imperfect. Such bounded rationality is an important condition for learning. Learning can only take place in circumstances in which agents have an imperfect understanding of the world in which they operate (Dosi and Marengo, 2000). Furthermore, we assume that to the extent that different people have developed in different social and physical surroundings and have not interacted with each other, they will see the world differently. Hence their cognition will differ resulting in a greater or lesser cognitive distance (Nooteboom, 1999a, 2000). Cognitive distance reflects diversity of knowledge that yields a potential for Schumpeterian novel combinations to emerge (Johnson, 1992). So, novelty can thus be perceived as to originate from the (re-)combination of existing and diverse parts of knowledge.

In line with this view is the assumption that interaction emerges because actors are heterogeneous, not because they are similar and that it is by means of interaction that actors are able to combine and integrate complementary knowledge and capabilities. From this interaction common meanings and frameworks are constructed, which connect with a social constructivist view (Berger and Luckmann, 1966). According to this view, no objective knowledge of reality can be claimed and different views of this reality can exist (Nooteboom, 2000). From this social constructivist view follows a broad definition of knowledge as including perception, understanding and value judgements (Nooteboom, 2000), which are contingent upon institutions.

Institutions form a central notion in evolutionary theory.[1] Institutions can be seen as 'devices' which shape the way in which individuals perceive the world surrounding them (Johnson, 1992). As such, institutions influence social interaction and thus affect learning processes. According to Douglas (1986), 'people recognise, classify, remember and forget in accordance with institutions'. So, institutions select the transfer and retention of knowledge and information. In this study we adopt a broad definition of institutions as the 'sets of common habits, routines, established practices, informal and formal rules, laws and so on that regulate the relations and interactions between individuals and groups' (Dosi et al., 1988; Scott, 1995; Edquist and Johnson, 1997). Taken together, we conceive of institutions as a selection environment in which interfirm learning and innovation processes are embedded. From this social constructivist view of knowledge and learning follows an embedded view on interfirm networks: different institutional environments stimulate different types and levels of interaction, leading to different networks and learning patterns. To specify this embedded view of networks, the (National) Systems of Innovation approach may further inform us.

(National) Systems of Innovation

The notion of different actors, connected by interactive learning processes shaped by institutions, forms the basis for the (National) Systems of Innovation approach (Lundvall, 1992; Nelson, 1993; Edquist, 1997). This approach studies the relationship between institutions, organizations and innovation. A (national) system of innovation consists of elements and relationships which interact in the production, diffusion and use of new, economically useful knowledge. Although there exist different approaches to (national) systems of innovation, all have innovation processes and learning at their centre and consider technological and institutional change as evolutionary.[2]

The systems-element connects with the notion to incorporate all possibly relevant elements in a systemic way; to not only treat the elements constituting the system but also the way these elements interact. Such a system-based approach adds value in (moderately) complex systems in which system properties such as feedback become more important. In such a system of non-linear relationships among variables, it is less meaningful to differentiate between independent and dependent variables since changes in one variable are caused endogenously by others (Baum and Singh, 1994; Edquist, 1997).

So, this NSI-approach is relevant for our study as it enables us to deal with an embedded view of networks. More specifically then, to deal with the notion of circumstances and conditions that can differ among industries, we adopt the concept of a sectoral system of innovation (SSI) from Malerba (2002). He defines a sectoral system of innovation as 'composed of a set of heterogeneous actors carrying out market and non-market interaction for the generation, adoption and use of new and established knowledge and for the creation, production and use of new and established products'.[3] Following this definition, we see the following arguments why our use of the concept of a SSI is relevant to study networks of firms. First, according to this definition of a SSI, interaction among actors is crucial. This connects with our social-constructivist, interactionist ontology with regard to learning, as discussed above. Second, relations and networks form the core of a SSI and form an integral element of the learning and innovation processes within it (Malerba, 2002). This connects with our interest in the dynamic aspects of learning and innovation in networks of firms. Furthermore, the concept of a SSI points to the relevance of sectoral institutions such as among others, the knowledge base, appropriability conditions, opportunity conditions and so on (Malerba and Breschi, 1997). In this respect, it is the central claim that we make in this study, that to develop a dynamic understanding of the role of knowledge, learning and innovation in networks of firms, the role of such sectoral institutions needs to be considered. In this respect, we will abstract from the role of national and/or regional institutions and will also pay less attention to the spatial boundaries of networks.[4]

Research Aim

As argued, we see networks as being conditioned by the institutional environment of the SSI in which they are embedded. From our ontology it follows that different institutional environments stimulate different types and levels of social interaction, leading to differences in learning patterns. An interesting question now is which aspects of such learning patterns are present in different SSIs and which aspects are more idiosyncratic for a specific SSI. One important element of a learning pattern that we expect to be present in different SSIs is that outcomes of interfirm learning can also shape the institutional environment and may lead to path-creation, exerting considerable influence on the broader structure in which they are embedded (Mowery and Nelson, 1999). So, given our interest in the dynamic aspects of learning in networks of firms, we are interested in a two-way relationship between networks and their institutional environment.

Based on these considerations we propose formulating our research aim as follows, to determine:

- How the institutional environment of a SSI conditions interfirm learning,
- How outcomes of interfirm learning may affect institutional environment,
- And in how far this varies per type of SSI.

We argue that SSIs may greatly differ in terms of the properties of their knowledge base upon which learning and innovation are based (Malerba, 2002). More specifically, we assume that heterogeneous actors searching around similar knowledge bases and embedded in the same institutional environment share some common behavioural and organizational traits and develop a similar range of learning patterns and behaviour. Moreover, we assume that decisions and actions of firms are enabled as well as constrained by actions and knowledge of other firms in their SSI (Lundvall, 1992). So, there is a collective dimension to innovation in addition to an individual dimension (McKelvey, 1997). As we study networks from the perspective of a SSI, we are especially interested in this collective dimension, seeing innovation in networks as a collective learning process.

Rather than developing a detailed understanding of the structure of a SSI and the networks within it at a specific point in time, our interest entails the dynamics of aggregate learning and innovation patterns. This reflects our interactionistic ontology that to understand why a specific pattern of learning in networks develops, one needs to understand the dynamic processes that generated it. In line with this, we are interested in the changing nature of the relationships among firms, rather than in acts of individual firms. So, a network of firms forms our unit of analysis.

RESEARCH QUESTIONS

Following our ontology and research aim, in this section we will formulate our research questions.

As mentioned, institutions play an important role in learning processes. Obviously, there are institutions in wider society which do not affect learning and innovation and they will not be our object of study. We are interested in those institutions that provide incentives to learn and innovate as well as institutions that shape or influence the direction of these learning and innovation activities. This leads to our first two research questions:

1. Which institutions are relevant for interfirm learning?

and

2. How do these institutions condition interfirm learning?

In the literature on learning and innovation, institutions are often considered as exogenous. It is assumed that institutions determine the learning and innovation patterns in an industry (Pavitt, 1984; Nelson, 1993; Malerba and Breschi, 1997; Malerba and Orsenigo, 1996; Carlsson, 1997; 2002; Mowery and Nelson, 1999). In such an approach a rather deterministic stance is taken that resembles a traditional 'structure-conduct-performance view': an exogenous structure determines conduct which subsequently leads to a certain performance. This clearly ignores the notion that outcomes of such learning and innovation can also (substantially) affect the institutional environment. In terms of the evolutionary mechanisms, these studies strongly focus on how selection processes take place but do not investigate how this relates to variety nor how variety affects selection again. We consider that to be too limited when developing a dynamic understanding of learning and innovation in networks. Following our social constructivist, interactionist view of knowledge we argue that outcomes that result from the behaviour of firms can also change the institutional environment which has first shaped this behaviour. So, we argue that firms are not only shaped by their institutional environment but are also shapers of this same environment.[5] Outcomes of learning can cause changes in the institutional environment and hence lead to changes in the selection process. So, there is a dynamic relation between the generation of novelty (variety) and selection among alternatives. Or rephrased in terms of our research, there is a dynamic interplay between the institutional environment and institutionalized interfirm learning.

This connects with a discussion among sociologists on the relation between structure and agency or, rephrased, between the over- versus undersocialized conceptions of human action. The undersocialized view is committed to social atomism which claims that human behaviour can be identified independently of its social environment. Its methodological approach is individualism which is based on the assumption that individuals form the ultimate constituents of society and that only data about individuals are relevant for understanding human behaviour. Methodological individualism leads to 'upward conflation', that is making it difficult to recognize how economic action is enabled and constrained by the social structure in which actors are embedded (Archer, 1995). The oversocialized view on the other hand assumes that people follow customs, habits or norms in an automatic and unconditional way. Its methodological approach is collectivism which portrays individuals as unilaterally determined by the social structure. Methodological collectivism leads to 'downward conflation', i.e. 'considering individuals as indeterminate material unilaterally moulded by society, whose holistic properties have complete monopoly over causation, and which therefore operate in a unilateral and downward manner' (Archer, 1995: 3). As we consider the dynamic relation between selection and the generation of variety, we need to thread our way between upward and downward conflation by analysing how behaviour is embedded in its institutional environment as well as how behaviour gives rise to changes in the institutional environment.

Our third research question is therefore:

3. What are the outcomes of interfirm learning and how do they affect the institutional environment?

When studying learning and innovation according to these three research questions, which stress the dynamic aspects of interfirm learning, it seems to be appropriate to conceive of this dynamic the relation between institutional environment and interfirm learning as a co-evolutionary process. Underlying this co-evolutionary process are the three evolutionary mechanisms of selection, transmission and retention, and variety generation. These mechanisms function as interacting forces which drive the co-evolutionary process into its path-dependent direction. One evolutionary mechanism may dominate a specific phase of the co-evolutionary process and as such affect interfirm learning. In the case of substantial selection forces, the generation of variety may be hampered or even become blocked. When variety abounds, the exploitation of what has been discovered may be blocked. Transmission mechanisms used in a network of firms may affect both selection and variety. So, the specific combination of evolutionary mechanisms affects interfirm learning and therefore also has implications for networks with regard to modes of organization and coordination mechanisms. We are interested in how far this co-evolutionary process is present in different types of SSIs and in how far it differs between different SSIs. More specifically, we are interested in which elements of this co-evolutionary process are more SSI-generic and which elements are more SSI-specific.

As argued, the evolutionary approach as developed by Nelson and Winter (1982) provides the general framework for our study. This approach studies individual and collective cognitive processes and considers routinized behaviour as the central element in economic evolution. However, this approach tends to ignore the fact that from these processes conflicts and opportunistic behaviour may emerge. Therefore, in this research we aim to develop an understanding of on the one hand stimulating interactive learning processes as developed by evolutionary theory, NSI-approaches and competence-based approaches, and on the other hand, reconciling diverging interests among dependent firms as developed by transaction costs economics. Transaction cost economics is often criticized for being static (Lazonick, 1993; Groenewegen et al., 1995) and neglecting learning (Lundvall, 1993; Nooteboom, 2000). So, there is an analytical gap between governance perspectives and competence perspectives and an evident need to connect them (Williamson, 1999; Nooteboom, 1999d, 2000; Dosi and Marengo, 2000). In our research we want to develop an effort to combine these two lines of thought by analysing incentives, coordination and cognition related problems of interfirm learning and knowledge creation. Therefore, our fourth research question reads as follows:

4. What are the implications of the co-evolutionary process for networks of firms and their coordination, from both a competence and governance perspective?

With regard to this last question we need to add that we not only aim to describe these implications but also intend to explain them. This explanation should follow from our first three research questions that should enable us to explain why a specific combination of network structure and forms of coordination emerges in a SSI at a specific point in time. In Chapter 6 on methodology we will further elaborate on some of the issues that are relevant with regard to explanatory research.

OVERVIEW OF STUDY

Following our research questions, in this section we discuss the structure of our study and the build-up of this book.

Chapter 2 'Selection by the institutional environment' deals with research question 1: which institutions are relevant for interfirm learning? In this chapter we will unravel the institutional environment. To do so, we introduce a model of institutional levels that differentiates between the institutional environment on the one hand, and a level of embedded, institutionalized behaviour on the other hand. With regard to the institutional environment the model takes a nested view and makes a distinction between different levels of institutions. Based on this distinction, we identify those institutions that are relevant for learning and innovation in a SSI, based on the contributions by scholars from different bodies of literature such as evolutionary theory, NSI-approaches, industrial dynamics and social network theory.

Chapter 3 'Learning regimes' deals with research question 2: how do these institutions condition interfirm learning? This chapter builds on the analysis as developed in Chapter 2 by analysing the level of institutionalized interfirm behaviour. We differentiate between two types of institutionalized interfirm behaviour, namely interfirm learning behaviour and interfirm dependent behaviour. Interfirm learning behaviour takes a competence perspective, based on which we discuss how the identified institutions condition interfirm learning activities. From these activities originates interfirm dependency. Interfirm dependency then requires a governance perspective, based on which we discuss how the identified institutions condition this interfirm dependency. In order to be clear about these two different, but related forms of interfirm behaviour, we analyse both types separately before integrating them. To reconcile both perspectives, we introduce the concept of a learning regime.

The institutions of the institutional environment, as analysed in Chapter 2, and the elements of a learning regime, as analysed in Chapter 3, are not independent. On the contrary, there are many connections among these variables, creating systemic combinations of features. In this respect, Chapters 2 and 3 reflect a static view of the relation between the institutional environment and learning regimes and relate to the first part of our research aim, namely how the institutional environment conditions interfirm learning.

Chapter 4 'Co-evolution of institutional environment and learning regimes' deals with research question 3: what are the outcomes of interfirm learning and how do they affect the institutional environment? This chapter builds on the analysis in Chapter 2 and 3 and discusses the dynamic relation between a learning regime and the institutional environment. To study this dynamic interplay we will make use of a co-evolutionary approach. Co-evolutionary inquiry attempts to understand and predict how variables in the system respond to changes in other system variables or in changes to the structure of the system itself. As a way to structure this co-evolutionary process we use the concept of the 'cycle of knowledge' as developed by Nooteboom (2000). From the dynamic viewpoint of the 'cycle of knowledge', the systemic combinations can be considered as a specific 'point' at this cycle. In this chapter we analyse the transition of these systemic combinations over time. Such a transition can be considered as a 'movement' of such a systemic combination along the cycle. This reflects a dynamic view and relates to the second part of our research aim, namely to changes in the relation between institutional environment and learning regimes.

Chapter 5 'Implications of the co-evolutionary process' deals with research question 4: what are the implications of the co-evolutionary process for networks of firms and their coordination, from both a competence and governance perspective?

Chapter 5 focuses on the implications for networks of firms that follow from the co-evolutionary process. An important implication relates to the choice of the organizational mode that is best suited to deal with learning and innovation. So, we discuss which type of network is best suited to deal with which type of learning. Next we discuss the implications of the co-evolutionary process for the properties of the relations making up these networks and the way these relations are coordinated. This combination of network structure, relational properties and coordination mechanisms may affect the co-evolutionary process. It may speed up learning but can also have a negative effect.

Chapter 6 'Methodology' forms the basis for the empirical part of our research and focuses on the development of a sound methodology to arrive at scientifically accountable answers to our research questions. Our interest in the dynamic relation between institutional environment and learning regimes, and to analyse this in terms of a co-evolutionary process, calls for a methodology that enables us to capture both the process of selection and the generation of variety. The development of such a methodology forms an important focus of this chapter. Based on that, we then focus on issues of operationalization by specifying how we measure our key-constructs and how we select our research method. Finally, we discuss methods of data collection.

Chapter 7 'Multimedia' deals with the co-evolution of institutional environment and learning regimes in the multimedia system of innovation in the Netherlands over the period from around 1990 towards 2000. Chapter 8 'Pharmaceutical biotechnology' deals with the co-evolution of institutional environment and learning regimes in the pharmaceutical biotechnology system of innovation in the Netherlands over the period from the late 1980s towards 2001. Chapter 9 'Conclusions', is our final chapter in which the main conclusions are formulated, based on a confrontation between our theoretical framework and the empirical research.

Summing up, our research covers the following three objectives:

- To identify systemic combinations of institutional environment and institutionalized behaviour (learning regimes). These systemic combinations are static and reflect a specific point at the cycle of knowledge.
- To identify the transition of those systemic combinations over time, as a movement along the cycle of knowledge.
- To identify and explain the implications of those transitions in terms of network structure, relational properties and coordination mechanisms.

Chapter 2	Chapter 3	Chapter 4	Chapter 5
Selection by Institutional Environment	Learning regimes	Co-evolution	Implications from co-evolution

Theoretical framework

Chapter 9
Conclusions

Empirical testing

Chapter 6	Chapter 7	Chapter 8
Methodology	Multimedia	Biotechnology

CONTRIBUTION TO THEORY

As outlined, this study aims to develop an understanding of the dynamics of interfirm learning in networks of firms. By analysing learning processes in such networks, and the changes created within them, we aim to shed some more light on the mechanisms that generate variety. In this respect we go beyond the selection bias as present in most innovation studies by developing an attempt to acquire an endogenous understanding of the origins of novelty in networks of firms. As argued, this requires a synthesis between evolutionary economics and the NSI-approach on the one hand and concepts from social network theory on the other hand.

In evolutionary economics and the NSI-approach in particular, a key-role is attached to relations and interaction among actors (Lundvall, 1992; Edquist, 1997). This agreement on the importance of relations and interaction notwithstanding, in this literature an in-depth understanding of the structure and functioning of networks is still underdeveloped. For this we need to turn to the social network literature. This literature has developed various concepts and tools to analyse social networks from different angles (Granovetter, 1973; Coleman, 1988; Burt, 1992). Due to this strong focus on structural elements of networks though, the identification of relevant institutional conditions and how they influence the structure and functioning of networks has generally been ignored by social network theorists. As a consequence, there is a strong universalistic tone in this literature. By combining these two different strands of literature we aim to develop a more profound understanding of how the structure and role of networks varies with the institutional conditions in different SSIs. In doing so, we also contribute to the social network literature by showing that there is no such thing as a universally optimal network structure and that this optimality is subject to the specificities of the institutional environment in which the network is embedded.[6] So, combining these lines of thought enables us to address various puzzles such as in how far specific types of SSIs favour specific network structures and also which type of network structure favours which type of learning. Other questions that we address are for example what the effects are on learning and innovation when networks show very dense relations or, alternatively, very loose relations between firms.

Furthermore, this study is an attempt to reconcile two views on organisation, namely a competence-view and a governance-view. As argued, there is an analytical gap between both perspectives and an evident need to connect them (Williamson, 1999; Nooteboom 1999d, 2000; Dosi and Marengo 2000). So, in this study we also develop an effort to combine a competence view with a governance view.

In sum, this study is at the crossroads of two theoretical perspectives, to which we add some notions on governance as advanced by transaction cost economics (TCE). This is schematically portrayed in Figure 1.1.

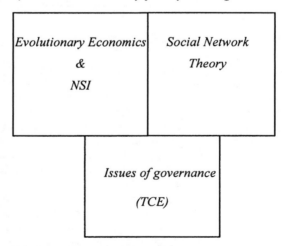

Figure 1.1 Combination of theoretical perspectives

In contrast with theoretical monism that is based on the conviction that the goal of science is to find a universally true theory, this combined use of different theories clearly reflects a theoretical pluralistic stance. Theoretical pluralism approves of a plurality of theories for a given set of phenomena which is based on the ground that any single theory inevitably gives a partial account (Groenewegen and Vromen, 1996). This is not for reasons of pragmatism but because theoretical pluralists are led by the idea that a deeper understanding of phenomena can be enhanced by using different theories instead of one. An important assumption here is though that theories do not contradict each other. To assess this, we need to go back to our ontology as articulated in 'ontology and research aim'.

The central premise in our ontology is that of bounded rationality. As argued, bounded rationality is an important condition for learning as this can only take place when agents have an imperfect understanding of the world in which they operate (Dosi and Marengo, 2000). In terms of Lakatos (1978), all three theoretical frameworks that we use in this study have as their 'hard-core proposition' this notion of bounded rationality and are in this respect compatible with our ontology. Furthermore, when considering social network theory, two important ontological premises that underlie social network analysis are that actors and their actions are viewed as interdependent, instead of independent, and that relational ties are channels for transformation of material and non-material resources (Wasserman and Faust, 1994). This connects with our ontology making our use of social network theory indeed legitimate for the purpose of our research. With regard to the issues of governance we can make the following observations. First of all, introducing such a governance perspective does not imply that we integrate TCE with our two main theoretical frameworks. That would be problematic. TCE explicitly takes an efficiency perspective by dealing with the question how differences in dimensions of transactions determine which governance structures most efficiently economize on transaction costs (Williamson, 1975). Moreover, TCE does not include learning and innovation, seeks equilibrium outcomes and is based on methodological individualism, negating the relevance of social embeddedness (Williamson, 1999). This is all incompatible with our ontology. As articulated in 'ontology and research aim', we acknowledge the profound role of institutions and assume selection to take place in relation to the distinctive structure of this institutional environment, reflecting the assumption of local optimality (Nelson, 1987; McKelvey, 1997) instead of universal optimality as assumed by TCE. So while rejecting TCE on a deeper level, we argue that on a more practical, instrumental level there are some notions that can provide an important complement to our study. As we will further argue in Chapter 3, engaging in interactive learning processes makes firms become dependent on one another. This dependency yields a risk of conflict and opportunism and we agree with Williamson in this respect that 'opportunism is so familiar that we often fail to acknowledge it and its consequences when we see it' (Williamson, 1999: 1098). The potential for opportunism and its consequences may severely affect interfirm learning and can therefore not be ignored. This is increasingly being acknowledged by scholars from both strands of literature, by Williamson himself (1999) as well as by Nooteboom (1999d, 2000) and Dosi and Marengo (2000).

So, our study is based on two theoretical pillars, namely evolutionary economics and the NSI-approach on the one hand and social network theory on the other hand. This reflects a competence view of learning. As argued, to reconcile this with a governance view, we add some notions on governance derived from TCE.

NOTES

1. At the heart of evolutionary theory is the notion of a process of endogenous change, in contrast with the static perspective of neo-classical equilibrium theory. These patterns of change are directly linked to learning processes which underlie technological advancements and innovations. These change processes are described in terms of the three evolutionary metaphors of variety, selection, and transmission and retention. Variety is the creation of novelty within a population. Selection occurs through competition among the alternative novel forms that exist. Transmission and retention involves those forces that perpetuate and maintain those forms that were selected in the past (Nelson and Winter, 1982). These evolutionary mechanisms should be seen as three continuous interacting forces which shape an evolutionary pattern of (technical) change.
2. Although there exist different approaches to (National) Systems of Innovation, they share their intellectual roots in evolutionary economic theory (McKelvey, 1997; Edquist 1997). The evolutionary characteristics of NSI's are that they put innovations and learning at the centre and that a historical perspective is natural. Furthermore they acknowledge the notion of non-optimality and consider institutions as a central explaining factor to learning and innovation (Nelson and Winter, 1982; Johnson, 1992).
3. This does not imply that products pertain to a sector in a narrow sense. Innovation can generate new (classes of) products that cross sectoral boundaries giving rise to changes in existing sectoral boundaries.
4. A concept that is closely related to a SSI is that of a Technological System (TS) as developed by Carlsson (1995, 1997, 2002; Carlsson and Eliasson, 2003). He distinguishes three dimensions of a TS, namely: (1) a cognitive dimension that defines the clustering of technologies resulting in a new set of technological possibilities; (2) an organizational and institutional dimension that captures the interactions in the network of actors engaged in the creation of these technologies; and (3) an economic dimension that defines the set of actors who convert technological possibilities into business opportunities, also referred to as a 'competence bloc'. The concept of a TS strongly emphasizes the role of (new) technology in explaining economic growth (Carlsson, 2002; Carlsson and Eliasson, 2003). Due to this strong focus on technology, one abstracts to some extent from other sectoral characteristics such as opportunity conditions, appropriability conditions, demand conditions and so on. For the purpose of our study, we consider these sectoral institutional conditions as important to include into our analysis, as we will argue throughout this book (see in particular Chapters 2, 3 and 4), and will therefore make use of the concept of a SSI.
5. This goes back to Veblen who took an interactionistic stance in the sense that actor and structure interact and mutually condition each other to the degree that explanation based on either actor or structure alone are unwarranted : 'both the

agent and his environment being at any point in time the outcome of the past process' (Veblen, 1898: 391).

6. Moreover, the notion of a universally optimal network structure would be difficult to reconcile with our evolutionary approach. According to evolutionary economic theory, "systems never achieve an equilibrium since the evolutionary processes in it are open-ended and path-dependent. We do not even know whether the potential best trajectory is exploited at all, since we do not know which one it is" (Edquist, 1997: 20). As argued in 'ontology and research aim', we see selection to take place in relation to the distinctive structure of the institutional environment, reflecting the assumption of local optimality (McKelvey, 1997). Hence the optimality of the network structure is subject to the specificities of this institutional environment so that this optimality is local instead of universal.

2. Selection by the institutional environment

Research Question 1: which institutions are relevant for interfirm learning?

INTRODUCTION

As argued in Chapter 1, we conceive of an institutional selection environment as consisting of different types of institutions. Interfirm learning and innovation processes are embedded in this institutional selection environment. This idea of embeddedness in the environment reflects the profound influence of institutions on the learning processes that take place among firms in an industry. Embeddedness refers to the contingency of interfirm relationships on the (social) institutions in which these relationships are embedded (Granovetter, 1985; Grabher, 1993; Whitley, 1994; Grandori and Soda, 1995).

In this research, we adopt a broad definition of institutions as the 'sets of common habits, routines, established practices, informal and formal rules, laws that condition the relations and interactions between individuals and groups' (Dosi et al., 1988; Scott, 1995; Edquist and Johnson, 1997). Taken together, these institutions form the institutional selection environment.

Structuring the notion of an institutional selection environment, in order to make this institutional environment more explicit we propose the following two steps. We structure our concept of institutions by means of an ordering principle. Our ordering principle follows from the assumption that networks in a SSI, for evolutionary survival, need to continuously adapt to changes in their institutional environment. Therefore, we propose as an ordering principle the adaptability of the various institutions. As a second step, we follow the suggestions made both by Nelson and Sampat (2001) and Nooteboom (2000) to conceptualize the notion of an institution as a process of institutionalizing. In doing so, we free ourselves from the need to identify types of institutions that may have relevance, to a greater or lesser extent, in any specific context. Not all institutions are relevant at the same time for all networks in a SSI. So, we can specify those institutions that are relevant at a certain moment in time and leave aside those which are not. A second implication by conceptualizing it as a process is that we can portray the institutional environment as a 'hierarchy of institutions' (Nooteboom, 2000). Some institutions are embedded in 'higher institutions' but at the same time embedding 'lower institutions'. Based on these two steps, adaptability as the ordering principle and a process of institutionalizing, we propose conceptualizing the institutional environment as a hierarchy of institutions structured by the ease with which institutions are able to adapt. See also Figure 2.1.

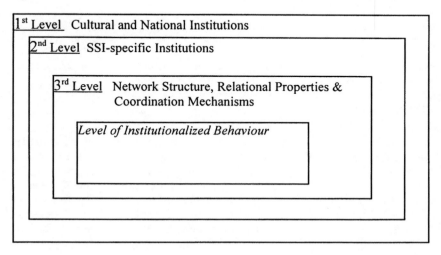

Figure 2.1 Schematic representation of the relation between the institutional environment and institutionalized behaviour

Unraveling the institutional selection environment, based on the above defined steps and considerations, we develop an attempt in this chapter to depict the institutions that form the institutional environment. Based on the contributions made by different scholars we will identify those institutions that are relevant for innovation processes in a SSI. We consider these different types of institutions as systemic features: they are mutually related and as such form a system, i.e. change in one institution will have consequences for others as well. Embedded in this institutional selection environment are interfirm learning processes that are conditioned by it, hence we see these interfirm learning processes as institutionalized behaviour (Lundvall, 1992). Following the logic of Figure 2.1, this chapter is structured as follows. First we briefly discuss the role of the institutions at the 1st level of the institutional environment. After that we deal extensively with institutions at the 2nd level of the institutional environment. Then we deal with the 3rd level in more detail. Finally, 'Systemic combinations of 2nd and 3rd level institution', we discuss some of the systemic relations that exist between these different institutional levels. The level of institutionalized behaviour, as portrayed by the rectangle in Figure 2.1, will be the topic of Chapter 3.

1st LEVEL INSTITUTIONS

The 1st level describes the cultural and national environment in which a SSI is embedded. As such, this level is generic for any SSI within it. This level contains various elements such as culture, the role of the state, the financial system, labour market institutions and so on. We consider this level, in terms of adaptability, as the most outer layer, that is change in this layer is highly incremental. Through its generic and encompassing character, it basically creates the selection environment for lower institutional levels as it enables and constrains these lower institutions, and in doing so, affects the embedded learning and innovation processes. As argued in Chapter 1, we are interested in the dynamic aspects of learning and innovation in networks, from the perspective of a SSI. So we have a special interest in the dynamic relation between sectoral and network institutions and therefore abstract from national institutions. We will therefore not further incorporate this level into our analysis but only mention it here for the sake of completeness.

2nd LEVEL INSTITUTIONS

Our 2nd level of the institutional environment is formed by those institutions that differ per type of SSI and can be highly idiosyncratic. These institutions are more adaptable than the institutions on the first level, which does not mean that change takes place quickly and easily. Change takes place in an incremental way but when pressures for change become manifest enough, institutions at this level can change relatively easily and quickly, compared with the 1st level. Given our research aim as formulated in Chapter 1, we will focus here on those SSI-specific institutions that are relevant for interfirm learning and innovation processes. To do so, we will first identify these various relevant types of institutions ('Identifying 2nd Level Institutions') based on which we then discuss how these institutions are related ('Systemic Combinations of 2nd Level Institutions').

Identifying 2nd Level Institutions

We see the following elements as the institutions that are specific to a SSI namely the knowledge base, appropriability conditions, opportunity conditions, demand conditions and competition.

Knowledge base, as argued in Chapter 1, we consider interfirm learning to be specific to a SSI. As a consequence, SSIs may greatly differ in terms of the properties of their knowledge base upon which learning and innovation are based. We see the following properties as relevant:

- Tacit vs. codified, tacit knowledge is embodied in people and context-specific that makes it difficult to formalise and transfer to others. Codified knowledge is made explicit through documents, standard operating procedures, technical norms and so and can therefore be (relatively) easily transferred to others by a formal, systematic language (Polanyi, 1966).
- Systemic vs. stand-alone, knowledge is systemic when it consists of an integration of different scientific and/or engineering disciplines required for innovation (Teece, 1986), forming part of a larger system. Knowledge is stand-alone when it can be considered to be as (relatively) isolated from other knowledge (Malerba and Breschi, 1997).
- Level of diffusion, knowledge, in either tacit and/or codified form, can pertain to an individual or a single firm indicating a low level of diffusion. Knowledge can also be widely diffused among firms in a SSI, indicating a high level of diffusion.
- Generic vs. specific, the knowledge may be of a generic nature or specific to certain application domains (Malerba and Breschi, 1997).
- Cumulativeness, cumulativeness indicates the probability of innovating at time $t+1$ is conditional on innovations at time t or on previous periods and experiences. It indicates the level of continuity in innovative activities (Malerba and Breschi 1997).
- Rate of change, the development of knowledge can range from very slow in stationary environments and increase towards high speed in turbulent environments (Lundvall, 1992).[1]

Opportunity conditions, opportunity conditions indicate the presence of clear incentives to undertake innovative activities (Marsili, 2001).

- Level, a high level of opportunities indicates that potential innovators may come up with (technological) innovations in easier ways and thus provides powerful incentives for firms to undertake innovative activities. A low level indicates that the ease with which (technological) innovations can be achieved is limited and thus provides weak incentives to undertake innovative activities (Malerba and Breschi, 1997; Marsili, 2001).
- Variety, a rich variety in opportunity conditions is associated with ample potential for diversity in (technological) solutions, approaches and activities. Low variety indicates that this potential for diversity is limited, for example after the emergence of a dominant design when the focus shifts to improve existing products and processes (Malerba and Breschi, 1997).
- Source, the source of opportunity may differ per type of SSI and can vary from scientific breakthroughs in academia, technological progress in R&D,

improvements in production or other functional disciplines within firms to external sources such as users and/or suppliers (Malerba and Breschi, 1997).

Demand, as argued by various scholars, demand may provide powerful incentives to firms for undertaking innovative activities (von Hippel, 1988; Porter, 1990; Lundvall, 1992). We see the following properties of demand as relevant:

- Size and growth, growth and size are interrelated and should be seen in relation to the investments firms make and the possibilities to secure a sound return on that investment. Size of demand yields contingencies for economies of scale and experience effects.
- Homogeneous vs. differentiated, a more homogeneous demand base in combination with a large size, may lead to standard setting by means of a dominant design. When demand has a high level of differentiability, customers require a more tailored solution that sets conditions for economies of scope. In that case, more than one standard may be adopted.
- Advanced vs. standard, this relates to the extent in which customers are critical and demanding in their requirements. Some demanding customers may act as lead-users (von Hippel, 1988) and provide powerful incentives for firms to come up with innovative solutions. In this respect, the level of advancement also sets conditions for experience effects (Porter, 1990). In addition, there is a relation with price-elasticity as more advanced demand may generally be prepared to pay a premium versus more standard demand.

Appropriability, appropriability relates to the possibilities of protecting an innovation from imitation and thus appropriating the rents from innovative activities.

- Level of appropriability, a high level of appropriability suggests that effective ways exist to protect against imitation. Low appropriability denotes limited possibility to protect from imitation and coincides with widespread knowledge spillovers (Malerba and Breschi, 1997).
- Means of appropriability, ways to protect innovations range from secrecy, patents, continuous innovations, standards, accumulated tacit knowledge and control of complementary assets (Teece, 1986).

Competition, competition relates to the competitive conditions in which learning and innovation take place. We see the following properties as relevant:

- Intensity, highly competitive conditions coincide with low entry barriers, high exit barriers and low concentration rates. Low competitive intensity indicates high entry barriers, low exit barriers and medium to high concentration rates.
- Dimensions, competition can take place on costs and/or on non-cost elements such as quality, flexibility, innovation, or on all of them (Bolwijn and Kumpe, 1989). In general, competition based on costs (low price) relates to more homogeneous and standard demand that lowers possibilities for firms to differentiate whereas more advanced demand relates to competition on quality, flexibility and/or innovation.
- Individual vs. group-based, competition can be among individual firms but can also take place between networks of firms. This latter case is also referred to as 'group-based competition' (Gomes-Casseres, 1994) and puts pressure on firms within such a group to cooperate and innovate.

Systemic Combinations of 2nd Level Institutions

As argued, the identified institutions are not separate or independent; on the contrary, there are various possible connections. To give some general examples with regard to 2nd level insitutions:

- When knowledge is mainly tacit and highly cumulative, appropriability takes place by means of accumulated tacit knowledge
- When knowledge is mainly codified, appropriability (may) takes place by means of patents
- Codified knowledge generally coincides with a high(er) level of diffusion, whereas tacit knowledge generally coincides with a low(er) level of diffusion
- A widely diffused knowledge base (may) coincides with high entry and strong competition on price
- A low level of knowledge diffusion (may) coincide with low entry and limited competition
- Appropriability by standards (may) induce group-based competition
- A high rate of change limits spill-overs of knowledge as by the time others could absorb this knowledge, it has become obsolete
- In an exploration setting with a high rate of change of the knowledge base, opportunities are generally diffuse and competition is limited
- In an exploitation setting with a low rate of change of the knowledge base, opportunities are generally well defined and competition is (relatively) intense.

According to our scheme in Figure 2.1, the 2nd level is embedded in the 1st level, implying that the 1st level is of higher order than the 2nd level. Of course it will depend on the type of SSI whether this will always be the case. For

SSIs that are clearly located within national boundaries, national institutions may indeed provide the larger context for lower institutions. However for a SSI that crosses national boundaries or approaches a global scale, the selective effect of 2nd level institutions on learning and innovation may exceed the effect of 1st level institutions. We will not further elaborate on this but refer to some studies that have developed interesting attempts to shed more light on this as for example by Malerba and Breschi (1997), Mowery and Nelson (1999), Marsili (2001) and Nelson et al. (2002).

Following the logic of our scheme in Figure 2.1, the 2nd level functions as the selection environment in which the 3rd level is embedded, the subject of the next section.

3rd LEVEL INSTITUTIONS

We consider this 3rd level as the intermediate level between the outer institutional environments, formed by the 1st and 2nd level, and institutionalized behaviour formed by embedded, interfirm learning processes. By intermediate we mean that the institutions at the 1st and 2nd level select 3rd level institutions that most clearly fit with them, in view of the embedded learning and innovation processes. More specifically, we conceive of the 3rd level as consisting of 3 elements, namely the characteristics of the network structure, the properties of the relations making up this network and the mechanisms through which these relations are coordinated.[2]

This paragraph is built up as follows. In the next section we make some general comments on social network theory and argue why it is relevant for our research. Next we discuss network structure and the properties of the relations making up a network. Finally we discuss various coordination mechanisms that may be employed in these network relations.

Social Networks

As argued by different scholars, outcomes of evolutionary processes are affected by networks and by the patterns of relations within them (Lundvall 1992; Baum and Singh, 1994; McKelvey, 1997; Carlsson, 1997 and 2002; Malerba and Breschi, 1997). Networks have been analysed from a variety of angles as schools of thought vary with different disciplines. A first school takes an interpersonal perspective and emphasizes the non-economic bases of social exchange. They are primarily concerned with the relations that individual actors have with one another and is referred to as the 'ego-centric perspective' on networks (Sandefur and Laumann, 1998[3]; Lesser, 2000). A second school takes a more structural approach and focuses on the configuration, number and quality of ties (Burt, 1992; Nahapiet and Ghoshal, 1998). This approach stresses a person's relative position within a network rather than his direct relationships with others in the network. Still others focus on the institutional nature of networks and define them as a distinct organisational alternative to markets and corporate hierarchies (Williamson, 1985; Powell, 1990). Other seminal contributions have been made by Granovetter on the distinction between strong and weak ties (1985) and Coleman on social capital (1988).

Our goal now is to understand how a network is structured and what function it has in the context of interfirm learning and innovation. To do so, we will make use of some concepts and tools as developed by social network analysis. Two important ontological premises that underlie social network analysis are that actors and their actions are viewed as interdependent, instead of independent, and that relational ties are channels for transformation of material and non-material resources (Wasserman and Faust, 1994). This connects with our ontology as articulated in Chapter 1, making our use of social network theory indeed legitimate for the purpose of our research.

The starting point for social network analysis is that relations among actors, or nodes, are the building blocks of networks (Knoke and Kuklinski, 1982). In an economic context, this web of interfirm relations enables and constrains the direction and various forms in which economic relationships can develop (Granovetter, 1985), also referred to as structural embeddedness. This embeddedness then is assumed to have important behavioral consequences for the individual firms as for the network as a whole (Wasserman and Faust, 1994).

When studying social networks, an important issue is the level of analysis. Knoke and Kulinkski (1982) differentiate between four levels of analysis, ranging from egocentric networks, dyads, triads and the complete network level. We will take the complete network as our level of analysis and will analyse it according to the following three dimensions:

- Structure of relations, i.e. network structure
- Content and form of relations
- Coordination mechanisms

Network Structure

Network structure refers to the general structure of relations making up a network. We consider the following structural features as relevant:

- Size, network size, also referred to as network volume, relates to the total number of ties that is present in a network (Knoke, 1999).
- Density, proportion of present ties to the total number of possible ties (Knoke, 1999).
- Structural holes, disconnections, or absent ties, between actors (Burt, 1992).

- Centrality, centrality refers to the extent in which there are actors in the network with relatively many ties (Knoke 1999).

These structural features of networks are not separate or independent as there are various, possible connections among them. To give a few, general examples:

- A network that is large in size may generally not have a very high level of density and will probably show structural holes
- Closure indicates a high level of density
- A network with many structural holes indicates a low level of density
- A network with many structural holes may have a high level of centrality. Actors that span these structural holes, so-called 'middle actors' (Burt, 1992), may occupy a central position in the network.

To these structural elements, which originate from social network analysis, we add two other elements that originate from industrial dynamics (entry/exit) and from innovation theory (cognitive distance):

- Entry/exit refers to the rate of entry and exit over a given period of time. We add this dimension as it gives an indication of the dynamics in the network that has over time consequences for the more 'static' structural elements mentioned above. A high entry/exit rate will increase/decrease the network size over time with subsequent consequences for density, structural holes, closure and centrality.
- Cognitive distance, cognitive distance refers to differences in categories of cognition (Nooteboom, 2000). We add this concept to our analysis as it complements the structural view, as described by the above elements, with a cognitive view of a network. Given the central focus of our research on knowledge and learning, we consider this an important feature of a network.

Relations

The building blocks of a network are formed by relations. In the context of our research, relations among firm or interfirm relations. These relations have two dimensions (Knoke and Kuklinski 1982): relational content and relational form.

Relational content, relations between firms can entail different elements, that is the relational content differs (Knoke and Kuklinski, 1982; Wasserman and Faust, 1994). Obviously, firms may have different relational content in relations with different firms. The engagement in frequent economic transactions does not need to imply that these transactions are knowledge intensive; transactions can entail mainly the exchange of standard products or services without any knowledge exchange whatsoever. Given our central focus on knowledge and learning we are primarily interested in those relations in which knowledge is exchanged, either in tacit or codified form and in varying levels of intensity (see next section on 'relational form' for our definition of intensity). Knowledge that is exchanged may entail different elements and can range from knowledge on technology, production processes, organizational practices, customers, markets, competitors, suppliers and so on.

Relational form, relational form refers to the properties of the relations independently of the specific contents. Relations that are quite distinct in content may exhibit identical or highly similar forms. We differentiate among the following:

- Formality, formality refers to the level of formalization due to formal contracts (Grandori and Soda, 1995).
- Durability, durability refers to the length of a relationship in time (Granovetter, 1973).
- Intensity, intensity refers to the frequency of contacts (Granovetter, 1973).
- Intimacy, intimacy refers to the level of agreement and trust between social actors (Granovetter, 1973).
- Symmetry, symmetry refers to the extent in which relations are parity-based in terms of power (DiMaggio and Powell, 1983; Grandori and Soda, 1995).

Coordination Mechanisms

Interfirm cooperation yields the problem of making sure that desired behaviour is indeed accomplished, requiring coordination mechanisms. Following our definition of networks as introduced in Chapter 1, we take a broad view on coordination mechanisms as 'not limited to price, exit and background regulation' (Grandori, 1999). In addition to Grandori's definition, we also follow her framework for identifying different kinds of coordinating mechanisms.

- Communication, decision and negotiation mechanisms, these are generally cheap and widely used mechanisms, present in all kinds of networks.
- Social coordination and control, these mechanisms relate to the functioning of groups norms, reputation, trust and peer control in networks.
- Integration and linking pin roles and units, lateral roles and responsibilities can be key-mechanisms for coordinating across functional and/or organizational boundaries.

- Common staff, in the case of a wide scope of interfirm cooperation and/or a high number of participating firms, coordination becomes important and may be based on dedicated staff. Examples are franchises and associations.
- Hierarchy and authority relations, these mechanisms may be used, although seldom exclusive, instead of lateral communication, negotiation and other more parity-based mechanisms (although often in a mixture of both).
- Planning and Control mechanisms, planning & control systems aim to 'deliver' desired behaviour by monitoring input, throughput or output of the cooperation.
- Incentive systems, such mechanisms are common in cooperation activities that are informationally complex and in which contribution or performance is difficult to measure. Rearranging property rights often form an effective mechanism to realign objectives so that interests converge.
- Selection systems, these mechanisms relate to who gets access to the networks based on specific selection mechanisms that can be either informal or formalized.
- Information systems, these mechanisms can be powerful integrators for managing interfirm cooperation due to their potential for fast exchange of information at low costs.

In general, these coordination mechanisms are used in a mix and it depends on the institutional conditions which specific combination of coordination mechanisms is selected.

SYSTEMIC COMBINATIONS OF 2nd and 3rd LEVEL INSTITUTIONS

As argued, the 3rd level of network institutions is embedded in the 2nd level of the institutional environment, making both levels interdependent. In other words, there are various linkages between them, creating systemic combinations of 2nd and 3rd level institutions. This connects with the relation that we can observe between innovation theory and the Systems of Innovation approach on the one hand and concepts of social network theory on the other hand. We will now further elaborate upon this and will develop a typology of networks that forms a synthesis between these two bodies of literature. Based on that we formulate a hypothesis.

Relation between innovation theory and social network theory, as argued in Chapter 1, we follow the basic principles from evolutionary theory and the Systems of Innovation approach. An important notion herein, is the system-concept of connectivity that refers to the intensity and type of connections among the various actors in the system (Carlsson, 1997). The general idea is that no or only a weak connection among actors hampers system performance in terms of innovation as interaction and learning do not sufficiently take place. When there is substantial connectivity among actors, fruitful opportunities for learning and innovation would arise. On the other hand, too much connection may again constrain learning and innovation, especially if no outsiders are allowed, indicating low external connectivity. In other words, connectivity is proposed as a key-concept when understanding the functioning and performance of a system of innovation (Carlsson, 1997). The equivalent of connectivity between actors is specified by 'density', one of the central concepts in social network theory. As defined in 'Network Structure', density refers to the proportion of present ties in relation to the total number of possible ties in a network.[4] The distinction between strong and weak ties as argued by Granovetter (1985) differentiates between high density relations on the one hand and low density relations on the other hand. In his theory on 'structural holes', Burt (1992) argues that (groups of) actors can show a low level of density in their relations, creating structural holes. Middle actors are those who close these holes by forming a connection among these disconnected actors.   Also Coleman's work on social capital (1988) deals with density. Depending on the density of ties, he distinguishes two types of networks, open vs. closed. An open network structure implies that there are very few connections among actors, whereas in the case of a closed network all are connected (closure). Following this notion of 'connectivity' in innovation theory, or density in social network theory, we are able to consider some systemic combinations of 2nd and 3rd level institutions along a general taxonomy of network types. We distinguish among the following three types:

- Compartmentalized networks (low density)
- Loosely connected networks (medium density)
- Strongly connected networks (high density)

Compartmentalized networks, networks can be compartmentalized in the sense that (groups of) actors are disconnected from each other. In general, this network structure does not accommodate learning and innovation between such 'compartments'. Due to the compartmentalized structure firms do not interact, allowing for a large cognitive distance and hence difficulties in absorbing new information or knowledge. Although the network may contain large amounts of information or knowledge, its potential use may be limited because opportunities for its recombination are constrained. In this type of network there are limited ties among (groups of) actors and many structural holes. As defined, structural holes entail 'disconnections between players in the arena' (Burt, 1992: 2) and provide opportunities for information access, timing, referrals and control. In this way, Burt explains competitive advantage as a 'matter of access to holes' (Burt, 1992: 2). His claim is that firms that are positioned between different networks by occupying a structural hole will be more profitable as they have better access and control over opportunities. A compartmentalized network can be considered as having a low level of density. As there are only limited relations among actors, the network is open to anyone who aspires to enter. As argued by Coleman, such a structure inhibits the build-up of social capital, consisting of a mix of trust,[5] reputation and sanctions ensuring trustworthiness (Coleman, 1988).[6] For social capital to develop, actors need to be connected so that they can interact in order to learn about the behaviour, intention and reputation of others in the network.

Strongly connected networks, the opposite of a compartmentalized network structure, are formed by a strongly connected network structure in which there are many linkages and frequent interaction among the involved actors. These are Granovetter's strong ties that are characterized by durability, high frequency of interaction, reciprocity and possibly intimacy (Granovetter, 1973). From this high density and strength in relations strong 'social cohesiveness' results, facilitating the build-up of social capital that resides in the presence of dense social ties (Coleman, 1988; Baker and Obstfeld, 1999). An important form of social capital is the potential for information that inheres in social relations. Social relations, also when maintained for other purposes, are important means to acquire information (Coleman, 1988). This connects with theories on innovation and learning: dense ties among firms accommodate a small cognitive distance that enhances mutual understanding and facilitates the transfer of tacit knowledge (Cohen and Levinthal, 1990; Nooteboom, 2000). Another form of social capital are norms that can have an important regulating effect on firm behaviour (Coleman, 1988). The effectiveness of norms will depend on the structure of the social relations. As argued by Coleman (1988), when network density is high or approaching closure, this enables the effective functioning of coordination mechanisms such as social norms, peer control and reputation. Whether this is beneficial depends on the institutional environment in which the network is embedded. In terms of our model, it depends on the 2nd level institutions.[7] When knowledge is mainly tacit, dense ties among firms accommodate a small cognitive distance enhancing easy transfer of this tacit knowledge. Also in the case of a systemic knowledge base, a dense structure offers advantages. The integration of different knowledge disciplines can only be done efficiently when firms share a common understanding, have sufficiently close relations and sufficient trust in one another. When appropriation takes place by means of complementary assets, firms also need relational and cognitive closeness in order to be able to coordinate the relationship. In such networks the dense, integrated nature may be further enhanced by coordination mechanisms such as planning and control systems, selection systems regulating access and information systems. All these benefits accrue to a dense network structure as long as change occurs incrementally. When change in 2nd level institutions becomes more radical, these benefits disappear and it may appear that there is a danger in dense structure as well. Such a network may retain the exclusivity of incumbents whereby existing norms and reputation regulate behaviour too strictly. To deviate from the established way of doing things may be highly discouraged by these prevailing norms stressing conformity. In such a situation, it may be difficult for outsiders to enter as reputation may act as a formidable barrier that further blocks renewal. This results into 'lock-in' (Arthur, 1988) or 'inertia' (Nooteboom, 2000), a situation in which established firms become blind in a way that they ignore exposure to other practices (for example other markets or new technologies) outside their immediate geographic, cognitive environment and/or cultural environment. Others have labelled this situation as 'overembeddedness' (Uzzi, 1997; Uzzi and Gillespie, 1999) or 'social liability' (Gargiulo and Benassi, 1999).

A loosely connected network, a more intermediate form, is a network with a loosely connected structure. In such a network structure actors are connected to others but the intensity may vary. There may be stronger relations to more inside actors and weaker relations to more outside actors. Relations that are based on the frequent and durable exchange of codified and/or tacit knowledge, can be labelled as a strong tie. Weak ties are formed by relations with a lower level of intensity and durability and may be coordinated by mechanisms such as lateral roles, linking pin units or incentive systems to realign objectives. Especially these weak ties may give access to other networks and as such form an important source of diversity (Granovetter, 1973). Diversity, or variety, is one of the central elements in evolutionary theory (Nelson and Winter, 1982). Variety on the level of a network affects the opportunities for communication and interaction among different actors (McKelvey, 1997; Nooteboom, 2000). These different sources of knowledge outside a firm are critical for innovation, implying that firms should maximize weak ties in their network. But we should not take this argument too far, for managerial and for cognitive reasons. First, there will be a limit on the number of weak ties that firms, in addition to their strong ties, are able to manage. An argument from a cognitive point of view is that the chance of misunderstanding increases when cognitive diversity becomes too big. Based on these considerations, there seems to be general agreement among (innovation) scholars that loosely connected networks, built up of strong and weak ties, provide fertile soil to nurture learning and innovation (for exmaple Grabher, 1993; Smith Ring and van de Ven, 1994; Carlsson, 1997; Nooteboom, 2000; Malerba, 2002).

A hypothesis: an interesting question now is whether there is something like an 'ideal level' of strong and weak ties in a network that could be specified *exante*. Following our social constructivist view of knowledge and learning, our answer is that it varies with the conditions set by the institutional environment in which a specific combination of strong and weak ties is selected, making it difficult to specify such a 'desired mix' of strong and weak ties. Following Granovetter's argument though, on the 'strength of weak ties' as an important source of diversity (1973), we can be more precise on the role of weak ties in the context of innovation. We propose the following hypothesis 1: when change in 2nd level institutions becomes more radical, there is an increasing need for weak ties to deal with this variability in conditions.

Whether such weak ties are easily 'available' again depends on whether knowledge is widely diffused. If so, there may be more potential partners to choose from, making selection a relatively easy task. When knowledge is not widely diffused, not only finding a knowledgeable partner becomes difficult but also relational risk may be generated due to potentially one-sided dependency. Such a governance-perspective will be further dealt with in Chapter 3.

NOTES

1. Rate of change should not not be confused with radicalism. A high speed of change is typically associated with radical innovations and a low speed of change with incremental innovations. However, incremental change may also be fast, whereas radical change may be slow. Obviously 'fast' and 'slow' are subjective notions and should therefore be interpreted with care, also because their connotation differs per type of SSI. A period of let's say two years for the development of an innovation may be considered long in one SSI and may be (very) short in another SSI.
2. This level can also be referred to as 'institutional arrangements' as is usually being done in TCE (Williamson, 1985) but also by some innovation scholars (for example Carlsson, 1997).
3. Sandefur and Laumann refer to this egocentric perspective as in which 'an individual's social capital is characterized by his/her direct relationships with others and the other people and relationships that he/she can reach through to those to whom he/she is directly connected' (1998: 484).
4. Connectivity is also used in social network theory but with a different connotation than in innovation theory. It refers to the extent in which all actors in a network are connected, through direct ties and/or indirect ties. A low level of connectivity then indicates that there are (groups of) actors with no connections to others, whereas a high level indicates that all actors can be reached, either directly or through others.
5. Although not mentioning this explicitly, Coleman basically refers to trust-in-intention rather than trust-in-competence (Nooteboom, 2002).
6. See for an overview of the literature on social capital Coleman 1988, Leenders and Gabbay (1999) and Lesser (2000).
7. At this point we leave 1st level institutions out of the analysis, although these can certainly condition the benefits of a densely connected network. For example, as argued by Fukuyama (1995), the absence of a reliable legal infrastructure in Italy has led firms to develop dense social relations within regional networks, which has facilitated the emergence of the Mafia (Sicily) and Camorra (Naples).

3. Learning regimes

INTRODUCTION

In Chapter 2 we addressed our first research question and have identified which institutions in the institutional environment are relevant for interfirm learning and innovation. In this chapter we will address our second research question, namely: how do these institutions condition interfirm learning?

In Figure 2.1, we have schematically depicted the relationship between the institutional environment (formed by three institutional levels) and institutionalized behaviour (formed by interfirm learning processes). As argued in Chapter's 2 Introduction, the rectangle in this figure is not an institutional level but represents a level of 'institutionalized learning behaviour'. This behaviour is institutionalized in the way that it is enabled and constrained by institutions at the 1st and 2nd and 3rd level of the institutional selection environment. So, this level of institutionalized learning behaviour represents the embedded interfirm learning and innovation processes and forms the topic of this chapter.

To deal with this level of institutionalized learning behaviour we introduce in this chapter the concept of a learning regime. A learning regime reflects the notion that interfirm learning is dependent on the specific set-up of the institutional environment in which it is embedded. To further analyse this, we start in, learning regimes: a competence perspective, with a competence-perspective based on which we discuss how a learning regime is conditioned by relevant institutions in the institutional environment. Solely relying on such a competence-view would create an impression of interfirm learning as a process of firms merely giving and sharing knowledge as this would enhance mutual learning and understanding. Obviously, this is only one side of the coin. The other side is that engaging in such interactive learning processes makes firms become dependent on one another. This dependency yields a risk of conflict and opportunism and may possibly influence the way firms interact. This connects with a governance-perspective. Governance forms a central element in transaction costs economics, which explicitly acknowledges opportunism. 'Opportunism is so familiar that we often fail to acknowledge it and its consequences when we see it' (Williamson, 1999: 1098). The potential for opportunism as well as its consequences may affect interfirm learning and innovation and therefore needs to be integrated into our analysis.[1] In learning regimes: a governance perspective, therefore, we analyse a learning regime from a governance-perspective. Based on that we then integrate it in the section 'Relational risk in different learning regimes' with our competence-view of a learning regime.

LEARNING REGIMES: A COMPETENCE PERSPECTIVE

In this paragraph we take a competence-perspective and introduce the concept of a learning regime. Next we discuss the differences between a learning regime and a technological regime.

The Concept of a Learning Regime

As argued in Chapter 1 we assume that heterogeneous actors that search around a similar knowledge base and that are embedded in the same institutional environment share some common behavioural and organizational traits and develop a common range of learning patterns and behaviour. Based on this, we have proposed differentiating between a collective dimension to innovation and an individual dimension (McKelvey, 1997). As we study networks from the perspective of a SSI, we are especially interested in the collective dimension. We see innovation as a collective learning process and are interested in aggregate learning and innovation patterns in SSIs, both in the process of interfirm learning and in its outcomes.

Following our analysis in Chapter 2, we argue that this collective pattern of interfirm learning is the result of the enabling and constraining effect of the institutional environment. In addition, following our social constructivist view of knowledge and learning, we argue that differences in institutional environments stimulate different sorts and amounts of social interaction and thus lead to differences in types of learning. These differences in institutional environments may not only affect what is learned but also how it is learned.

In this context we introduce the concept of a learning regime. A learning regime reflects the notion that learning varies with the conditions in which it is embedded. So, we see a learning regime as dependent on the specific set-up of the institutional environment. In this respect, our concept of a learning regime reflects the collective dimension of innovation. It helps us to understand this collective dimension of innovation in a more explicit way by decomposing it into various elements. From a competence-perspective we see the following elements as relevant:

- Object of learning: what is being learned
- Learning process: how this learning process is being carried out
- Actors: who is involved
- Input: what knowledge, resources and capabilities are needed
- Output: what is the result.

To get a further understanding of the combination of elements making up a learning regime, we differentiate between two archetypes of a learning regime. The differentiation between these two archetypes of learning regimes follows the notion as developed by March (1991) that evolutionary survival depends on the trade-off between exploration and exploitation. Exploitation involves the efficient utilization of existing resources and competencies. For interfirm learning this requires stability, standardization and routinization. Exploration implies a need for constant renewal of resources and competencies. For interfirm learning this requires breaking away from continuity, standards and routines. Exploitation is required for survival on the short term, exploration for survival on the long term. As a consequence, both are characterized by different learning regimes, as outlined in Table 3.1.

Learning regime in exploration, a learning regime has the 'discovery' of new knowledge as its object of learning. The learning process is by searching: activities that are explicitly aimed at the generation of new knowledge in order to increase the knowledge stock. Generally this builds on insights into the limits of the existing knowledge base and requires the development of new capabilities as inputs. The output of this learning regime is formed by new knowledge, new ideas and beliefs, different kinds of demo's, experimental products as well as new (technical) standards, new procedures, new routines and so on. This connects with Argyris and Schon's double-loop learning (1978 and 1996). Double-loop learning is concerned with changes to underlying mental frameworks such as theories in use, assumptions, organizational strategies and norms as well as the way in which competencies and environments are construed. This requires a capability of remaining open to environmental changes and of dismissing existing, underlying values and assumptions.

Learning regime in exploitation, a learning regime in exploitation focuses on one or a few specific elements of the existing knowledge base and focuses on improving or correcting these elements, its object of learning. The way of learning is by repetition: activities focused on constantly improving the existing knowledge base in a routine manner. This learning requires the development of refined problem solving capabilities to systemically monitor deviations and correct when necessary, as inputs. The output of this learning regime is formed by an improved understanding of specific issues, improved products, process improvements, improved problem solving skills, adapted technical norms, changed formal procedures and so on. This connects with Argyris and Schon's single-loop learning (1978 and 1996). Single-loop learning is a form of 'instrumental learning' that is concerned with the detection and correction of errors without altering underlying values and assumptions (Argyris and Schon, 1978 and 1996).

Table 3.1 Archetypes of learning regimes from a competence view

COMPETENCE VIEW	EXPLORATION	EXPLOITATION
Learning object	new knowledge base	specific elements of existing knowledge base
Learning process	expansive searching	repetitive activities
Actors	new combinations of actors	existing combinations of actors
Input	- insights into limits of existing knowledge base - new capabilities	refined problem solving capabilities
Output	- new knowledge - new ideas and beliefs -demo's, experimental products	- improved understanding of specific issues - product adaptations - process improvements - technical norms

As said, these are two archetypical forms of learning regimes and other, more intermediate types can be identified as well. We will deal with this more extensively in Chapter 4.

Differences between a Learning Regime and a Technological Regime

Our concept of a learning regime is related to the concept of a 'technological regime' although there are some clear differences between them. Nelson and Winter (1977) introduced the notion of a technological regime. According to them, 'the sense of potential, of constraints, and of not yet exploited opportunities, implicit in a regime focuses the attention of engineers on certain directions in which progress is possible, and provides strong guidance as to the tactics likely to be fruitful for probing in that direction. In other words, a regime not only defines boundaries, but also trajectories to those boundaries (1977: 57). This is comparable to the notions of technological paradigms and technological trajectories as developed by Dosi in analogy with Kuhn's concept of scientific paradigms (Dosi, 1982). He defines a technological paradigm as a 'pattern of solution of selected technological problems, based on selected principles derived from natural sciences and on selected material technologies' and a technological trajectory as the 'pattern of normal problem solving activity on the ground of a technological paradigm'. After being introduced by Nelson and Winter, and later Dosi, this concept of a technological regime has been used and further specified by others such as Georghiou et al. (1986), who defined a technological regime as a 'set of design parameters which embody the principles which will generate both the physical configuration of the product and the process and materials from which it is to be constructed. The basic design parameters are the heart of the technological regime, and they constitute a framework of knowledge which is shared by the firms in the industry'.

Underlying the notions of technological regime and technological trajectory is the central idea that relevant elements of technological development such as design options; heuristics and technical modes are shared among the involved actors and guide their interactions, resulting in a specific pattern of technological development. This connects with our interest in what we labelled in Chapter 1 as the 'collective dimension' of interfirm learning in networks.

As can be understood from these definitions, the concept of a technological regime has an interest in the 'contents' of a technology and hence in the products, processes, engineering practices and technical parameters associated with the particular technology. Changes in this technology can take place along certain paths, but it is implied that these paths themselves remain unchanged. In addition, the idea of a 'framework of knowledge that is shared by the firms in the industry' (Georghiou et al., 1986) suggests that a technological regime is limited to an industry that he defines by its main products and processes, implying that users, suppliers and others are considered as outside the industry.

We see two clear differences between our concept of a learning regime and a technological regime. First, our concept of a learning regime clearly acknowledges the distinction between exploration and exploitation. As argued in section; the concept of a learning regime, there are profound differences between both contexts with clear implications for the elements making up a learning regime such as its learning object, learning process etc. The concept of a technological regime more reflects an exploitation context as it 'defines boundaries and also trajectories to those boundaries' (Nelson and Winter, 1977: 57), whereas in exploration the primary object of learning is to change those boundaries, deviate from the existing trajectories and search for new ones. A second difference is that our concept of a learning regime acknowledges the 'dark side' of interfirm learning: by engaging in interactive learning processes, firms become more dependent on one another, yielding relational risk. The possibility of relational risk influences interfirm learning and may sometimes even prevent learning from emerging in the first place. So, whereas the concept of a technological regime clearly takes a competence perspective, our concept of a learning regime combines this with a governance perspective. Such a governance-view will now be further dealt with in the next section.

LEARNING REGIMES: A GOVERNANCE PERSPECTIVE

This paragraph takes a governance-perspective of a learning regime. In order to do so, we will first discuss the concept of relational risk and the various elements by which it is built up. As next step, we will relate these elements to our model of the institutional environment (Figure 2.1). Finally, we will integrate these elements into our concept of a learning regime.

Elements of Relational Risk

Relational risk has two dimensions: the size of loss to a firm due to accidents or opportunism by the other network partner(s) and the probability that such loss will occur (Nooteboom, 1999c). The first dimension of relational risk depends on the individual firm confronted with such risk. As the individual firm level is beyond the scope of our research, we will not further elaborate on this dimension. The probability of loss due to relational risk is determined by the institutional conditions in which a network of interfirm relations is embedded. We will therefore concentrate on the probability of the occurrence of loss due to relational risk.

Four elements of relational risk, an important notion in the literature on interfirm learning and innovation is that when firms dispose of the same knowledge, there is no potential for learning. Only when firms come from different cognitive backgrounds can new combinations of knowledge be created and the potential for learning emerges (Dosi et al., 1988; Nooteboom, 2000). Still then, learning among heterogenous actors can only take place when information and knowledge are transferred efficiently and when this knowledge and information can be retained (McKelvey, 1997). This requires that firms grow sufficiently cognitively close in order to be able to learn and to prevent misunderstandings. To grow cognitively close, firms need to make specific investments, both in terms of mutual understanding and in trust. From these investments, dependency arises which may result in hold-up. Hold-up refers to a situation in which the investments a firm has made can only be recouped in the relation with its specific partner. When a common cognitive framework among firms has developed, it becomes easier to learn from the other partner and knowledge may thus spill over. From a competence perspective such knowledge spillovers are desirable as they basically provide the reason why firms can learn from one another in a network. From a governance perspective however, spillovers can be problematic as they may lead to acts of freeridership. Freeridership is a general notion that refers to the room for a firm to benefit from the partner's efforts without making a full contribution (Nooteboom, 1999c). In our research we analyse freeridership in the context of learning and innovation. So we take a more narrow view on freeridership and interpret it as the room for firms to benefit through knowledge spillovers that originate from other partners' efforts. Figure 3.1 schematically outlines our argument.

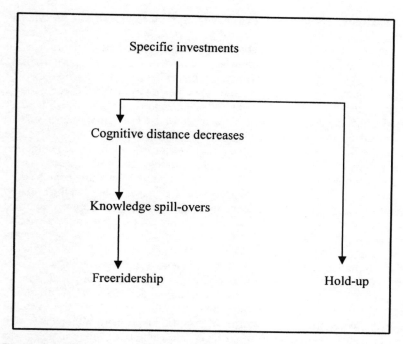

Figure 3.1 Governance perspective of a learning regime

In terms of our institutional level model (Figure 2.1), all four elements of relational risk pertain to the level of institutionalized behaviour, the rectangle in our figure. Taken together these elements make up a governance perspective of a learning regime. They therefore need to be analysed together although originating from different institutions in the institutional environment. The figure also indicates from which level of the institutional environment these four elements of relational risk originate. This will be now further elaborated upon in the next section.

Relational Risk Conditioned by the Institutional Selection Environment

To discuss the various elements that constitute relational risk we differentiate between specific investments and hold-up on the one hand and spillovers and freeridership on the other hand.

Specific investments and hold-up, the need to make specific investments, originates at the 2nd level of the institutional environment, especially from the nature of the knowledge base. More specifically, specific investments are a function of the level of diffusion of knowledge, the level of systemicness and the tacitness of knowledge. The level of specific investments will be higher when knowledge has not diffused, pertaining to individuals or a single firm.

This may require substantial investments in order to absorb this knowledge, irrespective of whether it is codified or tacit. When knowledge is systemic this requires substantial investments in understanding adjacent knowledge bases. In addition, a systemic knowledge base may imply that appropriability takes place by means of complementary assets. Appropriability by means of complementary assets also requires specific investments (Teece, 1986). Assets from both sides need to be adjusted, requiring again investments in mutual understanding and trust. The level of specific investments is also determined by the tacitness of knowledge. Tacit knowledge rests in people and only spills over in close interaction between them. In that case interaction requires investments in mutual understanding and also trust. These investments range from investments in learning about the knowledge base of the other firm, its organizational procedures, its people as well as the build up of trust (Nooteboom, 2000). Especially when knowledge is tacit and specific in scope, such investments may become highly specific to a particular relation. Another form of specific investments is formed by 'opportunity costs', that is by spending time, money and people for a particular relationship other opportunities may be missed. According to transaction cost literature, specific investments can take a variety of forms: physical, human, site-specific, dedicated assets, brand name capital and temporal (Williamson, 1996). Given our focus on learning and innovation in this research, we will not further elaborate on these forms of specific investments although we will include them in the analysis when their role cannot be ignored. So, in the remainder of this research, we limit ourselves to those investments that are required to create cognitive closeness, these are specific cognitive investments. Table 3.1 summarizes this discussion by presenting the extreme cases to clarify our argument. Of course, more intermediate forms are more likely to be observed in practice.[2] Figure 3.2 summarizes our argument. So, the need to make specific cognitive investments originates at the 2nd level of the institutional environment. Such investments may generate a potential problem of hold-up. Following our institutional level model, institutions at the 3rd level (network structure, interfirm relations and coordinating mechanisms) can reinforce the need for such investments and as such increase the probability of a situation of hold-up.

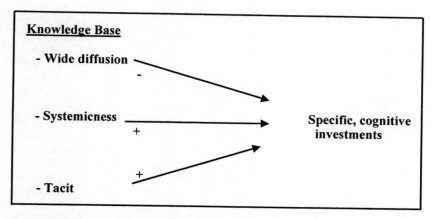

Figure 3.2 Relation between properties of the knowledge base and specific cognitive investments

Firms that occupy a central position in a network of a-symmetric relations can demand from others (suppliers, customers or competitors) to invest in understanding their particular knowledge base, organizational procedures, people, information systems etc. This understanding may yield exit barriers for the dependent actors, thereby creating a problem of hold-up.[3] When these relations are (mainly) formal, the need to invest into such cognitive, specialized assets can be formalized into contracts. For the dependent firm, this may be difficult when relations are a-symmetric but may become easier when relations are more symmetric. In the latter case, the need for specific investments can be negotiated before being formalized into an agreement in order to prevent hold-up. However, (detailed) contracts that limit the risks of hold-up are not desirable from an innovation point of view. The outcomes of learning and innovation are by definition uncertain which makes it difficult to specify those outcomes upfront. In addition, a contract needs to be monitored which, again, to a large extent is determined by the nature of the knowledge base: when knowledge is tacit and subject to radical change, monitoring may be very difficult. In addition, there is a relational argument that says that detailed contracts aimed at the prevention of opportunism are a signal of distrust (Nooteboom, 2000). This is especially the case when relations are (mainly) informal and coordinated by informal mechanisms such as social norms and reputation, putting a strong limit on the use of contracts. So, in the case of informal relations, and which are also symmetric, investments in mutual understanding and trust can only be recouped when relations are durable enough.

Spillovers and freeridership, as argued, firms make specific investments in order to develop a common cognitive framework that facilitates mutual learning and as such accommodates for knowledge spillovers. Whether knowledge can spill over depends, first of all, on the nature of the knowledge itself (2nd level). When knowledge is tacit, the risk of spillover is smaller than in the case of more codified knowledge. Tacit knowledge rests in people and only spills over in close interaction between them. On the other hand, when tacit knowledge does spill over, the possibility of freeridership rises as the use of tacit knowledge by the freeriding firm, is (more) difficult to monitor. Codified knowledge spills over rather easily by means of documents, blue prints, information systems and so on. On the other hand, its use by the freeriding firm is more easy to monitor. Also the rate of change in the knowledge base determines whether others have the ability to absorb the knowledge (Cohen and Levinthal, 1990; Nooteboom, 2000). In the case of a high rate of change of knowledge, recipient firms need time to be able to absorb new knowledge but then it may have become obsolete already. So, a high rate of change lowers the possibility of knowledge spillovers. In addition, appropriability conditions may condition knowledge spillovers as well. The possibility of using patents puts limits on the use and imitation of knowledge by others. Or when appropiation takes place by means of complementary assets (Teece, 1986): when the absorbing firm does not control these, the knowledge it absorbs may be rather useless, even when there is cognitive proximity. Again we claim that 3rd level institutions can reinforce or limit the risk of knowledge spillovers and thus influence whether freeridership may occur. These are the following elements: direction of the relation and density of the network structure.

Direction of the relation, in the case of horizontal relations, firms may often be direct competitors. When knowledge spillovers are enhanced, from the type of knowledge and/or appropriability conditions, and no governance mechanisms are in place, freeridership may become a likely phenomenon. Using a contract may be a way to prevent this, but its limits have already been discussed. An alternative may be evasion by keeping knowledge secret and by avoiding close interaction and specific investments (Nooteboom, 2000). Another option is integration which may be very effective in controlling spill-over but may also prove to be (very) expensive; not only the direct costs of acquisition but also the actual integration into the mother-firm. In the case of vertical relations, the direct risk of knowledge spillovers such as in horizontal relations, may be limited. However, the risk may here be more indirect: when a customer or supplier (depending on the position one occupies) also has a relation to a direct competitor of yours, knowledge can spill over to that competitor and may lead to freeridership. Or, alternatively, when the supplier or customer decides to forward/backward integrate he becomes a direct competitor and the relation turns from a vertical into a horizontal one.

Density of network structure, the potential for knowledge spillovers and the chance of freeridership is further conditioned by the density of the network structure. In Chapter 2 ('3rd level institutions'), we defined density as the number of ties that are present as a proportion of the total possible number of ties (Knoke, 1999). In the case of a non-dense network there are few relations among firms, which limits possibilities to cross the cognitive distance present in the network and hence to the development of a common understanding. This will constrain room for spillovers as a common infrastructure facilitating such spillovers, such as technical standards or a shared (technical) language, may be lacking. From a governance-perspective, such a network does not accommodate the build-up of social capital such as the functioning of social norms, social control, sanctions, trust and reputation mechanisms. This limits the possibilities for the control of opportunistic behaviour by others. So, if knowledge does spill over in a non-dense network structure, there is a high chance of freeridership. A dense network structure entails many relations present in the network and as such enables to cross cognitive distance that exists among the involved firms, accommodating for knowledge spillovers. From a governance-perspective, such a network also facilitates the functioning of social norms, reputation mechanisms, trust and sanctions and so on, which enable to control opportunistic behaviour by others. So, when knowledge spillovers occur in a dense network structure, there is a limited chance of acts of freeridership. Figure 3.3 summarizes our argument.

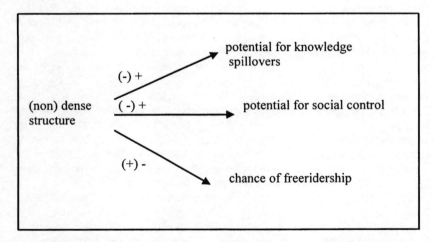

Figure 3.3 Relation between network density and the potential for spillovers, social control and freeridership

Obviously, possibilities for monitoring knowledge spillovers are largely determined by the nature of knowledge. When knowledge is codified, observability is generally easier than in the case of tacit knowledge. Codified knowledge may be easier to specify in a contract that can be used to prevent acts of freeridership. From the formal nature of such an arrangement follows that compliance is enforced by the legal system (Grandori and Soda, 1995). When spillovers are not clearly observable, it depends on whether social norms, control and reputation play a role prominent enough to compensate for a lack of formal enforceability.

RELATIONAL RISK IN DIFFERENT LEARNING REGIMES

Based on our analysis of relational risk and the way in which it is conditioned by the institutional environment, we will now integrate it into our concept of a learning regime, as developed in a section of Chapter 3 ('Learning regimes: a competence perspective').

Our analysis of relational risk has made clear that four elements are relevant in interfirm learning: cognitive closeness, spillovers, possibilities for freeridership and chance of hold-up. When following our earlier archetypical differentiation between two learning regimes with a focus on exploration or exploitation, the added elements of relational risk have the following values, as outlined in Table 3.2.

Exploration, in an exploration-oriented learning regime the cognitive distance among firms will in general be large. This large cognitive distance limits the potential of spillovers. This is further reinforced by the fact that knowledge is primarily tacit in this learning regime and can only spill over in close interaction between people, by poaching of key-people or by a take-over. On the other hand, when knowledge does spill over, its tacit nature makes it difficult to monitor such spillovers and also to observe its use by the absorbing firm. This opens up possibilities for freeridership. As argued in section 'Relational risk conditioned by the institutional environment', firms need to make specific, cognitive investments that increases the chance of hold-up. When cognitive distance among firms lowers, due to their joint searching activities, knowledge becomes more generic to the network, increasing the potential for spillovers but lowering the possibilities for freeridership. In general, knowledge becomes more codified that enhances spillovers but also enables to monitor its use by the absorbing firm.

Exploitation, in an exploitation-oriented learning regime the knowledge base is codified and more widely diffused across the network that makes cognitive distance among firms low or fairly moderate, enabling a medium to high level of spillovers. Among firms within the same network, chances of hold-up are small as the cognitive distance among firms is generally small(er) so that specific, cognitive investments will also be limited. In addition, the fact that knowledge is more widely diffused across the network also makes that specific investments can be recouped in relations with a larger number of partners. At the same time, from a viewpoint of outsiders, knowledge is specific to the network that makes cognitive distance with such outsiders large(r), creating a high(er) chance of hold-up in relations with them. However, due to a drive to larger scale and the presence of standards in exploitation there may be specific investments needed in production facilities, distribution channels, brand names and so on, with a long economic life. This may then create a potential for freeridership and/or hold-up, but now for non-cognition related reasons.

Table 3.2 Archetypes of learning regimes from a competence and governance view

COMPETENCE VIEW	EXPLORATION	EXPLOITATION
Learning object	new knowledge base	specific elements of existing knowledge base
Learning process	expansive searching	repetitive activities
Actors	new combinations of actors	existing combinations of actors
Input	- insights into limits existing knowledge base - new capabilities	refined problem solving capabilities
Output	- new knowledge base - new ideas and beliefs - demo's, experimental products	- strengthened knowledge base - product adaptations - process improvements - technical norms
GOVERNANCE VIEW		
Cognitive distance	medium to large	low to medium
Potential for spillovers	small to medium	medium to high
Potential for freeridership	- low if limited spillovers - higher if ample spillovers	- cognition related: low-medium - non-cognition related: potentially high
Chance of hold-up	- high if high specific investments - low if low specific investments	- cognition related: low inside network; high outside network - non-cognition related: potentially high

Dynamic view of a learning regime, as argued, these two types represent archetypical forms of a learning regime and reflect a static view. Obviously this does not reflect reality. As it entails learning, a learning regime is by its nature dynamic, in two senses. Firstly, there are dynamic relations among the elements making up a learning regime. One or two of the elements can change while the learning regime remains by and large the same, or alternatively, more elements change leading to a change of the learning regime. For example in an exploration-oriented learning regime: a large cognitive distance limits the potential of spillovers but may give rise to possibilities for freeridership and may increase the chance of hold-up. When cognitive distance lowers, due to explorative learning, the potential for spillovers increases, opportunities for freeridership lower as do chances of hold-up. In this way, a learning regime can change in nature and turn into another type of learning regime. In terms of the archetypical forms described above, from exploration to exploitation and vice versa. Secondly, there is a dynamic relation between a learning regime and the institutional environment in which it is embedded: changes in the level of the institutional environment affect a learning regime whereas outcomes of a learning regime can also affect the institutional environment. Such dynamic aspects of learning regimes and the dynamic relationship with the institutional environment will be the topic of Chapter 4.

NOTES

1. This relates to a discussion on the analytical gap between governance perspectives and competence perspectives and the need to connect them (Williamson, 1999; Nooteboom, 1999d and 2000; Dosi and Marengo, 2000).
2. From the point of view of the central actor this may seem to be an advantageous situation but this does not always need to be the case. In the 1980s Japanese *keiretsu* networks tended to be closed. It used to be common practice that suppliers had dedicated assets and knowledge of which the use exclusively accrued to the large central firm. Increasingly these large Japanese firms have become aware of the necessity of learning, also among their suppliers. For this reason, Toyota has decided to allow these suppliers to use these assets in other markets in order to stimulate knowledge sharing and learning. In this case the central actor, for its own sake, opened up the network in order to stimulate spillovers by exposing its dependent suppliers to different practices (Grabher, 1993).
3. In our discussion above we have focused on how the characteristics of the knowledge base determine the level of specific investments. The level of investments also depends on one's absorptive capacity. If knowledge is close to one's core competence, absorption will be easier than when it entails a completely new field. Absorptive capacity may also benefit from a large R&D-capacity. When the knowledge involved is highly codified, it may be raised by maintaining R&D in areas outside the focus of the firm. As found by Granstrand, Pavel and Pavitt (1997), this explains the empirical phenomenon that firms continue to engage in some R&D activity in areas that they have outsourced. When knowledge is more tacit, the hypothesis is that absorptive capacity is raised by cumulative experience in communicating and interacting with agents who think differently (Nooteboom

and Gilsing, 2002). The level of absorptive capacity though pertains to the firm level. As our focus is on the network level, this issue of absorptive capacity will be further left out of the analysis.

4. Co-evolution of institutional environment and learning regimes

Research Question 3: what are the outcomes of interfirm learning and how do they affect the institutional environment?

INTRODUCTION

In Chapter 2 we identified the various types of institutions that are relevant for interfirm learning, followed by an analysis in Chapter 3 of how they condition this learning. In this chapter we will build on this by discussing the main outcomes generated by interfirm learning and how these outcomes again affect the institutional environment. So, the focus of this chapter is on the dynamic relation between the institutional environment and learning regimes. This differs from the dominant approach taken in the literature on learning and innovation in which the institutional environment is often considered as exogenous; assuming that institutions determine the learning and innovation patterns in an industry (Pavitt, 1984; Dosi et al., 1988; Nelson, 1993; Whitley 1994 and 1999; Malerba and Breschi, 1997; Mowery and Nelson, 1999). This reflects a rather deterministic stance with a clear focus on processes of selection. We consider that to be too limited when developing a dynamic understanding of learning and innovation in SSIs as it ignores that outcomes of such learning and innovation can also affect the institutional environment. Hence a dynamic analysis implies that we not only analyse how selection processes take place but also how this relates to the generation of variety and how this variety affects selection again.

Given the importance we attach to variety, we take a special interest in the outcomes of interfirm learning. An innovation is an important outcome of a learning process but there are other relevant outcomes as well. Following our social constructivist view of knowledge (as including perception, understanding and value judgements), we argue that learning outcomes are formed by new knowledge, new ideas, changed beliefs, adapted or newly created institutions, changes in the design of the network structure and adaptations to coordinating mechanisms. So, we explicitly take also such non-technological outcomes into the analysis.

To study this dynamic interplay between the institutional environment and a learning regime, we will make use of a co-evolutionary approach. Co-evolutionary inquiry attempts to predict how variables in the system respond to changes in other system variables or in changes to the structure of the system itself. The goal of co-evolutionary inquiry is to understand how the structure of direct interactions and feedback within systems gives rise to their dynamic behaviour (Baum and Singh, 1994). When describing this process of co-evolution, we run the risk of describing all possibly relevant institutions that would make such a description overcomplete. We refer to what we argued earlier about conceptualizing the notion of an institution as a process of institutionalization (Chapter 2) in order to free ourselves from the need to identify all different types of institutions that may have relevance under all conditions. So, when analysing this co-evolutionary process, we will mention those institutions, which are relevant at a certain point in this process and leave aside those that are not.

As a way to structure this further, we propose to use the concept of the 'cycle of knowledge' as developed by Nooteboom (2000), which describes a heuristic of discovery. It starts from the notion developed by March (1991) that evolutionary survival depends on the trade-off between exploration and exploitation. Exploitation is required for survival in the short term and involves the efficient utilization of existing resources and competencies. Exploration is required for survival in the long term and involves breaking away from continuity, standards and existing routines. This cycle is supposed to apply to all levels: of people, organizations and innovation systems and intends to explain the difference between radical and incremental innovation; between second order and first order learning; between exploration and exploitation (Nooteboom, 2000), see also Figure 4.1.

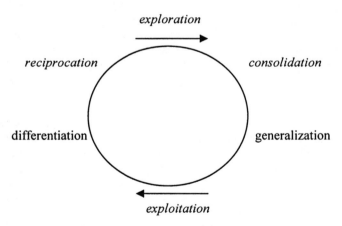

Figure 4.1 Cycle of knowledge (Nooteboom, 2000)

Following the logic of this cycle, we will analyse the co-evolutionary process in three steps:

- In exploration
- Towards exploitation
- Back towards exploration.

In the last section we will summarize by means of four hypotheses.

EXPLORATION OF NOVEL COMBINATIONS

A radical innovation starts with breaking away from an established way of doing things. Such an event is often initiated by a technological discontinuity, which often marks the beginning of a newly emerging knowledge base. This embryonic knowledge base is highly tacit and often located at a local firm level, bound up in specific assets and people (Nelson and Winter, 1982). The search process is highly empirical as opposed to more rational and driven by technological opportunities rather than demand (Stankiewicz, 2002).[1] In this search process firms often need to rely on other firms in order to exchange knowledge and establish connections with complementary knowledge or assets. Another reason for collaboration is to spread and share risk.

In making use of knowledge held by others, both existing ties and new ties are important. The advantages of existing, strong ties lie in their cognitive closeness and trust, which help to exchange and complement newly emerging, largely tacit knowledge, in so far as available in established fields of practice such as for example the use of existing distribution channels or suppliers of raw materials for new products. On the other hand, during the phase of exploring novel combinations, the new knowledge base requires novel linkages with 'outsiders'. These weak ties may give access to other networks and as such form an important source of diversity (Granovetter, 1985). This connects with innovation theory those opportunities for learning which increase when firms come from different cognitive backgrounds (Dosi and Marengo, 2000). However, when cognitive distance is (too) large, chances of misunderstanding increase, which lowers the potential for learning (Nooteboom, 2000).

In the relations with these weak ties cognitive distance is large, and trust still needs to be built up. For this, firms need to make specific investments in mutual understanding (not only of knowledge but also of new organizational procedures and people) and the building of trust. At this stage, the network structure will be dense, small and locally embedded, more or less operating in seclusion. In view of novelty and tacitness of knowledge, ties are generally characterized by mutual openness and frequent interaction on a variety of issues, ranging from technology, organization and potentially also future market demand, the availability of competent suppliers and so on. Specific investments may be needed to build up mutual absorptive capacity and relation-specific trust. However these investments have a short economic value, and thereby require only limited duration of relations. In such networks informal relations may also play a substantial role. Skilled people such as engineers or scientists may have informal ties to one another, which facilitate also the spill-over of firm-specific, tacit knowledge (Dahl and Pederson, 2003).

Concerning forms and instruments of governance, we already noted in Chapter 3 that formal contractual safeguards are problematic in innovation. As a result, the more radically new exploration/innovation is, the more one can only use more informal instruments such as relation-specific trust, and transfer of reputation. Due to the specific and tacit nature of knowledge in this phase, monitoring the input and contribution of the involved firms is only possible by means of close interaction among a limited number of people. Therefore, the size of these newly forming exploration networks is generally small. While risks of hold-up are limited due to limited specific investments, the generally high mutual openness in knowledge sharing on various issues yields a potential risk of spillover. However, this risk is limited by the high degree of tacitness of knowledge, in exploration, and the fact that knowledge may have changed before it can be used for competition.

Whereas firms within these exploration networks may grow cognitively closer due to their explorative learning activities, cognitive distance between these networks may be large, creating a compartmentalized structure among the various exploration networks. This makes the generation of collective action difficult, which further reinforces this compartmentalized structure. Such exploration networks may operate in relative isolation from established networks because the existing institutional environment can be highly selective and may hamper this variety generation processes, for two reasons. One has to do with vested interests. Firms occupying a central position in these existing networks, and whose interests are threatened, may try to undermine the legitimacy of the new technology (Aldrich and Fiol, 1994). They may try to block new entrants so that novel combinations may not be further explored. A second reason has to do with the fact that an innovation has to prove itself first before the existing institutional environment will be prepared to make the investments needed for adopting it. Especially when knowledge is systemic, the effects of the new finding can be highly disruptive so that the costs for adaptation may become substantial. In other words, the benefits of novelty should outweigh the costs of change.

To the extent that the exploration of novel combinations 'violates' institutions in the existing institutional environment, it needs to find a niche outside the reach of these established institutions, in 'allopatric speciation' (Eldredge and Gould, 1972; Nooteboom, 2000).[2] The exploration of new knowledge may then only continue when the 'heroic, Schumpeterian entrepreneur' keeps on pursuing his vision and ignores this selection by the existing institutional environment. Within these developing exploration networks a new learning regime emerges, characterized by expansive searching with the new knowledge base as its primary object of learning. Increasingly it becomes clear who is participating, what are the new aims and purposes and which new combinations of resources are required. Coordination of these searching processes is generally light and takes place by means of direct communication and social coordination and control mechanisms that increasingly function as selection mechanisms of who gets access to the newly forming network (Rosenkopf and Tushman, 1994). In addition to social norms, some first tentative, shared concepts and technical norms may also develop. These reduce cognitive distance, thereby improving mutual understanding among the directly involved firms and hence enabling further learning. In addition to social and technical norms, other outcomes are formed by all kinds of demos, experimental products as well as new (technical) standards, new procedures and new interorganizational routines. So, outcomes from this new learning regime mainly affect the new knowledge base, and other internal institutions, rather than outside structures and institutions.

In general it is difficult to appropriate, and knowledge changes rapidly. By the time a new product has been developed commercially, the knowledge it represents may have become obsolete already, making customers less willing to pay a premium or to make specific investments. It may then be more rational not to go for full appropriation but rather to stay connected with one's exploration network and to 'live and let live' in order to keep up to date with the rapidly changing knowledge base. So, in this phase of exploration, competition is no real issue and demand is hardly present.

Exploration: summing up, exploration is characterized by volatility or 'chaos' of experiments in multiple directions, without clear criteria for selection. The newly emerging institutional environment is highly embryonic and consists of a (very) few selection forces at this moment in the cycle. Variety abounds in this phase as many explorative learning processes result in all kinds of ideas, prototypes and demos, few of which are ready-to-market products or processes. So, variety is especially formed by learning results and mainly consist of new knowledge that is highly tacit and very specific to a limited number of firms. In terms of our 3-level model of the institutional environment (Figure 2.1), there is a strong feedback to the newly emerging knowledge base (2nd level) and selection by this knowledge increases over time.

In terms of our 3-level model of the institutional environment, we can define exploration now as follows:

- Main selection comes from the newly emerging knowledge base
- Limited selection by coordination mechanisms such as social norms and reputation
- Variety abounds and mainly affects the new knowledge base.

Schematically:

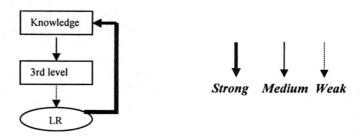

Based on the above analysis of the co-evolutionary process in exploration, we can formulate the following hypotheses.

Hypothesis 2a: In the phase of exploration of novel combinations variety abounds, there is little selection by the newly emerging institutional environment and feedback by outcomes of a learning regime mainly affects the development of a new knowledge base.
Hypothesis 2b: Novelty in exploration originates in allopathic speciation, at the periphery of the existing network where selection from the centre is less strong.

TOWARDS EXPLOITATION: CONSOLIDATION AND GENERALIZATION

Based on the testing and some first use of newly developed products and demos, insights into potential application areas grow. Increasingly, firms start to focus on trying to develop demand in order to match the newly emerging knowledge base to potentially new markets. As a consequence, the new knowledge gains in cognitive legitimacy (Aldrich and Fiol, 1994). Still, the absence of a dominant design constrains the broad diffusion of knowledge. Over time different paths of development may emerge, leading to a potential break-up into different networks developing along different paths. Hence outside competition, in a race to establish a market standard, may begin to emerge (Mowery and Nelson, 1999).

In the emergence of novel networks, novel strategic targets, and novel supply chains, a new institutional environment also starts to emerge. This institutional environment gets more and more a selection character: the involvement of demand and the combination of social and technical norms increasingly direct the searching activities and in doing so, delineate the boundaries of the new knowledge base. As a consequence, exploration of novel combinations slows down and variety decreases as outcomes of the learning regime such as newly generated ideas, knowledge and products increasingly need to fit into the emerging selection environment. The rate of change decreases and knowledge becomes more widely diffused across a larger number of firms. This enlarges possibilities to recoup earlier made specific investments as more potential partners become available now. As cognitive distance decreases and the codification of knowledge increases, knowledge spillovers become a more common phenomenon within the growing network of involved firms.

Consolidation takes place when a 'dominant design' is selected (Abernathy and Utterback, 1978). Dominant institutional selection forces are the knowledge base, demand and appropriability conditions (Malerba and Breschi, 1997). When the new knowledge base has substantial public benefits, government involvement can also have a substantial selective effect (McKelvey, 1997).

The effect of a dominant design on interfirm learning is substantial. It involves the establishment of a new paradigm and entails a common understanding of selected problems and the general search direction for appropriate solutions (Dosi et al., 1988). It is in this clarity provided by a dominant design and in the elimination of competing standards that stability is created. Firms find guidance in identifying required resources and competencies on which they can base further learning activities (Stankiewicz, 2002). As a result, the rate of change of the knowledge base slows down, uncertainty decreases and standardization becomes now a central issue. A learning regime becomes confined to the selected boundaries of the knowledge base and it mainly focuses on incremental improvements.[3] In defining such improvements, demand plays an increasingly important role (Stankiewicz, 2002).[4,5] Competition intensifies and generally provides incentives to focus on cost reductions. Firms that cannot compete on price or that have not adopted the dominant design drop out.[6] So, the institutional environment has become highly selective and provides numerous incentives to engage in interfirm learning processes aimed at strengthening and formalizing the dominant design. With this, standards based on which new knowledge can be assessed are selected. The knowledge base becomes predominantly codified, diffuses more widely and turns into a collective asset (Malerba and Breschi, 1997).

Due to increased competition on price, there is a need to utilize economies of scale, and this opportunity arises since, due to decreased uncertainty on the part of customers, the market has enlarged. As a result, there is increase of scale, a shakeout of producers, and resulting concentration. In addition, there is an increase in specialization that makes relations entail more specific knowledge on a narrower range of issues. This drive for efficiency requires the elimination of redundant relations, yielding a less dense network structure. Reduced uncertainty and codified, diffused knowledge on a narrower range of issues enable the specification of contracts and the monitoring of compliance. This favours the use of contracts, with less relation-specific trust, which enables more arms-length, less personalized relations. This, together with a less dense structure, enables a larger size of the network. In other words, attention shifts to new forms of organization to enable efficient production and distribution, for exploitation of the new paradigm, and to respond to increased price competition due to novel entrants joining the bandwagon. Hence a division of labour arises, regulated by formal contracts with built-in incentives to follow the dominant design, which further reinforces this organizational form. All this contributes to the emergence of a dominant design of organization for production and of supply chain structures, to yield 'dominant organizational logics' (Bettis and Prahalad, 1995), and 'industry recipes' (Spender, 1989). Important characteristics of this dominant organizational form are that, in general, relations among firms become more hierarchy and authority based. Also durability of relations increases as specific investments are made, other than specific cognitive investments, such as in specialized machinery, storage facilities, specialized employees and so on. Coordination mechanisms enhance integration such as planning and control systems, (formal) procedures, and standard modes for problem solving, information systems and so on. In other words, new organizational institutional arrangements arise, next to a new technological paradigm (Freeman and Perez, 1989).

As a result, variety decreases and mainly consists of adaptations to standardized products, (formalized) social norms, newly formed industry associations and collectively defined issues. So, the focus of a learning regime here is on the efficient exploitation of existing resources and competencies that results in incremental, order-creating (technical) change. Critical (technical) issues are defined collectively, legitimate procedures are established and common norms and values emerge from the learning regime. Actors that reinforce these issues become more prominent such as standards bodies, professional societies and industry associations (Rosenkopf and Tushman, 1994).

After the emergence of dominant designs in technology and organization, and adapted institutions, networks no longer need to hide in seclusion and local embedding, since they are now legitimized. Networks get dis-embedded from local environments and will tend to extend their markets internationally, for both inputs and outputs. This expansion is facilitated by new transmission and retention routines and procedures for problem solving, standards bodies, professional societies and industry associations. This expansion to new contexts of application is called the stage of generalization.

Exploitation: Summing up

The institutional environment provides incentives to transmit and retain the dominant design in the learning regime. This manifests itself by strong selection forces such as demand, competition, formalized control systems, technical standards and so on, allowing for incremental improvements. In terms of our 3-level model of the institutional environment (Figure 1, Chapter 2), we can define exploitation as follows :

- A strong selection by 2nd level institutions such as competition and demand
- A strong selection by 3rd level institutions such as social norms and/or formal control
- Limited feedback of learning outcomes to the institutional environment

Schematically:

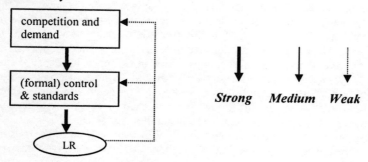

Based on the above analysis of the co-evolutionary process from exploration towards exploitation, we can formulate the following hypotheses.

Hypothesis 3a: In consolidation selection by newly formed 2nd level institutions such as the knowledge base and demand has become strong, whereas selection by 3rd level institutions is emerging.
Hypothesis 3b: The increasing selection by 3rd level institutions manifests itself by an emerging dominant organisational form that enables a division of labour.
Hypothesis 4: In the phase of exploitation there is a strong selection by the existing institutional environment with limited feedback by outcomes of a learning regime.

TOWARDS EXPLORATION: DIFFERENTIATION AND RECIPROCATION

The phase of exploitation is generally characterized by a strong drive to achieve further economic growth based on the existing knowledge base and learning regimes. Scale effects are enabled by the fact that essential transmission and retention mechanisms are highly institutionalized by means of technical norms, formalized procedures for problem solving, standards bodies, professional societies and industry associations. In this respect, a competitive position has been built up and further growth may be obtained by the application of the dominant design in different contexts. This leads to the phase of differentiation: the application of the dominant design into a context that, although related, is different from the context from which it originates.[7] The application of the knowledge base in these different contexts often requires adaptation to demand and institutions of that context. Especially when knowledge is systemic, adaptations can become more complex when complementary (non-technological) processes also need to be adjusted in order to make the dominant design fit into the new context. In that case, knowledge needs to be embedded in local tacit knowledge. However, such incremental adaptations, in differentiation, may turn out to be insufficient. They do not further improve efficiency but rather create additional complexity, adding extra costs. This is an important event as now insights develop into the limits of the existing dominant design and its dominant mode of organization, providing a rationale for more radical change. Through these insights seeds for a new path of exploration are sown and as a result, uncertainty increases and instability is created.

To explore the new opportunities then requires the break-up of the existing learning regime and the opening up of the existing, densely connected network structure towards outside ties.[8] Such outsiders, coming from another context, may dispose of knowledge on 'solutions' to the identified limits of the knowledge base. It may turn out that in some respects these local practices perform better in the novel context, so that one tries to incorporate such elements in imported practices, or indeed adopts local practices while incorporating elements from the existing dominant design. This is the phase of reciprocation.

Moving to reciprocation requires the dominant organizational form to be adapted before new knowledge can be adequately accessed and locally absorbed. So, a process starts that forms the mirror image of the process that occurred earlier towards exploitation, after the establishment of a dominant design. There, the new dominant design led to the emergence of a dominant organizational form. Here, the entrance of outsiders to the existing network ensures that the dominant organizational form is changed first, before the dominant design can be adapted. So, towards exploitation selection of the dominant knowledge base, at the 2nd level of the institutional environment, leads to selection of the dominant organizational form, at the 3rd level. Towards exploration, variety in this dominant organizational form, at the 3rd level, creates variety in the existing knowledge base, at the 2nd level. Hence the phase of reciprocation marks the transition from selection to variety as the main driving evolutionary mechanism, at different levels of the institutional environment. At the 3rd level of the institutional environment, variety is formed by an opening up of the dominant organizational form towards outside sources of knowledge, resulting in a mix of strong and weak ties. At the 2nd level, variety is formed by ideas about directions for new exploration, originating from insights into limitations of the existing knowledge base and dominant design. The most important learning outcome of this 'reciprocal learning' is the insight that for a full utilization of the adopted practices a more fundamental restructuring is required. This provides indications for the integration of elements from various practices into a novel combination.

Based on the above analysis of the co-evolutionary process from exploitation towards exploration, we can formulate the following hypotheses:

Hypothesis 5a: From differentiation to reciprocation the insights into the limits of the existing knowledge base strongly affect the 3rd level and 2nd level of the institutional environment.

Hypothesis 5b: From differentiation to reciprocation the dominant organisational form opens up towards outside sources of knowledge, resulting in a hybrid structure of strong and weak ties.

This analysis of this process of institutionalization provides us with insights in how the co-evolution of network structures, interfirm learning processes and changes in the institutional environment takes place. We have described how the actors by means of their interaction in these interfirm learning processes, socially (re-) construct the institutional environment. In addition, we have described how the interfirm learning processes are facilitated and constrained by the institutional environment and how the outcomes of these learning processes, in various degrees, again affect the institutional environment.

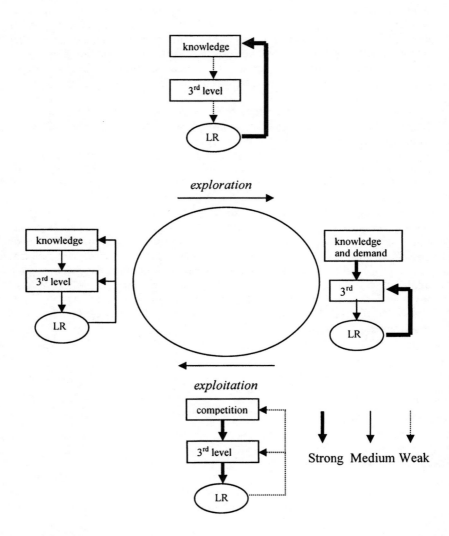

Figure 4.2 Schematic relation between cycle of knowledge and institutional level model

SUMMARY: FOUR HYPOTHESES

In this chapter, we have described the co-evolutionary process between institutional environment and learning regimes based on the cycle of knowledge. Following Figure 4.2, we can summarize our analysis of this co-evolutionary process by developing the following hypotheses:

Hypothesis 2a: In the phase of exploration of novel combinations variety abounds, there is little selection by the newly emerging institutional environment and feedback by outcomes of a learning regime mainly affects the development of a new knowledge base.

Hypothesis 2b: Novelty in exploration originates in allopathic speciation, at the periphery of the existing network where selection from the centre is less strong.

Hypothesis 3a: In consolidation selection by newly formed 2nd level institutions such as the knowledge base and demand has become strong, whereas selection by 3rd level institutions is emerging.

Hypothesis 3b: The increasing selection by 3rd level institutions manifests itself by an emerging dominant organizational form that enables a division of labour.

Hypothesis 4: In the phase of exploitation there is a strong selection by the existing institutional environment with limited feedback by outcomes of a learning regime.

Hypothesis 5a: From differentiation to reciprocation the insights into the limits of the existing knowledge base strongly affect the 3rd level and 2nd level of the institutional environment.

Hypothesis 5b: From differentiation to reciprocation the dominant organizational form opens up towards outside sources of knowledge, resulting in a hybrid structure of strong and weak ties.

These hypotheses describe the co-evolutionary process between institutional environment and learning regimes in a general way. How this co-evolutionary process manifests itself in a particular SSI is dependent upon SSI-specific institutions. Therefore we have not mentioned all possibly relevant 2nd and 3rd level institutions as these will differ per type of SSI.

NOTES

1. This context of exploration closely resembles the concept of a 'discovery-driven' technological regime, characterized by a strong focus on learning-by-doing in which serendipity plays a keyrole (Stankiewicz, 2002).
2. In general the new knowledge base will for a substantial part be based on scientific knowledge. In this respect, such a secluded niche may be formed by universities

and governmental institutions that can act as important incubators of radical new technology (Stankiewicz, 1990; Duysters, 1995).

3. Learning becomes, what is referred to in the literature on organisational learning, 'single loop'. Single loop learning aims to optimise within existing structures and is primarily concerned with the identification and correction of errors (Argyris and Schon, 1978, 1996).

4. This context towards exploitation resembles the concept of a 'design-driven' technological regime, characterized by a well-structured search process that is more focused on demand-driven, incremental improvements and efficiency (Stankiewicz, 2002).

5. With regard to the role of demand, Carlsson stresses that in upscaling an innovation to a mass-market, users should dispose of sufficient 'receiver competence', i.e. the ability to understand its added value to them and to use it (Carlsson, 1997; Carlsson and Eliasson, 2003).

6. At the same time, the strong focus of most (large) firms on dealing with the mass market may create niches of more sophisticated demand that opens up potentially attractive opportunities for specialized (smaller) firms. In the literature this phenomenon is also referred to as a process of 'niche-elaboration' (Pianka, 1978).

7. This connects with the notion of 'local search' as mentioned by Nelson and Winter (1982). Local search reflects the idea that firms search in related areas with which they are familiar instead of totally unrelated areas. Underlying this is the idea of the relative inertia of firms, as advanced by population ecologists such as Hannan and Freeman (1984) that firms are better at doing more of the same than at adapting to change.

8. As argued, this analysis of the co-evolutionary process pertains to a sectoral level. In other words, it is not said that all firms present in a SSI will make such a shift as conjectured here, on the contrary. In general, incumbent firms are characterized by (strong) inertia that prevents them from changing, due to sunk costs in specialized equipments, personnel and so on. It is found that even under such conditions of change as considered here, incumbent firms may even increase investments in the existing knowledge base and dominant design rather than absorbing signals that point to the relevance of new, outside knowledge (Porter 1990, 1998).

5. Implications of the co-evolutionary process

Research Question 4: what are the implications of the co-evolutionary process for firms with regard to the configuration of networks, the properties of interfirm relations and coordination mechanisms?

INTRODUCTION

Following our nested view of the institutional environment as developed in Chapter 2, changes in the 2nd level of the institutional environment have implications for 3rd level institutions formed by network structure, relational properties and coordination mechanisms. In addition, outcomes of a learning regime can also affect these 3rd level elements of the institutional environment. So, as analysed in Chapter 4, changes in 3rd level institutions can occur through selection by the institutional environment or through variety generated by outcomes of a learning regime. This chapter therefore focuses on the implications of the co-evolutionary process for network structure; the properties of the relations making up this network and the way these relations are coordinated.

This chapter is built up as follows. The next section discusses various concepts and insights on social networks as advanced in the social network literature. The third section deals with the need for trade-offs in a network when balancing a competence view and a governance view, and how these trade-offs vary with the environmental context. Based on this we discuss the implications of the co-evolutionary process for the optimality of the network structure, relational properties and coordination mechanisms. To do so, we differentiate between a setting of exploitation in section 'Exploitation' and next 'Exploration'. Admittedly, this distinction is sharp, which is on purpose in order to clarify our argument. Of course, in practice the long-term continuity of firms depends on how they combine both these processes instead of focussing on either one of them (March, 1991; Nooteboom, 2000).

SOCIAL NETWORKS

The focus of this paragraph is on social networks. We start with a brief review on networks as developed in innovation theory. Then we turn to the literature on social networks as we discuss the contributions of three influential scholars, namely the work of Granovetter, Coleman and Burt. Next we discuss the importance of the joint consideration of density and strength of ties in order to develop a more in-depth understanding of networks that has relevance from a learning and innovation perspective.

Notions on Networks from Innovation Theory

One of the key messages from innovation theory is that learning and innovation take place within networks of firms and non-firm actors (Lundvall, 1988, 1992; Grabher, 1993; McKelvey, 1996; Carlsson, 1995; Oerlemans, 1996). So, networks are considered as important by innovation scholars although a systematic analysis and understanding of networks is lacking. When differentiating between various types of networks, the general distinction is made between densely connected networks, loosely coupled networks and open networks. But a systematic comparison of the strengths and weakness of each of these forms in the context of the learning and innovation has not been made. So, insights into the question under which conditions networks should have more integrated or more disintegrated structures tend to be underdeveloped. In this respect, it comes as no surprise that suggested solutions to solve hindrances in learning and innovation processes are quite general and often refer to the abstract notion of 'interaction' or 'system connectivity' (Malerba and Breschi, 1997; Lundvall and Borras, 1997; Edquist, 1997). Obviously, interaction plays a key role in interactive learning but we consider this too general a statement. As our analysis in Chapter 4 has made clear, interaction and learning differ considerably in the various phases of the co-evolutionary process and also varies with different types of networks and with different combinations of coordinating mechanisms. The agreement on the importance of networks notwithstanding, these notions are underdeveloped in the literature on learning and innovation. For a deeper understanding of networks we need to turn to the social network literature.

Social Network Theory

Networks and relations among actors are the primary object of analysis in social network theory. In this paragraph we discuss the contributions of three influential scholars in particular, namely the work of intensive, frequent and possess informational resources which one already has. Strong ties produce and are governed by relational trust and norms of mutual gain and reciprocity, which grow through a history of interactions (Rowley et al., 2000; Lesser,

2000). Granovetter associated these strong ties with a dense network structure. In view of the debate among Granovetter, Burt and Coleman, each of their considerations lead to different conclusions with respect to the optimal network structure. As we will argue, the question is not who is right, but who is right under which conditions.

Granovetter: the distinction between strong and weak ties was introduced by Granovetter (1973). Strong ties are formed by relations which are frequent and intense interaction between many actors, much of the information circulating in the system is redundant. Weak ties are formed by relations with persons one is loosely connected to. As they operate in different networks, weak ties offer the advantage of providing access to different information. So, in theory, the more weak ties one has, the wider scope of accessible information. Still, neither type is preferred as both have different qualities and it depends on the conditions which of the two a firm may favour (Rowley et al., 2000).

Burt (1992) focuses on the efficiency of networks and stresses that there are costs associated with maintaining contacts. According to Burt an efficient network structure is characterized by non-redundant contacts and brokerage opportunities. It is not considered rational to increase the number of linkages within an existing network as, according to Burt, redundant contacts carry the same information. Therefore, firms should aim to have non-redundant contacts that are complementary and do not overlap, so called structural holes. Structural holes are 'disconnections between players in the arena' and provide opportunities for information access, timing, referrals and control. In this way, competitive advantage is explained as a 'matter of access to holes' (Burt 1992: 2). A strategic actor can build efficiency into its network by acting as a bridging tie, that is an actor who connects structural holes. Such a structure minimizes redundancy, thereby creating brokerage opportunities and access to different kinds of information. In this respect Burt made a clearer conceptual separation between the strength and the density of ties than Granovetter. It is the dense structure, apart from the strength of ties, which yields redundancy, when the aim is access to new knowledge. In dense networks one needs to expend many resources on the maintenance of ties (even if they are weak), while there is a high chance that ties in this dense structure carry the same information and hence form 'redundant contacts'. So, efficiency can be obtained from maximising the nonredundancy of contacts so that time and energy are saved for developing new contacts to unconnected people (Burt, 1992). In doing so, access can be created to valuable information held by unknown others.

Coleman (1988) relates the structure of a network to the level of social capital which can emerge between network actors.[1] On the relationship between social structures and social capital Coleman (1988) comments as follows: 'All social relations and social structures facilitate some forms of social capital; actors establish relations purposefully and continue them when they continue to provide benefits. Certain kinds of social structure, however, are especially important in facilitating some forms of social capital' (p. 329). In this respect Coleman points at the benefits of dense networks for their potential with regard to the build-up of social capital.[2] This social capital is not only built up of information but also facilitates the functioning of norms and sanctions, which may form effective ways to coordinate a relationship. Social norms on how to behave 'properly' can be highly prescriptive and deviating from them may be unattractive due to reputation effects, which are generally strong in dense networks (Coleman, 1988; Grandori and Soda, 1995). In this way social capital functions as a social control mechanism to pre-empt firms from opportunistic behaviour (Grandori and Soda, 1995; Rowley et al., 2000). Betrayal becomes more costly as it not only affects the relation with the trustor but, through reputation mechanisms, also the relations with other ties (Coleman, 1988).

Who is right under which conditions? Unlike their universalistic tone, the considerations of Granovetter, Burt and Coleman lead to different conclusions with respect to the optimal network structure. Granovetter stresses the importance of weak ties in order to increase the potential scope of accessible information. Burt stresses the importance of efficiency and proposes a structure rich in structural holes, spanned by 'middle actors' who have ties to unconnected alters. Both the considerations of Granovetter and Burt clearly refer to the competence side of relations. Coleman (1988) proposes a dense structure that enables the build-up of reputation and social capital, in the form of trust and social norms. These considerations have relevance from a governance-perspective of relations. So, it seems that there is no such thing as a universally optimal network structure. Due to the strong focus on structural elements of networks such as centrality, density, structural equivalence, structural autonomy and so on (Knoke and Kuklinski, 1982; Wasserman and Faust, 1994), the identification of relevant conditions and how they influence the structure and functioning of networks has generally been ignored by social network theorists. This is increasingly being acknowledged, among others by Coleman who stated that 'social relationships that constitute social capital for one kind of productive activity may be impediments for another (Coleman, 1994: 177). Also Burt (1998) suggests that his view is not necessarily contradictory to Coleman's as networks and social capital are valuable for different populations and purposes. Recently some studies have tried to shed more light on this and have indicated that the optimality of the network structure is indeed dependent upon the environmental context (Rowley et al., 2000; Ahuja, 2000; Duysters and Hagedoorn, 2003). In line with this, we argue that the context has profound implications for how a network is structured and how it functions in view of a division of labour among its members. Hence the optimality of the network structure is liable to be a function of the context. Before further elaborating on that, we analyse two characteristics of networks more in-depth as this enables us to develop a more profound understanding of networks that is relevant in the context of learning and innovation. This will be further examined in the next section.

Density and Strength of Ties

In this sub-paragraph we focus on two characteristics of networks that are important when developing a more in-depth understanding of networks from a learning and innovation perspective: the density of ties and the strength of ties. In doing so, we deviate from the insights as advanced by social network theorists in two ways. Firstly we argue that, unlike the discussion in social network theory, the understanding of the optimality of the network structure benefits from a joint consideration of density and strength of ties. Secondly, we argue that we need to differentiate between different dimensions of strength of ties as networks can vary in different dimensions of tie strength, depending on the context. We will discuss both issues in turn now.

Joint consideration of density and strength, the discussion on the importance of the strength of ties (Granovetter) versus the density of ties (Burt) is not so relevant from a learning and innovation perspective. We argue that in such a context the understanding of the network structure benefits from a joint consideration of the strength of ties and the density of ties. To further substantiate this we need to differentiate between cognitive variety and cognitive distance. Cognitive variety refers to how many different individual cognitive frameworks are present in a network, cognitive distance refers to the difference between any of them (Nooteboom, 1999b). The density of ties is relevant as it indicates the potential for cognitive variety present in a network. A large number of ties present in a network, as a percentage of the total possible number, provides the possibility of having access to many different types of knowledge held by others. Depending on the cognitive distance between these different frameworks, ties need to vary in strength in order to cross this distance. So, the strength of ties is relevant as it indicates the potential to absorb this knowledge.

Strength of ties, to further specify this relation between the strength of ties and the potential to absorb outside knowledge, we need to differentiate between different dimensions of strength. As recognised by Granovetter, the strength of ties entails a linear combination of amount of time, emotional intensity, intimacy (mutual confiding) and the reciprocal services, which characterize the tie (Granovetter, 1973: 1361). So, next to the amount of time, the combination of emotional intensity, intimacy and reciprocal services provide a good indication of the strength of the relation, especially in personal networks. In this respect, these four dimensions have a general meaning when developing an understanding of the strength of ties. However, in a context of learning and innovation these dimensions of strength are too general and require a more detailed elaboration. So, these four dimensions need to be adapted, which we will do by combining a competence and a governance perspective. We propose the following four steps. First we propose to keep the amount of time and will refer to this as the duration of the relationship. This is relevant from both a governance and competence perspective. The duration of the relation is important to recoup specific investments made in the relationship that are needed to develop a common cognitive framework. Second we propose to adapt emotional intensity to intensity in terms of frequency of contacts. The level of frequency indicates the potential for the transfer of tacit knowledge and thus the chance of spillovers. A high level of frequency enables an easy transfer of tacit knowledge and thus a high chance of spillovers, whereas a low level of frequency decreases the potential of the transfer of tacit knowledge and may thus prevent spillovers. Third we propose to adapt intimacy or mutual confiding to openness, that is the willingness to share knowledge in view of mutual learning as well as in view of relevant relational risks of spillover and legitimation. Our fourth step deals with reciprocal services, that deals with the level of 'give-and-take' in shared activities. This is a more slippery notion and may lead to misinterpretation. In this respect, we observe that Granovetter's first three dimensions basically refer to the properties of the ties, whereas this dimension of reciprocal services may also provide an indication of the relational content of ties. Such a more explicit indication of relational content may have relevance from an innovation point of view. As argued, in the case of systemic knowledge firms need to operate in a more or less orchestrated fashion that may require interaction on many elements. A stand-alone knowledge base allows for more leeway, and interaction on fewer elements may be needed. Hence for the understanding of the strength of ties some indication of the relational content seems to be relevant. We therefore propose to adapt reciprocal services to the breadth of the relational content, by which we mean the extent to which the relation between firms deals with a wide or narrow scope of issues. This is also relevant from a governance perspective as a wider scope generally provides more potential for spillovers than a more narrow scope.

Bringing in the context, following the discussion above, networks can differ in their combinations of density and strength of ties. Our central argument now is that the optimality of any combination is dependent on the context in which the network is embedded. In Chapter 3 we made the general distinction between a context of exploration and of exploitation. Our dynamic analysis in Chapter 4 made clear that from exploration to exploitation the main co-evolutionary processes are standardization and routinization, within a context of increasing stability. Organization theory then informs us that under such conditions, more integrated organizational structures are the preferred mode of organization (Lawrence and Lorsch, 1967). As we will argue in section 'Exploitation', this enhances integration and tighter forms of coordination, largely coinciding with a non-dense structure of strong ties. From exploitation to exploration, the main co-evolutionary processes are characterized by experimentation and deviation from existing standards and routines within a context of (increasing) instability. According to Lawrence and Lorsch (1967), to deal with such conditions requires more loose organizational structures. As we will discuss in section 'Exploration', this enhances disintegration and more loose and informal forms of coordination, largely coinciding with a dense network structure built up of ties with low strength. We will further analyse this more in-depth by relating the combination of density and strength of ties to the context of exploitation and exploration. Before doing so we first discuss the need for trade-offs in a network when reconciling a competence perspective and a governance perspective.

Combining a Competence and a Governance Perspective

As discussed in Chapter 3, our concept of a learning regime integrates a competence view with a governance view. In this paragraph we build on this analysis by analysing how the environmental context of a network conditions the various trade-offs between these two perspectives. The environment creates uncertainty with which firms need to cope in terms of hazards, restrictions and demands put on them and on their network. In this respect, we introduce the notion of a 'network strategy', which we define as 'those decisions and actions that firms need to make in order to balance a competence and a governance perspective in view of environmental uncertainty'.

To further elaborate on this, we differentiate between three types of environmental uncertainty: complexity, variability and dependency.

Environmental uncertainty: complexity, generally speaking, uncertainty due to complexity arises from accomplishing a difficult task. It may, for example, stem from a systemic knowledge base. In general, such a knowledge base requires standards on the interfaces as well an (basic) understanding of adjacent technology areas, creating complexity. In that case other firms are needed and the basis for a network emerges. To reduce uncertainty due to complexity, in the case of systemic knowledge, the design of the network structure should be so that relations are durable and (partially) exclusive. Such a network structure of strong ties then offers two advantages to reduce complexity. It accommodates efficient and quick coordination, and it enhances knowledge spillover (also tacit) that furthers mutual learning and understanding.

Environmental uncertainty: variability, uncertainty due to variability arises from changes in the institutional environment such as for example change in demand or the advent of a new technology. In general, changing conditions in the environment requires the entrance of outsiders to the network. These outsiders give access to other networks with different cognitive perspectives and may form an important source of diversity (Granovetter, 1973). And this diversity is needed when dealing with variability in conditions. So, when uncertainty due to variability increases, relations with weak ties enable to cope with change.

Environmental uncertainty: dependency, engaging in a network for the purpose of learning and innovation creates dependency, on strong ties and on weak ties. This dependency yields relational risk, which again influences possibilities for learning. As argued, a dense network structure in the case of a systemic knowledge base reduces uncertainty due to complexity. But it also creates dependency on these strong ties. The network configuration as described above (durable, dense and exclusive relations) also offers two advantages to cope with dependency. First, it allows for recouping specific investments, which are made to grow cognitively close, and as such prevents hold-up. In addition, it allows for the build up of social capital, which also puts limits on freeridership. However, there is one big drawback of such a network structure, which is its inability to cope with uncertainty due to variability. The accumulated social capital of a network of strong ties may then turn into lock-in (Arthur, 1989; Nooteboom, 2000) or social liability (Uzzi, 1997; Gargiulo and Benassi, 1999; Leenders and Gabbay, 1999). Weak ties are now needed but also create dependency on them.

Network strategy, in sum: a network strategy deals with combining a competence and a governance perspective in view of environmental uncertainty. More specifically we argue that, within an evolutionary context, a network strategy needs to fulfill three functions based on the three types of environmental uncertainty. Table 5.1 provides a schematic overview.

Table 5.1   Types of environmental uncertainty and related function of network strategy

TYPE OF ENVIRONMENTAL UNCERTAINTY	FUNCTION OF NETWORK STRATEGY
Complexity	Coordination
Variability	Adaptation
Dependency	Safeguarding

A network strategy should fulfil these three functions by crafting a mix of coordination mechanisms that matches the three types and varying levels of environmental uncertainty. Obviously, these three separate functions do not need to be congruent; on the contrary, they may conflict. Each function pursues different objectives and hence selects different coordination mechanisms. So, in developing a network strategy, there are trade-offs to be made. These trade-offs are contingent upon the institutional conditions in which a network is embedded. As said we make a general distinction between two types of contingencies, namely an exploitation setting and an exploration setting.

EXPLOITATION

In this paragraph we discuss the implications of an exploitation setting for the optimality of the network structure in terms of density and strength of ties. Based on that we discuss an appropriate network strategy in such a network. We finish by summarizing and by formulating three hypotheses.

Non-dense Structure of Ties Strong in Durability

As argued in Chapter 4, a setting of exploitation is characterized by standardization and routinization, creating stability with some incremental change. Dominant designs have emerged, and technological and market uncertainty have decreased. Here, considerations of efficiency are crucial, since competition has shifted to competition on price, with new entrants in the emerging market. Due to increased competition on price, there is a need to utilise economies of scale, and this opportunity arises due to decreased uncertainty on the part of customers: the market has enlarged. As a result, there is an increase of scale, a shakeout of producers, and resulting concentration. A learning regime develops with a focus on refining existing innovations and improving existing competencies. As analysed in Chapter 4, this requires a search-process that is well structured around a limited search space. As a consequence, there is an increase in specialization so that relations entail more specific knowledge on a narrower range of issues. These requirements for information and the search-process are better obtained from strong ties (Granovetter, 1973). More precisely, ties are generally strong in terms of durability as this enables the continuous search for and development of specific information and knowledge around selected topics. Furthermore, investments shift to large-scale production, distribution systems, and brand name, which are all long-term. The drive for efficiency requires the elimination of redundant relations. This yields a less dense structure. The increased codification of knowledge furthers diffusion without the need for relation-specific investments of mutual understanding. This enables a less dense structure, since now one can identify what competencies are and will remain relevant, who has those competencies, and who is likely to survive in the industry. The increased competitive pressure narrows the potential for trust and creates a need for contracts. At the same time, reduced uncertainty and more codified, diffused knowledge on a narrow range of issues enable the specification of contracts and the monitoring of compliance. As a consequence, ties show generally lower strength in terms of frequency of contacts, mutual openness and breadth of relational content.

Potential benefits and risks of a non-dense structure of ties strong in durability, following the discussion above, such a non-dense network of ties which are strong in terms of durability enable members to specialize in a specific task so that they only need to coordinate with their immediate, direct ties. The long-term and frequent interaction between these strong ties result in a limited cognitive distance among firms so that this exchange of context-specific, tacit knowledge can indeed take place efficiently.[3] Such a network structure enables a clear separation of tasks in a stable division of labour. This presupposes though a high level of centrality in this network by one or a few members. Only the presence of such a central firm can ensure that the activities in the various parts of the non-dense network are coordinated and integrated in a stable way. In this respect, a non-dense network of strong ties is highly efficient as knowledge can reside within specialized firms and coordination can take place by one or a few firms in the core of the network. Furthermore this makes it possible to take a structured approach to innovation, generally resulting in incremental adaptations. From a governance-perspective, the advantage of durable ties lies in the possibility to recoup specific investments that are made in view of specialization and the development of specific knowledge on a narrow range of issues. Obviously, there are also risks associated with this network structure. From a competence perspective there is a chance of overload from the side of the central firm. Its coordination role makes that all information generated in the various parts of the network move through it. Especially in the case of a high level of complexity, large bodies of information and knowledge may be generated that cannot be handled by the central firm alone. Another risk is that such a network may not be capable enough to deal with (radical) change. Due to the high level of centrality of the core firm, knowledge and information cannot move freely so that their rapid recombination may be inhibited. This requires more direct ties among the various members that would increase density and turn this network into a more densely connected network of strong ties. In addition, interaction of high frequency over a long(er) period of time decreases the cognitive distance that lower the potential for innovation, creating a risk of lock-in (Arthur, 1988) or inertia (Nooteboom, 2000).[4] Risks from a governance-perspective relate to both freeridership and hold-up, especially from the side of non-central members in the network. Due to its central position the core firm may occupy a powerful position. As a result, it may be tempted to freeride on the efforts of the dependent, non-central members. In addition, it may force these members to make specific cognitive investments as well as other forms of specific investments such as dedicated assets, human, physical, site-specific and so on. This creates a potential problem of hold-up on the side of non-central members. Table 5.2 summarizes our argument.

Table 5.2 Potential benefits and risks of a non-dense network of ties strong in durability, in exploitation

	COMPETENCE PERSPECTIVE	GOVERNANCE PERSPECTIVE
POTENTIAL BENEFITS	- functional specialization - efficiency	possibility to recoup specific investments
POTENTIAL RISKS	- low potential for rapid recombination of knowledge - lock-in	- hold-up - freeridership

Network Strategies in Exploitation

We now further analyse how to balance a competence perspective and a governance perspective when developing a network strategy in a setting of exploitation. Obviously, these trade-offs are also firm specific and in this respect dependent on firm-specific characteristics such as such a firm's position in the network structure, firm specific knowledge and capabilities, its ambitions with regard to innovation, etc. As argued, the individual firm level is beyond the scope of our research and we therefore confine ourselves to the possible set of options for network strategies and the trade-offs among them from which firms can choose.

In a setting of exploitation, as argued in Chapter 4, uncertainty due to complexity is fairly low due to a more codified and widely diffused knowledge base. Compared to exploration, the rate of change is much lower resulting in low(er) uncertainty due to variability. In addition, initial weak ties have turned into ties that are strong in terms of duration. So, environmental uncertainty in exploitation is fairly low and dependency mainly rests in relations with strong ties. These general environmental characteristics lead to the following trade-offs among network strategies.

The codification of knowledge and the presence of (technical) standards make it possible to monitor and value both inputs as outputs by other firms, lowering possibilities for freeridership. The coordination function favours a network strategy of contracts, which outline specific mechanisms such as personal communication, decision and negotiation procedures, planning and control systems, information systems and so on. Contracts may increasingly be complemented by relational contracts, which mirror informal understandings and habits (Smith Ring and van de Ven, 1994). Such contracts are also desirable from a safeguarding perspective as they lower possibilities for freeridership. A further advantage of relational contracts is that they allow for flexibility and low set-up costs (Nooteboom, 1999b).[5] Such a network strategy of formal contracts and informal, relational contracts enhance the need for coordination, safeguarding as well as for adaptation. In this respect, the three functions are mutually reinforcing. Although an important assumption here is that interests converge.

When interests diverge, uncertainty due to dependency rises and a different situation develops. Conflict of interests requires coordination by means of formal, obligational contracts (Grandori, 1997). However, when contracts are too detailed they may signal distrust (Nooteboom, 2000), which is undesirable from a safeguarding perspective. In addition, they limit flexibility and hence do not allow for adaptation. Also from a coordination perspective, detailed contracts can bring disadvantages. More tacit parts of the knowledge base are difficult to monitor and value, thus putting limits on the possibility for input and/or performance control by means of contracts. In that situation, realignment of objectives by means of (partial) integration may be an option (Grandori, 1997), enhancing both coordination and safeguarding. However, for adaptation this option may be less attractive as it creates a potential for hold-up as well as social liability.

Relevance of Burt's structural holes argument, in such a network, Burt's recommendations to create or improve efficiency are especially relevant. Given the small cognitive distance in this network there is a high chance that strong ties carry the same information and hence form 'redundant contacts'. Given the costs associated with maintaining contacts, Burt suggests that firms can create efficiency in the network by disposing of such redundant contacts and selectively maintain relations with a limited set of firms. In this respect, Burt's suggestions are adequate in an exploitation setting, at least as a general strategy in structuring a network.[6] More specifically then, the question becomes who should be selected and who should be disposed of by reaching him through others. Burt proposes to 'minimalise information-redundancy among contacts' as the primary design and selection principle. This implies that those contacts that are well informed and provide access to other, information-rich networks should be selected. Although understandable from a viewpoint of improving efficiency, Burt's theory does not give any guidance from a competence-perspective nor from a governance-perspective: in how far is the central actor who spans a structural hole sufficiently competent, now and in the future, and in addition, can he be trusted? To assess this may again require relations with the actors who were initially disposed of and who are now reached through this central player. In general, insights into who and how to select for cooperation is a fairly unexplored issue in the literature.

Summary and Hypotheses

Towards exploitation the main co-evolutionary processes are standardization and routinization with a focus on improving existing competencies and the search for context-specific knowledge. Under such conditions a network is selected of low density and of ties that are strong in terms of durability but show lower strength in terms of frequency of contacts, mutual openness and breadth of issues covered. This combination of density and tie strength means that firms can develop a deep understanding of selected topics in view of incremental innovations. A network strategy aimed at integration and coordination takes place by contracts and other formal control mechanisms, possibly complemented by 'relational contracts' that are reflected in the use of more informal mechanisms such as reputation, trust-in-intention and social norms. A risk of such a network is a heavy inward-looking orientation that blocks renewal, resulting in lock-in.

We can now rephrase these conclusions in terms of our evolutionary approach by means of the following hypotheses:

Hypothesis 6a: In exploitation the institutional environment will select non-dense networks of ties that are strong in durability but show low(er) strength in terms of frequency of contacts, mutual openness and breadth of issues covered.
Hypothesis 6b: In exploitation the institutional environment will select coordination mechanisms that enhance integration such as contracts and formal control mechanisms, possibly complemented by informal mechanisms such as reputation, trust-in-intention and social norms.
Hypothesis 7: A potential risk of such a network is a heavy-inward looking orientation that results in lock-in.

EXPLORATION

In this paragraph we discuss the implications of an exploration setting for the optimality of the network structure. Based on that we discuss an appropriate network strategy in these types of networks. We finish by summarizing and by formulating three hypotheses.

Dense Structures of Ties with Low Strength

As argued in Chapter 4, a setting of exploration is characterized by a shift away from established routines and competencies so that existing knowledge and proven practices become less relevant. So, a learning regime develops characterized by a constant search for new information on many potential alternatives. Such an exploration setting poses an important challenge for firms. On the one hand firms need to develop an in-depth understanding of the newly emerging field whereas on the other hand they need to keep a broad focus and maintain access to various possible options. Searching through its existing strong ties enables the firm to develop such a deep understanding but decreases chances for finding new information as cognitive distance in this network is limited. This implies the importance of different or new sources of knowledge outside this existing network through establishing linkages with weak ties (Granovetter, 1973). This connects with arguments made by various innovation scholars who stress the fact that different sources of knowledge outside a firm are critical for the innovation process (Lundvall, 1992; Carlsson, 1997; Malerba, 2002). In line with this argument we can make the conjecture that when environmental uncertainty due to variability increases, the need for weak ties becomes stronger. However, there is a maximum of weak ties that firms are able to handle, for two reasons. First, the time and resource obligations to strong ties puts a limit on the possibilities to create and maintain relations with weak ties (Rowley et al., 2000). A second argument is that too many weak ties may increase the chance of misunderstanding when cognitive distance among the various ties is (too) large (Nooteboom, 2000). Learning among heterogeneous actors can only happen when information and knowledge are transferred efficiently and when this knowledge and information can be retained (McKelvey, 1997), which requires some overlap in cognition.

So, an exploration setting requires weak ties although they should be seen in relation to the existing strong ties that firms have.[7] It is in the mix of strong and weak ties that firms can make new combinations of what is already known and what is new, yielding a dense structure. This connects with information theory, which argues that the chance for 'information noise' reduces while the demand for more exact information increases, when accessing multiple and redundant contacts (Shannon, 1957). In this respect, the existing strong ties facilitate triangulation among their multiple weak ties and thus better assessing the value of the obtained information and knowledge (Rowley et al., 2000). Following our contingency-argument, the 'desired mix' of strong and weak ties depends on the environmental context.

Potential benefits and risks of a dense network with low strength of ties, a network of high density indicates a high number of ties as a proportion of the total possible number of ties in a network. The existing ties needed for triangulation are mostly strong but especially the relations with new or weak ties are characterized by low strength, being generally non-durable with limited interaction on a few issues with limited openness. These weak ties give access to other networks and as such form an important source of diversity (Granovetter, 1985). The combination of high density and low strength indicates that there are many connections among different firms but for a limited period of time, with low frequency and possibly with limited openness and/or entailing a few issues. From a competence-perspective this brings the advantage of a rapid recombination of ties that enables an effective exploration of novel combinations. Especially in the case of a systemic knowledge base such a network offers the possibility of exploration through the rapid recombination of different technologies. From a governance-perspective it brings the advantage of a rapid transfer of reputation, especially with regard to competence rather than with regard to intentional trustworthiness. However, there are also risks associated with this network structure. From a competence perspective there are two potential risks. Recombining different types of knowledge through various weak ties may create a risk of misunderstanding when cognitive variety becomes too big. In addition, this process of recombination of knowledge may often require specific investments in order to make these different types of knowledge fit with one another. This is generally a more tacit process and requires some duration of the relation in order to recoup such a specific investment. When the strength of ties is too low in terms of durability then firms may show less inclination to engage in exploration that may negatively affect knowledge creation. As a consequence, from a governance perspective there is a risk of hold-up. When specific investments are made in the relation with weak ties, the generally short duration of the relation may prevent this investment from being fully recouped. As such this knowledge may possibly be used in relation with others to compensate for a hold-up problem but the rapid transfer of reputation in the network also puts limits on the possibility of such acts of freeridership. In addition, the rapid recombination of ties creates a (large) potential for knowledge spillovers although this will be conditioned by the level of codification of knowledge; the more codified, the higher this potential risk. Table 5.3 summarizes our argument.

Table 5.3 Potential benefits and risks of a dense network with a low strength of ties, in exploration

	COMPETENCE PERSPECTIVE	GOVERNANCE PERSPECTIVE
POTENTIAL BENEFITS	rapid recombination of knowledge	rapid transfer of reputation
POTENTIAL RISKS	- risk of misunderstanding - insufficient creation of new knowledge	- hold-up - potential for spill-overs

Network Strategies in Exploration

We now further analyse how to balance a competence perspective and a governance perspective when developing a network strategy in a setting of exploration. Obviously, these trade-offs are also firm-specific and in this respect dependent on firm-specific characteristics such as such a firm's position in the network structure, firm specific knowledge and capabilities, ambitions with regard to innovation, etc. As argued, the individual firm level is beyond the scope of our research and we therefore confine ourselves to the possible set of options for network strategies and the trade-offs among them from which firms can choose.

As analysed in Chapter 4, initially in exploration the newly emerging systemic knowledge base is highly tacit and cognitive distance among firms is large. The coordination function asks for direct mutual adjustment 'in real time' which requires coordination mechanisms such as direct personal communication, group problem solving and group decision-making. Relations should be durable and (partly) exclusive, both for reasons of coordination (to lower cognitive distance) as for reasons of safeguarding (to prevent hold-up). In addition, both functions require that the network size is kept limited: due to the specific and tacit nature of knowledge, its exchange (coordination) as well as monitoring the input and contribution of the involved firms (safeguarding) is only possible by means of close interaction among a limited number of people. The adaptation function requires low set-up costs and flexibility due to a high rate of change in exploration. This may favour more short-term relations but this may be undesirable from a coordination and safeguarding point of view. A solution could be to create additional relations with other weak ties to remain flexible: lateral relations by means of liaison roles and linking pin units, initially coordinated by transfer of reputation and trust-in-competence. This enlarges network size which may increase the chance that interests diverge. As argued, relations with weak ties may give rise to acts of freeridership and to prevent this, safeguarding prefers coordination by reputation on past performance and trust-in-intention, with the benefit of limited monitoring (Nooteboom, 2000). But in the relation with weak ties this trust cannot be built from scratch and needs to develop as the relation grows. Contracts only have a (very) limited use, especially in the early phase of exploration, as there is little known on the value of inputs and outputs. In addition, too many weak ties may generate social liability (freeridership and hold-up), which is undesirable for both coordination and safeguarding. This latter function may consider evasion but this may be undesirable again from an adaptation perspective as weak ties are needed to cope with (rapid) change. An alternative network strategy may be formed by mutual self-interest (e.g. non-equity alliance), although, only when interests with a weak tie(s) converge. When interests diverge and when knowledge is close to one's core competence, realignment of objectives by rearranging property rights may be more appropriate such as by means of joint-ventures and other equity-alliances (Grandori and Soda, 1997).

Relevance of Burt's structural holes argument, another question here is the relevance of Burt's recommendations for creating efficiency in a network. As argued, a setting of exploration with volatile and (highly) uncertain conditions means that existing knowledge and competencies become increasingly less relevant. The search-process is concerned with exploring which new technologies are most useful to invest in as much as with finding out who is capable and trustworthy in this new field, making selection of the right partner a difficult task. This applies especially in a Schumpeter Mark I regime in which a new technology breaks with the existing dominant design and in which non-incumbent firms form the primary driving force. As argued in chapter 4, variety in exploration originates in 'allopatric speciation' (Eldredge and Gould, 1972; Nooteboom, 2000), at the periphery of the existing network where selection from the centre is less strong. In such a setting, selecting those partners with vested interests in existing technologies and that, by spanning structural holes, occupy a central position in the network may then prove to be an unwise strategy. In this respect, as we have suggested, a more viable strategy is to build relations with different types of weak ties that bring in different cognitive perspectives as a basis for learning. In addition, we mentioned the importance of triangulation of different external sources of knowledge that is only possible through multiple, redundant contacts. So, in exploration redundancy should not be reduced but rather be considered as an inevitable phenomenon. This was confirmed empirically in a recent study by Hagedoorn and Duysters (2003) on networks of firms in the international semiconductor industry. From this study the authors concluded that firms in unstable environments had indeed benefited from learning through multiple, trusted contacts.

In conclusion: in a setting of exploration, access to new knowledge is more important than the most efficient route to that knowledge. In other words: it is important who you reach, not how you reach, which contradicts Burt's proposition that actors should optimize both these aspects of their network.

Summary and Hypotheses

Towards exploration the main co-evolutionary processes are characterized by experimentation, deviation from existing standards and the increasing obsolescence of existing routines. In such changing conditions more dense, redundant forms of networks are preferred of strong and weak ties that enable a rapid recombination of different types of knowledge ties as well as the triangulation needed for that. An appropriate network strategy is then formed by a combination of a rapid transfer of reputation, trust-in-competence and mutual self-interest.

We can now rephrase these conclusions in terms of our evolutionary approach by means of the following hypotheses:

Hypothesis 8a: In exploration the institutional environment will select a dense network structure of strong and weak ties as the dominant mode of organization.

Hypothesis 8b: In exploration the instituitional environment will select coordination mechanisms that enhance variety-in-cognition such as a rapid transfer of reputation, trust-in-competence and mutual self-interest.

Hypothesis 9: A potential risk of such a network is the possibility of misunderstanding that results in chaos.

NOTES

1. See for an overview of the literature on social capital Coleman, 1988; Leenders and Gabbay, 1999; Lesser, 2000.
2. Coleman mentions 'closure' as a specific structure of dense networks in which all actors are directly connected to one another.
3. This is confirmed by empirical research such as for example Uzzi's study (1996) on the New York apparel industry. He found that firms that were connected through strong ties were able to quickly exchange 'fine-grained' knowledge on products and market-developments.
4. Others have labelled this situation as 'overembeddedness' (Uzzi, 1997) or 'social liability' (Gargiulo and Benassi, 1999).
5. This flexibility is of a different order than flexibility within exploration. In exploitation flexibility refers to adaptations within the constraints of the existing knowledge base, accomplished by the existing network. Flexibility in exploration entails the creation of a new knowledge base which requires the creation of (totally) new networks.
6. See a longitudinal study by Ahuja on networks in the international chemicals industry for an empirical test and (partial) confirmation of these claims by Burt (Ahuja, 2000).
7. This issue seems to be a bit overlooked in the literature in which the choice for strong and weak ties is often approached in terms of 'either or'. An interesting attempt to jointly consider them is made by Rowley et al. (2000).

6. Methodology

INTRODUCTION

This chapter forms the pivot of our research in the sense that it discusses how we relate our theoretical concepts, as developed in the preceding chapters, to empirical testing. Therefore, the focus of this chapter is on the development of a sound methodology that enables us to arrive at scientifically accountable answers to our research questions. We start by discussing our hypotheses as developed in the preceding chapters. Next section, we formulate our basic methodological starting points. After that we discuss the implications of these starting points for our research design. Based on our research design we finally discuss methods of data collection and the operationalization of our key-variables.

STRUCTURING OUR HYPOTHESES

In this section we collect our hypotheses as formulated in earlier chapters in order to indicate their relation to our research questions. To do so, we refer to Chapter 1 where we concisely summarized what our research aims to do, namely:

- To identify systemic combinations of institutional environment and learning regimes. These systemic combinations are static and reflect a specific point at the cycle of knowledge.
- To identify the transition of those systemic combinations over time, as a movement along the cycle of knowledge.
- To identify and explain the implications of those transitions in terms of network structure, relational properties and coordination mechanisms.

As can be noted from this concise summary of our research, the first two elements aim to describe the systemic combinations of learning regimes and institutional environment as well as how they change over time. Based on this we then aim to identify and explain the implications of those changes for the combination of network structure, relational properties and coordination mechanisms. At this point it is important to discuss our interpretation of 'explanation' as there are some different interpretations in the literature. The more general interpretation is the deductivist model of explanation (Lawson, 1997). According to this deductivist model of explanation, the 'explanandum' (what must be explained) must be deduced from a set of initial and boundary conditions plus universal laws of the form 'whenever event x then event y'. Following this deductivist logic, explanation and prediction then become almost similar terms. Explanation entails the deduction of an event after its occurrence, prediction prior to its occurrence (Lawson, 1997). In this way explanation entails formal relations but not causal relations. In our study we follow a different interpretation of explanation. Our approach to explanation can perhaps best be formulated in terms of understanding why a specific combination of network structure, relational properties and coordination mechanisms develops. This entails an explanation that differs from the deductivist model in the sense that it aims to explain causal relations instead of formal relations. Our description of the systemic combinations of the institutional environment and learning regimes (the 1st element as formulated above) and the changes within them (the 2nd element as formulated above) should enable us to develop an understanding of the causal relations between the institutional environment and the embedded learning regime. The methodological implications of this combination of descriptive and explanatory research will be further discussed in Research Design.

We will now discuss how our hypotheses cover these three issues. In doing so, we keep to the general distinction that we made between exploration and exploitation, and categorize our hypotheses accordingly.

Exploitation-related hypotheses: our hypotheses that relate to exploitation are the following:

Hypothesis 3a: In consolidation, selection by newly formed 2nd level institutions such as the knowledge base and demand has become strong, whereas selection by 3rd level institutions is emerging.

Hypothesis 3b: In consolidation, the increasing selection by 3rd level institutions manifests itself by an emerging dominant organizational form that enables a division of labour.

Hypothesis 4: In the phase of exploitation there is a strong selection by the existing institutional environment with limited feedback by outcomes of a learning regime.

Hypothesis 6a: In exploitation the institutional environment will select non-dense networks of ties that are strong in durability but show low(er) strength in terms of frequency of contacts, mutual openness and breadth of issues covered.

Hypothesis 6b: In exploitation the institutional environment will select coordination mechanisms that enhance integration such as contracts and formal control mechanisms, complemented by informal mechanisms such as reputation, trust-in-intention and social norms.

Hypothesis 7: A potential risk of such a network is a heavy-inward looking orientation that results in lock-in.

These exploitation-oriented hypotheses are related to the three main issues of our research in the following way:

- To identify the transition of those systemic combinations over time, as a movement along the cycle of knowledge: hypotheses 3a, 3b, 4.
- The implications of those transitions in terms of network structure, relational properties and coordination mechanisms: hypotheses 6a, 6b, 7.

So, with regard to exploitation, we can say that hypotheses 3a, 3b and 4, covering the second issue, deal with the general pattern of co-evolution between institutional environment and learning regimes. The hypotheses 6a, 6b and 7 covering the third issue, deal with how this general pattern settles in network structures, relational properties and coordination mechanisms. Furthermore, the possibly negative consequences of hypotheses 6a and 6b are covered by hypothesis 7.

Exploration-related hypotheses: our hypotheses that relate to exploration are the following:

Hypothesis 1: When change in 2nd level institutions becomes more radical, there is an increasing need for weak ties to deal with this variability in conditions.
Hypothesis 2a: In the phase of exploration of novel combinations variety abounds, there is little selection by the newly emerging institutional environment and feedback mainly affects the development of a new knowledge base.
Hypothesis 2b: Novelty in exploration originates in allopatric speciation, at the periphery of the existing network where selection from the center is less strong.
Hypothesis 5a: From differentiation to reciprocation the insights into the limits of the existing knowledge base strongly affect the 3rd level and 2nd level of the institutional environment.
Hypothesis 5b: From differentiation to reciprocation the dominant organizational form opens up towards outside sources of knowledge, resulting in a hybrid structure of strong and weak ties.
Hypothesis 8a: In exploration the institutional environment will select a dense network structure of strong and weak ties as the dominant mode of organization.
Hypothesis 8b: In exploration the institutional environment will select coordination mechanisms that enhance variety-in-cognition such as a rapid transfer of reputation, trust-in-competence and mutual self-interest.
Hypothesis 9: A potential risk of such a network is the possibility of lack of selection that results in chaos.

These exploration-oriented hypotheses are related to the three main issues of our research in the following way:

- To identify systemic combinations between institutional environment and learning regimes. These systemic combinations are static and reflect a specific point at the cycle of knowledge: hypothesis 1.
- To identify the transition of those systemic combinations over time, as a movement along the cycle of knowledge: hypothesis 2a, 2b, 5a.
- The implications of those transitions in terms of network structure, relational properties and coordination mechanisms: hypotheses 5b, 8a, 8b, 9.

So, with regard to exploration, we can say that hypotheses 2a, 2b and 5a covering the second issue, deal with the general pattern of co-evolution between institutional environment and learning regimes. The hypotheses 5b, 8a, 8b and 9 covering the third issue, deal with how this general pattern then settles in network structures, relational properties and coordination mechanisms. Furthermore, our hypotheses are related in the following way: combining hypothesis 1 and hypothesis 5b leads to hypotheses 8a and 8b, of which the possible negative consequences are covered by hypothesis 9.

So, the three issues of our research are adequately captured by our hypotheses, both for exploitation and exploration.

METHODOLOGICAL STARTING POINTS

In this section we develop some methodological starting points, according to the following two steps. First we will discuss the dynamic relation that exists between our concepts of an institutional environment and a learning regime. This understanding then has implications for how the time dimension will be incorporated into our analysis, which will be considered next.

Dynamic interplay between institutional environment and institutionalized interfirm learning: as argued in Chapter 2, we follow the suggestions made by both Nelson and Sampat (2001) and Nooteboom (2000) to conceptualize the notion of an institutional environment as a process of institutionalizing. In doing so, we free ourselves from the need to identify all different and specific types of institutions, which may, to a greater or lesser extent, have relevance; not all institutions are relevant at the same time. So, we can actually mention those institutions, which are relevant at a certain moment in time and leave aside those which are not. A second implication by conceptualizing it as a process is that we can portray the institutional environment as a 'hierarchy of institutions' (Nooteboom, 2000). Some institutions are embedded in 'higher institutions' but at the same time embedding 'lower institutions'. Hence higher institutions select lower institutions, which can then be considered as the units of selection. These lower institutions again act as the selection environment for even lower institutions and finally for institutionalized behaviour that we have conceived of as a learning regime. Figure 6.1 schematically portrays this relationship between the institutional environment and a learning regime.

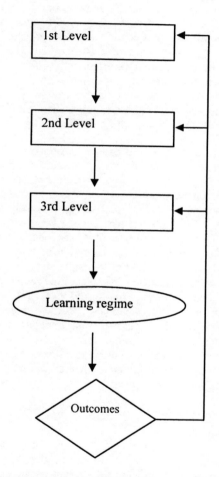

Figure 6.1 Schematic relation between institutional environment and learning regime

In this figure the rectangular boxes represent the various levels of the institutional environment. As argued, institutions at a higher level in the institutional environment select lower institutions and ultimately select upon a learning regime, as expressed by the S-arrows. The rectangle in Figure 6.1 represents our concept of a learning regime that generates a variety of outcomes, as portrayed by the toppled square box. These outcomes may again affect the institutional environment in varying degrees, as expressed by the F-arrows.[1]

When analysing this dynamic interplay between processes of selection and of variety generation, Archer's methodological principle of 'analytical dualism', as discussed in Chapter 1, is useful. It informs us on the importance of keeping the process of selection and the process of variety generation analytically separate and hence to make explicit whether causation is more attributable to the institutional environment (structural conditioning in terms of Archer) or to outcomes of a learning regime (structural elaboration in terms of Archer). To analyse then the dynamic interplay between institutional environment and learning regimes requires the careful treatment of time. So, for the purpose of our research the time dimension needs to be incorporated explicity.[2]

Incorporation of time: the effective incorporation of time in our analysis calls for a clear treatment of the past that requires studying sectoral systems of innovation in a longitudinal way. We do not aim to precisely identify at which point in time a process has started or ended. In the context of our research it is not very realistic that we can precisely identify such points in time, especially when studying past events. So, such a precise identification of specific points in time will be neither practically possible nor relevant for the purpose of our study. The incorporation of time is required insofar as it brings an understanding of the dynamic interplay between process of selection and variety generation. An exact time reconstruction would result in an overly detailed account. This would not fit with the purpose of our research as formulated in Chapter 1. As we argued, our interest is to understand the dynamic processes that generate aggregate learning and innovation patterns, rather than the development of a detailed understanding of the structure of a SSI and the networks within it at a specific point in time.

Based on these methodological starting points we now discuss the implications for our research design.

RESEARCH DESIGN

This section deals with the development of a design for the empirical part of our research. In order to develop this design we first distinguish among four basic forms of research, then discuss the choice of our research method and finish by the number of research units that we want to study.

Basic Research Form

The choice of the basic research form is largely determined by the available level of theory development of which four basic forms can be distinguished (Drew, 1980; Murdick and Cooper, 1982; Wijvekate, 1991):

1. Exploratory research
2. Descriptive research
3. Explanatory research
4. Testing research.

The less a problem has been researched, the more likely the basic research form is exploratory. Its primary analytical question is 'which variables are important to future research?'. When concepts, definitions, variables and research subjects have developed to some extent, the level of theory development is somewhat higher and the research may become more descriptive. Explanatory research can be conducted when a theory has become more substantial. This facilitates the selection of a number of independent variables which are expected to exert an explanatory effect on dependent variables. A set of explanatory studies may provide sufficient ground to conduct testing research where the primary analytical question then is how the dependent variables are related to the independent variables. The main difference with explanatory research is that a number of precisely formulated hypotheses are tested, often by using statistical techniques.

As it is our ambition to contribute to the development of a dynamic theory of interfirm learning, our research is especially of a theory-building nature. The question now is what is the level of development of our theory building.

Studying the dynamic relationship between institutional environment and learning regimes entails two multi-level issues: 1. the differentiation between an institutional environment and a learning regime and, 2. a hierarchical or nested view of the institutional environment as built up of different institutional levels. Multilevel theory entails a synthesis of various disciplines and hence requires to cut across various disciplines (Klein et al., 1999; Danserau et al., 1999). Especially research in the context of innovation and technological change may benefit from such a multidisciplinary approach (McKelvey, 1996). In this research we make use of the following 'theoretical lenses':

- The theoretical basis of our research is formed by evolutionary economic theory as developed by Nelson and Winter (1982)
- Concepts and variables as developed by the (National) Systems of Innovation literature (Lundvall, 1992; Nelson, 1993; Edquist, 1997; Malerba, 2002)
- Theories on learning (Argyris and Schon, 1978, 1996; Nooteboom, 2000)

- Social network theory (Granovetter, 1985; Coleman, 1988; Burt, 1992; Grandori, 1999)
- Theories on governance (Williamson, 1985; Nooteboom, 1999d, 2000; Grandori, 1997, 1999).

Using these theoretical frameworks implies that we do not start from scratch. Various concepts, definitions, variables, research subjects as well as methods of data collection and analysis are available from this variety of literature. So, our research cannot be considered as (fully) exploratory. On the other hand, using elements originating from different theoretical frameworks implies inconsistencies among them that does not make them readily available to our research. So, by crossing various theoretical boundaries, the level of theory development can certainly not be considered sufficient for rigorous testing either.

The aim of our research is to determine 'how the institutional environment conditions interfirm learning, how this changes over time and how this varies per type of sectoral system of innovation'. This indicates a descriptive basic form. By describing the dynamic interplay between the institutional environment and interfirm learning behaviour, we also attempt to explain why a specific pattern in this dynamic interplay develops. We then move from descriptive to more explanatory research. This is also what we intend as we want to develop an understanding of why a specific combination of network structure, relational properties and coordination mechanism emerges. In other words, by the description of the dynamic relationship between institutional environment and learning regimes we also attempt to explain how this dynamic relation settles in a specific combination of network form, relational properties and coordination mechanisms. So, the basic form of our research is descriptive with some clear explanatory elements in it.

Choice of Research Method

In general, basic forms of research correspond to certain basic research methods, as outlined by Table 6.1 based on van de Zwaan (1990: 44). The table is to be interpreted as a guiding tool in the choice of the research method and is only one of many possible classifications. Obviously, every research design has its own strengths and weaknesses, which should be considered jointly when choosing and crafting a particular research method.

From the table it follows that for a mainly descriptive research form with some explanatory elements a (longitudinal) case study is an appropriate research method. Such a research method based on case-studies is especially appropriate when the set of interactions among relevant variables is unclear (Eisenhardt, 1989; Yin, 1994). In this respect it is better to study a limited number of situations in-depth with a more generic model than using a (highly) specific model in which possibly relevant variables are absent (Swanborn,

1987). This brings us to four quality aspects, which are also relevant for a method based on case-studies (Swanborn, 1987; Yin, 1994).

Table 6.1 Affinities of basic research forms with research designs in the social sciences

Research Design	Basic Research Form			
	Exploratory	Descriptive	Explanatory	Testing
Experimental Research				
- laboratory			+	+++
- field			+	+++
Case study Research				
- momentaneous	+++	+	+	
- longitudinal	+	+++	++	
Comparative Research			++	
- momentaneous				
- longitudinal		++	++	++
Evaluation Research			+	+++
Simulation Research	++	++	+	+

First, construct validity relates to the question whether we measure what we intend to measure. So, operational measures have to be developed which assure that the variables cover the areas of interest correctly. This will be dealt with extensively in the section Data collection and analysis.

Second, internal validity is concerned with the verification of relations and causality among variables. To increase the internal validity one can make use of triangulation of data collection methods which entails combining various methods and data sources in order to compensate weakness of one method by the strength of another. Triangulation is especially useful when a research is aimed at theory-building (Swanborn, 1987) and in addition to provide stronger support for hypotheses and causality in case-studies (Eisenhardt, 1989).

Third, external validity deals with the generalizability of the conclusions. Generalizability is not a particular strength of a research method based on case-studies. At best, it can generate well-founded propositions. We will come back to this issue of generalizability in Chapter 9.

Fourth, reliability deals with a proper execution of the research and addresses two aspects. It relates to the question whether the same results would be obtained when the research is repeated. In addition, it relates to the question whether the same results would be obtained when the research is conducted by another researcher. How we deal with this issue of reliability, as well as with internal validity, will be dealt with in more detail in the section Level of aggregation and data collection methods, when discussing data collection methods and data analysis. An emphasis on reliability would require more effort per case-study which, given time constraints, may result in a smaller number of case-studies, negatively affecting generalizability. To increase generalizability one can choose to increase the number of cases and/or to make use of an embedded case-study containing multiple cases in it, if time and budget constraints allow. This then makes it possible to compare across cases which may lead to replication, enhancing generalizability. We will come back to this issue of generalizability in Chapter 9.

In acceptance of its limitations, our research method will be based on case-studies. Following the importance of the explicit incorporation of time we choose longitudinal case studies opposed to momentaneous case-studies.

Number and Selection of Case-studies

The number of case-studies and the way to select them depends on what we want to achieve. Our research aim stresses differences among SSIs. As argued in Chapter 1, we claim that interfirm learning is specific to a SSI. Hence our research questions focus on SSI specific institutions, insofar relevant for learning and innovation, and abstract from national institutions. By keeping the national context constant we can focus on differences among sectoral systems of innovation that enables us to verify the relationships among the relevant variables, enhancing internal validity. Furthermore, the criterion of internal validity indicates to study SSIs that are 'knowledge-intensive', so that assumed causal relations between the properties of the knowledge base and interfirm learning behaviour may be expected. So, we should select (at least two) different, knowledge intensive SSIs that are within the same national institutional context.

For the purpose of our study it is important to incorporate time into the analysis. Using triangulation for data collection methods implies that we will collect data by among others industry experts. But when relying on people's reflections and memory it is critical to study recent events. So, for reasons of construct validity and reliability, it is important not to go back too far in history.

Based on these considerations, we plead to study sectoral systems of innovation that show and have shown a (relatively) high level of dynamism with regard to interfirm learning and innovation within a limited period of time. In the context of the Netherlands two sectoral systems which clearly fit this profile are multimedia and biotechnology. Both these sectoral systems are known for their high innovation rate and for learning and innovation taking place in networks (Ministry of Economic Affairs, 1999; OECD 1999, 2001). Both sectoral systems are built up of numerous networks that engage in learning and innovation. In this respect, both contain multiple cases within them and may as such provide sufficient empirical 'feedstock' for the purpose of our research.

DATA COLLECTION AND ANALYSIS

This paragraph deals primarily with construct validity and reliability: our methods of data collection, the variety of data sources as well as the way in which we analyse those data. When discussing methods of data collection and analysis an important issue is the level of aggregation at which we want to study interfirm learning in the context of a sectoral system of innovation. Essentially, the purpose of study dictates the appropriate level of aggregation that subsequently dictates which data to collect and how to analyse those data. Therefore we will jointly consider the appropriate level of aggregation and data collection methods. Next we will discuss the operationalization of our key-constructs.

Level of Aggregation and Data Collection Methods

In the context of a SSI, the firm-level cannot always be considered as the most appropriate unit of analysis (Malerba, 2002). Depending on the purpose of analysis as well as the specific system under investigation, a higher or lower level may have more relevance. The purpose of our research is to study the dynamic interplay between the institutional environment and interfirm learning. If there is one central notion in our research it is that interfirm learning takes place in networks, suggesting networks should be the relevant level of aggregation.

Regarding the specific sectoral systems under investigation, multimedia and biotechnology, the following considerations are relevant. As explained in section Research Design, the argument for choosing these two sectoral systems of innovation relates primarily to the fact that both are characterized by substantial dynamism in terms of learning and innovation within a limited period of time. In fact, both sectoral systems involve the transformation of more traditionally defined sectors as by Mowery and Nelson (1999) into newly emerging sectoral systems of innovation. Such transformation processes clearly entail 'novel combinations' of previously distinct knowledge bases and is driven by newly forming links and dynamic complementarities among previously unconnected firms. In this respect, Malerba (2002) argues that a high level of aggregation is important in order not to miss out on things. In addition, in such uncertain and changing environments networks can be considered as the key organizational form in which interfirm learning takes place (Grabher, 1993; Lundvall, 1993; Grandori, 1999; Nooteboom, 2000). And it is through this learning that outcomes are generated that give rise to changes and transformation of a SSI.

Differentiating between sectoral level and network level: based on these considerations, we argue that the network level can be considered as the most appropriate level of analysis for our research. In addition, we differentiate between the network level and the sectoral level. We propose conceptualizing the relationship beween a SSI and interfirm networks as schematically depicted in Figure 6.2.

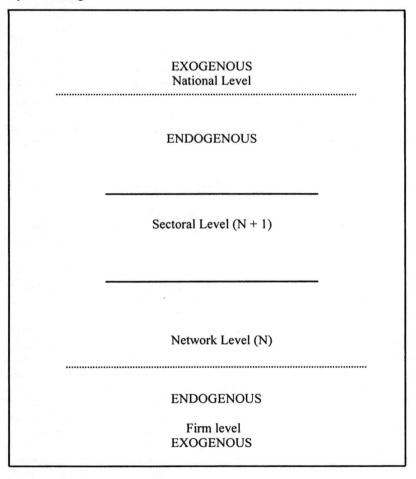

Figure 6.2 Different levels of aggregation

As can be understood from Figure 6.2, the network level can be considered as the relevant level of aggregation, corresponding to n. The sectoral level is considered as providing the institutional environment in which the networks are embedded, corresponding to $n+1$. This differentiation between the network level and sectoral level connects with our discussion in the section on the basic form of our research. As argued, the basic form is descriptive with some clear explanatory elements in it. Regarding the sectoral level we will take a descriptive approach that then enables us to explain on a network level why a specific combination of network structure, relational properties and coordination mechanisms is selected. So, following our methodological discussion earlier, we consider the network level and the sectoral level as endogenous. As a consequence, we consider both the national institutional environment and the individual firm level as exogenous.

Boundaries of a SSI: an other issue which we need to address here is how to determine the boundaries of a SSI. In this respect, it is relevant to mention two methods of identifying networks (Knoke and Kuklinski, 1982). A realist approach is based on the subjective perception of the involved actors. The identification of a network is determined by 'the limits that are consciously experienced by all or most of the actors that are members of the entity'(Knoke and Kuklinksi 1982: 22). A nominalist approach is based on the viewpoint of the researcher. Identification of a network is based on the application of his analytical framework used. As we clearly focus on a SSI, a sectoral system of innovation opposed to a sectoral system of production or distribution, we see learning and innovation as the relevant starting point for determining the boundaries of a SSI. More specifically, we consider the boundaries of a SSI to be determined by those interfirm networks whose relational content is made up of knowledge exchange, learning and innovation and given this, which parties are considered as relevant according to the involved actors. So, we take a two-step approach to identifying networks and the subsequent boundaries of a SSI: we start with a nominalist approach by only considering those networks with relevance from an innovation perspective, within these networks we study the relations among those firms that are considered to form part of such a network by the involved actors, which entails a realist perspective.[3]

Methods of data collection: given the breadth of information that we need, ranging from information on sectoral features, network characteristics and learning regimes, our primary source of information and data is formed by industry reports and studies. Given their (growing) importance to the Dutch economy, both industries have been extensively studied over the past 10–15 years. These studies were carried out by individual (scientific) researchers, specialised research institutes and consultancy firms. Clients of these studies ranged from the Dutch Ministry of Economic Affairs, the Dutch Ministry of Transport and Telecommunication, various industry associations, the OECD and others. Most of these reports cover (some of) the issues that we are interested in and, taken together, these reports enable us to draw an accurate picture of the co-evolutionary processes that have characterized both SSIs over the past 10–15 years. Using a variety of industry reports also enables to triangulate among them. Furthermore, we approach recognized industry experts with our analysis of the multimedia and biotechnology SSI. Their role is to check whether the analyses made are correct in terms of facts and completeness and may potentially come up with additional information. This combination of data collection methods enables us to triangulate between these two sources, which is important for internal validity and reliability.

For the analysis of the multimedia SSI in the Netherlands we have studied over 30 industry reports and around 15 articles in professional journals and newspapers, all of which have been published in the period from the early 1990's towards the early years of the new millennium. For biotechnology these numbers are 26 reports and 22 articles. Based on these reports and articles we have made an analysis of the evolution of both SSIs in the relevant period. Next we have asked recognized industry experts on multimedia or biotechnology to make a critical check on our analyses. For multimedia we have approached drs. Sven Malta and Pim den Hertog of Dialogic who have conducted numerous studies on the multimedia industry, both for various Dutch ministries and for the OECD (Paris).[4] For biotechnology we have approached Drs. Christien Enzing and Sander Kern of TNO-STB who have also conducted numerous studies on biotechnology for the Dutch ministry of Economic Affairs, the European Commission and the OECD (Paris).[5] Both groups of experts have read our analyses and have provided comments, most of which we have incorporated into our study. In addition, our analyses have been presented on various international conferences.[6] In addition, an earlier version of our analysis on biotechnology has been extensively commented upon by dr. Steve Casper of Cambridge University (UK), who has published widely on the biotechnology industry in among others Germany, the United Kingdom and the US.

The absence of reliable quantitative data sets on the exact number of firms and the properties of the relations among them in both multimedia and biotechnology means that we have to rely on this combination of qualitative data sources. This approach is in line with some of the recent work on SSIs that has been published by among others Maureen McKelvey, Luigi Orsenigo, Franco Malerba, Nicoletta Corrocher and others on behalf of CESPRI (Bocconi Univeristy, Milan).[7] Still, this makes an attempt to develop such quantitative data sets a worthwhile effort for future research as this would enable a more rigorous analysis of the sectoral and network dynamics in these two SSIs.

Operationalization of the 2nd level of the Institutional Environment

In this section we operationalize the various relevant variables in a qualitative way. Unlike quantitative data which can be recorded on a naturally occurring numerical scale, qualitative data can only be classified into categories

(McClave, 2000). Therefore we will make use of three categories of values which our variables may have, namely : low - medium - high.

First, we operationalize our variables of the 2nd level of the institutional environment. The variables of the 2nd level of the institutional environment consist of A. knowledge base, B. appropriability conditions, C. demand conditions and D. competitive conditions. Taken together, these variables form variables which, as a set, describe the 2nd level of the institutional environment.

A. Knowledge base:

- Level of tacitness (low, medium, high)
    - Extent in which knowledge is experience-based
- Level of codification (low, medium, high)
    - Extent in which knowledge is made explicit through documents, blueprints, standard operating procedures and so on.

We do not consider tacitness and codification as mutually exclusive variables, rather, we consider knowledge as consisting of varying combinations of both tacit and codified elements. We consider this mix to differ per type of SSI , per network within a SSI as well as to change over time.

- Level of diffusion within a SSI (low, medium, high)
    - A low level of diffusion indicates that knowledge pertains to a specific network of firms within a SSI
    - A high level of diffusion indicates that knowledge is widely shared among networks within a SSI.

- Level of systemicness (low, medium, high)
    - A low level of systemicness indicates that knowledge has a low degree of integration with different scientific and/or engineering disciplines
    - A high level of systemicness indicates that knowledge has a high degree of integration with different scientific and/or engineering disciplines. In this respect, the direction of the external sources is relevant:
        - Horizontal (competitors)
        - Vertical
        - Upstream (suppliers, academia)
        - Downstream (users, users of users).

- Rate of change (low, medium, high)
    - Level of cumulativeness of knowledge, that is extent in which there is serial correlation between innovations or more specifically, between interfirm learning activities; it represents the probability of innovating at

time *t+1* is conditional on innovations and interfirm learning activities at time *t* or periods before that.

B. Appropriability conditions:

- Level of appropriability (low, medium, high)
  - Extent in which innovation can be protected from imitation
- Means of appropriability
  - Secrecy
  - Accumulated tacit knowledge (e.g. learning curve)
  - Lead times
  - Complementary assets
  - Standards
  - Patents.

C. Opportunity conditions:

- Level of opportunity (low, medium, high)
  - Extent in which there are clear and powerful incentives for undertaking innovative activities
- Variety (low, medium, high)
  - Extent in which the opportunities are diverse or clearly defined
- Sources
  - Technology
  - Production
  - Demand.

D. Competitive conditions:

- Level of competition (low, medium, high)
  - Extent in which competitions is intense
- Origin of competition
  - Horizontal (i.e. competitors)
  - Vertical
    - Upstream (i.e suppliers)
    - Downstream (i.e. customers)
      - External (indication of 'group-based competition' cf. Gomes-Casseres 1994)
        - With other networks within same type of SSI in other locations
        - With other types of SSIs
- Dimensions along which competition takes place
  - Costs

- Quality
- Flexibility
- Innovation.

Taken together, these variables describe, as a set, the 2nd level of the institutional environment.

Operationalization of the 3rd level of the Institutional Environment

As argued in before, we take a nominalist approach to the identification of networks within a sectoral system of innovation. We focus on those interfirm relations whose relational content is (primarily) made up of knowledge exchange and learning. As a next step, we now further elaborate on which elements of these networks are relevant for our research.

Following our structural approach to networks, our interest lies in the structure of the relations among actors as well as in the properties of these relations. Based on our discussion of networks in the preceding chapters, we now list the relevant structural features of networks as well as how we want to operationalize these features. This set of variables consists of A. Network structure, B. Relational form and C. Governance of relational risk.

A. Network structure: structure of the relations among actors

- Size: number of members (bilateral - trilateral - multilateral (4+))
- Entrality: member(s) with relatively many ties: (low - medium - high)
- Density: number of ties related to total possible number of ties (low medium high)
- Structural holes: lack of ties between 'parts' (low - medium - high)
- Closure: level of exclusiveness, i.e. closed to outsiders (low - medium - high)
- Cognitive distance: difference in knowledge, experience and thought (low - medium - high)
- Entry: number of entrants (low - medium - high).

B. Relational form: properties of the relations among actors

- Formality: level of formalisation due to formal contracts (low - medium - high)
- Durability: length of relationship in time (low - medium - high)
- Intensity: frequency of contacts (low - medium - high)
- Mutual openness: extent in which knowledge and information moves freely between firms (low - medium - high)

- Breadth of relational : range of issues that is covered (low - medium - high)
  content

Next to these structural features and relational properties of networks, we also consider the governance of these networks. More specifically:

C. Governance of relational risk

Relational risk

- Strategic need: lack of alternatives (low - medium - high)
- Structure of interests: direction of interests (converging - parallel - diverging)
- Specific investments: level of specific investments (low - medium - high)

Governance

- Governance strategy
  - Evasion
  - Integration
  - Contracts
  - Mutual self-interest
  - Reputation (trust in intention, trust in competence)
  - Position in network structure
- Coordinating mechanisms
  - Direct communication
  - Social coordination and control mechanisms
  - Integration and linking pin units
  - Common staff
  - Hierarchy and authority
  - Planning and control
  - Incentive systems
  - Selection systems
  - Information systems

Taken together, these variables describe, as a set, the 3rd level of the institutional environment.

Operationalization of Learning Regime and its Main Learning Outcomes

In this paragraph we operationalize the variables that pertain to a learning regime and its main outcomes.

A. Elements of a learning regime

- Object of learning
  - User needs
  - Technology
  - Products
  - Process
  - Business model
- Learning process
  - Exploitation
    - Indicators:
      - Incremental adaptations
      - Learning to detect and correct errors from existing values and norms
      - Routinization/learning by doing (limited search)
  - Exploration
    - Indicators:
      - Radical adaptations
      - Learning to detect and correct errors in existing values and norms
      - Searching (expanded search)
- Actors
  - Type of actors in terms of their role in a learning regime
- Input
  - Knowledge, resources and capabilities needed
- Output
  - See B. learning outcomes
- Spillovers: level and direction of knowledge spillovers
  - Outside-in
    - From other networks within sectoral innovation system (low - medium - high)
    - From outside sectoral innovation system (low - medium - high)
  - Within network (low - medium - high)
  - Inside-out
    - Towards other networks within sectoral innovation system (low - medium - high)
    - Outside sectoral innovation system (low- medium - high)
- Freeridership: possibility for alter to benefit from ego's efforts without making a full contribution (low - medium - high)
- Hold-up: possibility that alter takes advantage of ego's dependency on alter (low - medium - high).

B. Learning outcomes

As argued in Chapter 3, interfirm learning generates outcomes which are idiosyncratic for a specific learning regime. We consider the following outcomes as relevant:

- New products/services
  - Level of newness
    - New to network
    - New to sectoral innovation system
    - New to the world
  - Elements of newness (either one or a combination of following elements)
    - Lower price
    - Improved quality
    - Faster delivery
    - Wide variety of customer choice
    - New function

- New processes
  - level of newness
    - New to network
    - New to sectoral innovation system
    - New to the world
- Elements of newness (either one or a combination of following elements)
    - Lower costs
    - Improved reliability
    - Increased speed
    - Higher flexibility.

Following our social constructivist approach, we consider cognitive understanding, perception and value judgements as elements of knowledge. As such new knowledge can also form an outcome of a learning regime. In this respect, we differentiate among various types of knowledge as relevant outcomes:

- New shared ideas and/or beliefs
  - Level of newness
    - New to network
    - New to sectoral innovation system
    - New to the world

- Elements of newness
  - New cognitive insights
  - Appropriability
  - Demand competition.

With regard to this overview of learning outcomes, two observations are relevant. A first observation is that this overview is a rather expansive list of outcomes of a learning regime. Because we only consider new outcomes (at T3 in Figure 6.3), it is (very) unlikely that all of these outcomes will occur at the same time. A second observation relates to spillovers, freeridership and hold-up that we have included as relevant variables in our set of a learning regime. In our set of outcomes, we do not include outcome-variables that explicitly relate to these three elements of a learning regime. Our argument is that we focus on learning outcomes, i.e. outcomes that form a direct indication of what has been learned by firms as members of a network. In this respect, we do not consider outcomes of freeridership or hold-up (for example mistrust among actors, financial loss, reputational loss and so on) as a direct indicator of what has been learned by firms. Still, we consider freeridership and hold-up as having a possible feedback effect on the institutional environment. We measure this feedback-effect by means of changes in the variables governance strategies and/or coordinating mechanisms. In addition, knowledge spillovers have a feedback-effect to the institutional environment as well. We incorporate this feedback-effect of knowledge spillovers into our analysis by means of changes in the cognitive distance among actors. Taken together, these variables describe, as a set, a learning regime and the main learning outcomes it generates.

NOTES

1. Archer considers this feedback effect as consisting of 'largely unintended consequences' (1995: 91). As we see a sectoral system of innovation as a collective emergent outcome of the interaction and co-evolution of the various actors which make up this system, we can agree up to point with the notion of 'unintended consequences'. However, we do not share Archer's view that the consequences of social interaction are 'only' unintentional. In the context of interfirm learning within a sectoral system of innovation, we argue that a more precise examination of social interaction reveals that it can have intentional consequences for structure as well. Although the selection bias of most innovation studies has tended to ignore this until now, there is clear evidence that firms may successfully pursue 'path-creation strategies' and can exert considerable influence on the structure in which they are embedded (Mowery and Nelson, 1999). So, we consider this feedback effect as built up of both unintentional and intentional consequences of a learning regime.
2. This distinctive recognition of time is made explicit by Archer through her two propositions of structural conditioning *pre-dating* action and structural elaboration

post-dating action. These two propositions are reflected implicitly by the evolutionary concept of path-dependency. This expresses the notion that the past is retained in rules, designs, habits and so on that guide present and future firm action (Arthur, 1988). Although evolutionary theory describes processes of change and as such acknowledges the temporal dimension, in most studies on innovation the careful treatment of time is underdeveloped.

3. Due to our focus on interfirm networks, we follow here the methodology for the identification of networks as developed within social network theory. There are alternative approaches to identifying the boundaries of an (sectoral) innovation systems. In chapter 1 we argued that the conept of a SSI is closely related to that of a TS (see note 4). See Carlsson (2002) for an extensive and fine overview of the methodological issues when identifying the boundaries of a TS, with relevance also for a SSI.

4. See for more details on both experts www.dialogic.nl

5. See for more details on both experts www.tno-stb.nl

6. The following conferences have been visited to present (parts of) our analyses on multimedia or biotechnology: DRUID-Winter Conference January 2000 (Copenhagen), MERIT ETIC-Conference October 2000 (Maastricht), EGOS July 2001 (Lyon), DRUID-Winter Conference January 2002 (Skoerping), CHIMES-Conference June 2002 (Rotterdam), Conference 'Empirical Research on Routines' November 2002 (Odensee), ERIM-Conference 'Competence Development in MNC's (1) January 2003 (Rotterdam), 'Competence Development in MNC's (2) May 2003 (Oslo) and EGOS July 2003 (Copenhagen).

7. This was under the Fourth Research and Technological Framework Programme, Targeted Socio-Economic Research (TSER) on European Sectoral Innovation Systems commissioned by the EU, March 2001.

7. The Dutch multimedia system of innovation

INTRODUCTION

The aim of this case-study is to analyse how the co-evolution of institutional environment and learning regimes in the Dutch multimedia SSI has taken place.[1] In this analysis we will take the moment of the adoption of the Internet, as the worldwide standard for on-line communication, as a starting point. Following our methodological considerations as outlined in Chapter 6, we need to study sectoral systems of innovation that have shown a high level of dynamism within a limited period of time. Therefore, our analysis of the multimedia SSI will range from the early 1990s until the early start of the new millennium, a period characterized by a high level of dynamism with regard to interfirm learning and innovation.

This chapter is built up as follows. In the first section we analyse learning regime 1 that dealt with technological exploration. In next section we analyse learning regime 2 with a focus on technological exploitation. Learning regime 3 engaged in business exploration. After that we analyse some of the differences between these three learning regimes more indepth. Finally we confront our hypotheses with our empirical findings, based on which we draw some conclusions. But we start by giving a brief overview of the period before the Internet was adopted.

Business side, three Dutch industries formed the basic building blocks for the emerging multimedia SSI around the early 1990s, namely the telecommunication industry, the information technology industry and the media industry. These various industries were 'worlds apart' in the off-line era. We will now first discuss some of the key characteristics of these three industries.[2]

The telecommunication industry in the Netherlands was dominated by various specialized suppliers such as Philips and some foreign firms such as Lucent, Ericsson, Siemens. A further key role was played by KPN, at the time a state-owned monopolist for distribution. In addition there existed a well-developed telephony-based services industry formed by call centres and firms specializing in transaction-based applications such as Electronic Data Interchange (EDI) and tele-banking (directie EDI, 1996).

A key characteristic of the information technology industry was its high growth rate in terms of number of firms, turnover and employment, mainly created through a strong focus on selling capacity, i.e. man-hours. There were relatively few firms that specialized in in-house development of software and this activity mainly pertained to small niches in which these firms found a relative strength, such as ERP-applications and financial transactions.

The media industry was characterized by a traditionally strong publishing and printing sector and a rapidly growing advertising industry (ATKearney, 1997). In addition, various strong firms were emerging in the field of TV-production such as John de Mol and Joop vd Ende, which later merged in Endemol. Moreover, there was a relatively well-developed industry that specialized in providing technical facilities. At the demand side there was a growing cable penetration (Booz Allen and Hamilton, 1997a).

Technology side, technological advancements in the fields of micro-electronics, miniaturization, compression-technology etc. led to increasing possibilities for digitization of information. Digitization made information easy to combine and to manipulate. The major implication was the change from analogue to digital representation, manipulation, storage and transportation of information (Bouwman and Propper, 1994). In addition, digitization spurred the convergence of three different technological fields that dealt with information processing, namely telecommunication technology, information technology and media technology (Dialogic, 1998). More specifically, this technological convergence could be described as a process of the convergence of transport utilities such as cable and telecommunication networks, interactive storage, manipulation and processing of information as well as devices to use or consume the information (Bouwman and Hulsink, 2000).

Before the advent of Internet, Philips and Sony played a pioneering role, in the early 1980s, when they introduced CD-rom. CD-rom technology was the first application of these converging technologies as it built upon the integration of media technology and information technology. Still, CD-roms did not require an integration with telecommunication technology as distribution of CD-roms took place through traditional channels such as bookshops, music stores, video stores, consumer-electronics outlets etc. So, the clear delineation of the various industries remained largely intact (directie EDI, 1996). This situation changed with the adoption of the Internet as the dominant design for on-line communication. This required integration with telecommunication technology in the technological convergence process resulting in a newly arising technological field labelled as 'on-line multimedia' (Dialogic, 1998). The essential difference with CD-roms was its on-line character enabling direct interaction between senders and users of information as well as its capacity to store, analyse and transport information anywhere, anytime, any place at negligible costs. This technological convergence fuelled an industrial convergence process formed by the gradual merging of telecommunications, IT and media industries resulting in a newly emerging multimedia value chain (directie EDI, 1996; Dialogic, 1998 and 1999). In Figure 7.1 an overview is given of this newly emerging multimedia value chain and the positioning of the three learning regimes along it.

LEARNING REGIME 1: EXPLORATION OF TECHNOLOGY

Before the advent of the Internet, the existing knowledge base was compartmentalized in separate technologies that co-existed: information, communication, audiovisual and data transmission technologies. These technologies were mostly stand-alone and most exploration was done by large, R&D-intensive firms. These firms were specialized suppliers of hard- and software such as Lucent, Ericsson, Philips, and Sony, which explored within the scope of their own knowledge domain (directie EDI, 1996; Bouwman and Jansen, 1996; Bouman and Bouwman, 2000). At the time there were various, competing standards for on-line communication but selection took place when the Internet developed as the dominant design. The arrival of the Internet yielded the insight that for its full utilization a more fundamental restructuring was required, in technological convergence. Digitalization provided a technical incentive and opportunity for this integration of technologies. Thus, the Internet, together with perspectives for digitalization, provided powerful incentives to actively search for convergence of these technologies, in new applications (Condrinet, 1998). This led to the entry of new firms that were small in size and formed by people with technological knowledge and a keen interest in exploring the potential for this technological convergence process.[3]

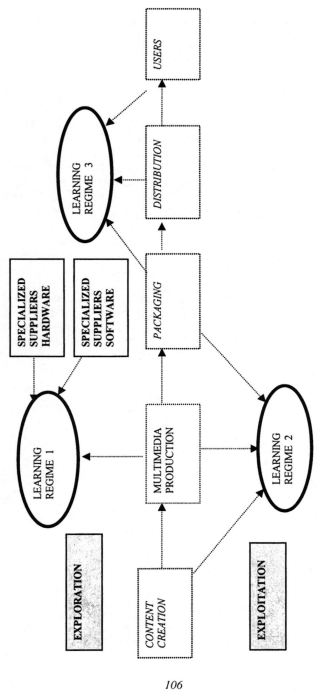

Figure 7.1 Positioning of learning regimes along multimedia value chain

In doing so, these new entrants complemented the search activities of the large, R&D-intensive firms. This yielded learning regime 1: technological exploration. This learning regime developed between small specialized multimedia firms and specialized suppliers of hard- and software. The outcome of these exploration and search activities was a change of the knowledge base, resulting in an increasingly systemic integration of technologies such as information technology, communication technology, screen display technology and language technology (Smeulders, 1999). Competition was hardly an issue yet and demand was highly embryonic and small (Schaffers et al., 1996). In this respect, learning regime 1 emerged in allopatric speciation: largely outside the sight of the established players in the media, telecommunication and ICT industry. Many of these existing firms remained very aloof as they did not recognize the potential impact of the Internet on their business in the early 1990s nor much more later on.[4] These new entrants were formed by spinoffs from these established firms as well as by new start-ups. In general, spinoffs were created by individuals, formerly employed by these existing firms, who were denied the possibility to explore these newly arising opportunities whereas start-ups were mostly created by a new breed of university graduates with no relevant antecedents in existing industries whatsoever (Schaffers, 1994; Beam-it, 1999).

The relations making up the networks in learning regime 1 were mainly informal and (relatively) symmetric (Dialogic, 1999). Although these relations became more intensive, the growing number of entrants led to an overall loosely coupled network structure. Increasingly, this network started to develop its own learning regime. Interfirm learning was 'double loop' and took place by much trial-and-error, with a great deal of tacit knowledge on which search directions to explore and how to explore them (Peelen et al., 1998). This resulted in a dense network structure with low centrality (Peelen et al., 1998; Jonkheer et al., 1999). Ties were strong in terms of frequency of interaction that was open on various issues, but of fairly short duration.[5] This combination of dimensions of tie strength created the possibility for an easy recombination of ties so that the systemic knowledge base could be explored rapidly. The main object of this explorative learning was the exploration of technological integration and later on also some first, new applications. Due to the increasingly systemic nature of knowledge, strong network externalities developed to effectuate technological integration: firms needed to cooperate in hard- and software, in joint development, where no single firm disposed of the necessary knowledge of all technologies (Schaffers et al., 1996). Firms' capabilities were mainly technology-oriented and centred around the ability to integrate key technologies. Entrance was governed by professional norms stressing technical novelty and reputation, creating a network made up of established R&D-intensive firms and new entrants (Wegberg, 1997; Peelen et al., 1998). Furthermore, governance within the network was based on trust-in-competence and the assumption of intentional trustworthiness with limited opportunism and freeriding, without extensive formal safeguards (Dialogic,

1999; Bouwman and Hulsink, 2000). This was further reinforced by firms' mutual technological dependence and the importance of reputation for the sake of future options for collaboration in unpredictable, emerging networks.[6] The notion of technological convergence was seen as the ultimate challenge for firms engaged in this learning regime and functioned as a sort of shared belief in which direction technological exploration should take place. This shared belief in the promises of technological convergence enabled firms to coordinate their relation in their network by a 'free-souls mentality' (Dialogic, 1999).[7,8] The combination of these prevailing coordinating mechanisms and this free-souls mentality selected for dense networks made up of short relations in which knowledge diffusion took place quickly and by direct communication between actors sharing a great deal of tacit knowledge, yielding mutual absorptive capacity (Leisink et al., 1998 and 2000; Bouwman and Hulsink, 2000). See also Table 7.1.

The outcomes of this learning regime were some first applications such as simple e-mail applications, websites and electronic games which propelled demand, causing some first users to become involved (directie EDI, 1996). Early demand was mainly formed by professional users in information-intensive industries such as banking and finance and also by large firms with dispersed activities like multinationals (directie EDI, 1996; Condrinet, 1998). Initially, between these users and multimedia production firms there was a considerable cognitive distance. From this a-symmetry of knowledge stemmed an interesting selection mechanism, with specialized multimedia suppliers selecting lead customers rather than the other way around (Dialogic 1999).

Table 7.1 Analysis multimedia innovation system: learning regime 1

2nd LEVEL INSTITUTIONS

Knowledge Base
Tacitness	High (search process)
Codification	Medium (technological knowledge)
Level of diffusion	Low
Level of systemicness	High
Rate of change	High

Appropriability conditions
Level	Low-medium
Means	Complementary assets

Opportunity conditions
Level	High
Variety	High
Source	Technology

Competitive Conditions
Intensity   Low
Dimensions   Innovation

3rd LEVEL INSTITUTIONS

Network structure
Size   Multilateral
Centrality   Low
Density   Medium - high
Structural holes   Low
Closure   Medium - high
Cognitive distance   Medium
Entry   High

Relational form
Formality   Low
Durability   Low
Intensity   Medium
Mutual openness   High
Breadth of issues covered Medium - high

Governance of relational risk
Relational Risk
Strategic need   High
Structure of interests   Converging - parallel
Specific investments   Medium

Governance
Governance strategy   Mutual self-interest
                         Trust-in-intention
                         Transfer-of-reputation
Coordinating mechanisms Social coordination and control
                         Professional norms
                         'free-souls mentality'

ELEMENTS OF A LEARNING REGIME

Object of learning	Exploration of technological convergence
Learning process	Information-intensive, interactive learning
Actors	Established R&D-intensive firms and new entrants (start-ups, spin-offs)
Input	Complementary assets in hard- and software (codified knowledge on various technologies, tacit knowledge on their integration and on directions for further exploration)
Output	Integration of distinct technologies and converging multimedia devices
Spillovers	
Outside-in	High (from outside Netherlands)
Within network	High (tacit knowledge on search)
Inside-out	High (to learning regime 2)
Freeridership	Low
Hold-up	Low - medium within network; high by users

These first users needed to invest in specialized personnel with the ability to deal with specific multimedia technology and its applications, making it difficult for them to enforce exclusiveness (Dialogic, 1999). So, at this point demand was a weak selection force, which entailed a general neglect of developing capabilities to deal with users and leading to relations with users at a large cognitive distance. The investments in specialized personnel made by users increasingly led to learning on their side, lowering cognitive distance to these specialized multimedia firms. Some turned into lead-users, and relations with specialized multimedia firms became more symmetric from the mid 1990s onwards (Bouwman and Hulsink, 2000). Then, exploration started to focus more on user-oriented features such as different kinds of user-interfaces, speak- and language technology and image processing. Thus, learning regime 1 changed in nature as the object of learning shifted from a sole focus on technological convergence in the early 1990s towards more user-oriented technologies from the mid 1990s onwards. This is in line with our analysis made in the preceding chapters that the institutional environment and learning regime form systemic combinations of features. A change in 2nd level institutions such as demand and opportunity conditions induced changes in 3rd level institutions (more symmetric relations and parity-based governance) and in various elements of a learning regime: the object of learning (from technology towards user-needs), required inputs (knowledge on technology and ergonomics), a lowering of cognitive distance and a smaller chance of hold-up by users.

LEARNING REGIME 2: TECHNOLOGICAL EXPLOITATION

As argued, learning regime 1 was embedded in technical networks with a strong focus on technological exploration. Increasingly, different elements of the knowledge base became more codified, enabling its wider diffusion, for example by means of downloadable software from the Internet (Schaffers et al., 1996). This led to the emergence of learning regime 2, pursued by networks with a focus on exploitation. The emergence of this learning regime 2 was further stimulated by a broadening customer base, built up of a growing mass-market which exerted a relatively simple, more homogeneous demand (directie EDI, 1996; Dialogic, 1998 and 1999).[9] This market was served, from around 1995 onwards, by a rapidly developing, new type of network. The vast majority of firms making up this new type of network were very small in size (often employing less than 10 people) and disposed of average technological capabilities, all of them trying to take advantage of the growing market for on-line applications (Leisink et al., 1998). Around 40 per cent of them were new entrants, the majority (approximately 60 per cent) had their major chunk of business in more traditional industries such as printing, advertising, audio-visual production, IT or pr/advertising (Jonkheer et al., 1999; Dialogic, 2000). In this respect, they had more familiarity with those aspects of multimedia that were closer to their traditional business (Dialogic, 1999).

Increasingly learning regime 2 further developed in this network. Compared with learning regime 1, learning in this learning regime 2 was more oriented to exploitation with a dual learning object: the understanding of customer needs as well as keeping up-to-date with the constantly changing technological knowledge as explored in learning regime 1.[10] In general, customers were formed by professional users that were formed by firms in a wide variety of industries that increasingly adapted multimedia-devices and its related services such as e-mail, websites, intranet-applications and so on.

In this learning regime a dominant network form arose reflecting a growing division of labour: communication with customers was done by a 'main-contractor' with a reliable reputation, surrounded by a stable set of firms with competences for solving various technical issues (Mijland, 2001a). The focus of this network was on a quick delivery of standard products such as e-mail and websites, enabled by an increasingly codified and diffused knowledge base, reducing cognitive distance between the involved firms

(Mijland, 2001b). This dominant mode of organizing consisted of a relatively non-dense network of ties as relations mainly existed between the core firm and the various supplying firms (Leisink et al., 1998 and 2000). These relations were durable, with frequent interaction[11] to accommodate the integration and delivery process, and in this respect mainly entailed specific issues that were related to this integration and delivery process. These supplying firms only had direct ties among one another when needed in view of the integration process (Leisink et al., 1998 and 2000).

So, the systemicness of the knowledge base in combination with demand for quick delivery of relatively standard products selected a relatively non-dense and stable network with high centrality that integrated all required, complementary skills. For appropiation then, the network needed to be able to deliver a 'turn-key solution' that required from the involved firms that they could understand one another well and could count on one another. So, the vast majority of these networks was built up of durable, mostly exclusive and relatively symmetric relations (Leisink et al., 1998 and 2000).[12] Governance was based on mutual dependence with contracts playing a limited role. Further coordination took place by reputation built on past performance and trust-in-intention, this latter explaining why most of the partners came from within a region. Reputation within this local network then acted as an important mechanism to prevent partners from freeriding and poaching.

Over the 1990s this network structure with largely exclusive and durable relations turned out to be self-reinforcing. When relations endured and experience accumulated, firms grew closer in terms of cognition and trust-in-intention and could therefore speed up their single-loop learning (Mijland, 2001). This further enhanced possibilities to appropriate, which reinforced the existing network structure and further deepened the learning regime embedded in this network. See also Table 7.2.

Table 7.2 Analysis multimedia innovation system: learning regime 2

2nd LEVEL INSTITUTIONS

Knowledge Base
Tacitness	High (how to organise the delivery process)
Codification	Medium - high (technological knowledge)
Level of diffusion	High
Level of systemicness	High
Rate of change	Medium

Appropriability conditions
Level	Medium
Means	Complementary assets
	Continuous improvements

Opportunity conditions
Level   Medium
Variety   Medium
Source   Demand / delivery process

Competitive Conditions
Intensity   Medium
Dimensions   Price
                             Flexibility

3rd LEVEL INSTITUTIONS

Network structure
Size   Multilateral
Centrality   High
Density   Low
Structural holes   Medium - high
Closure   Low
Cognitive distance   Low - medium
Entry   Low

Relational form
Formality   Low - medium
Durability   Medium - high
Intensity   Medium - high
Mutual openness   Medium
Breadth of covered issues   Low - medium

Governance of relational risk
Relational Risk
Strategic need   Medium
Structure of interests   Converging - parallel
Specific investments   High

Governance
Governance strategy   Mutual self-interest
                             Trust-in-intention
                             Limited use of contracts
Coordinating mechanisms   Reputation on past performance
                             Social coordination and control

ELEMENTS OF A LEARNING REGIME

Object of learning	User needs and outcomes of exploration in Learning regime 1
Learning process	Learning-by-doing
Actors	Established firms from adjacent industries and new entrants
Input	Complementary capabilities in technology and organization (codified knowledge on technologies, tacit knowledge on integration and organization of the delivery process)
Output	Internet applications such as websites, portals and other web-enabled applications
Spillovers Outside-in	High (from learning regime 1)
Within network	High (tacit knowledge on organization of delivery process)
Inside-out	Low
Freeridership	Low
Hold-up	High

There was a clear connection between learning regime 1 and 2: the continuous influx of spill-overs necessitated that firms in learning regime 2 maintained an open orientation to the exploration activities in learning regime 1 (Dialogic, 1999). As said, this formed an important object of learning in learning regime 2 whereas the other learning object was the identification of customer needs. This second learning object then nurtured the capability to communicate with users, where it is not feasible to make use of specialized technical language, a capability mainly absent in learning regime 1. So, this dual learning object of learning regime 2 made it possible to fine-tune the new multimedia practice as explored in learning regime 1 and to make full use of its potential. This then formed the basis to 'invade' the domain of established industries such as printing, advertising, audio-visual production, IT, media and telecommunication (Condrinet, 1998). So, whereas learning regime 1 emerged in allopatric speciation and induced the development of learning regime 2, this second regime basically formed the 'move back' in the existing institutional selection environment, as can be noted from the large-scale presence in learning regime 2 of (large) firms from existing industries. These large firms were prepared to make substantial investments in the newly arising field and this growing availability of capital enabled the rapid emergence of learning regime 3.

LEARNING REGIME 3: BUSINESS EXPLORATION

The combination of learning regime 1 and learning regime 2 provided the basis for the emergence of learning regime 3 from around 1997, with a focus on exploration of business opportunities for on-line services (Dialogic, 1999; Beam-it, 1999). Whereas exploration through learning regime 1 created the potential for a new field of multimedia, learning regime 3 made it possible to actually explore these business opportunities. It made multimedia-technology more widely available by creating the necessary tools (software, user-interfaces, content, distribution) at increasingly lower costs, an important condition for unlocking a potential mass-market. In contrast to learning regime 2 that primarily focused on intermediary users, this mass-market on which learning regime 3 focused was mainly formed by consumers (Booz Allen and Hamilton, 1997a). These consumers became increasingly interested in the Internet for different purposes, from using it as a source of information, communication, entertainment and purchases. So, the closing down of technological variety at the 'supply' side of the multimedia SSI, entering a phase of consolidation, enabled the opening up of variety through business exploration at the business/demand oriented side (formed by the value-steps of multimedia packaging, distribution and end-use).

Learning regime 3 emerged from the exploration of new business models that took place in a variety of ways. Some firms, especially Internet service providers as well as various publishers, opted for related diversification through in-house creation of new business models. Others made use of alliances, either equity or non-equity based, with firms already occupying a certain market position in the growing market for on-line services. For example the alliance between VNU, a publisher, and Ilse, a Dutch search engine (Barschot, 2000). But also the integration of successful start-ups by large firms such as the acquisition of Planet Internet, an Internet service provider by KPN, the Dutch national telco (Bouwman and Hulsink, 2000). Another type of network was that of a start-up backed by one or more venture capitalist(s) and/or informal investor(s) (Dialogic, 1999).

Towards the end of the 1990's though, the learning regime embedded in the network made up of 'start-ups and venture capitalists/informal investor', started to dominate. Its systemic combination of characteristics appeared to be more effective in exploring on-line business opportunities: a-symmetric relations among start-ups and venture capitalists/investors, these latter having a strong coordinating role by acting as linking pins and taking seats on the board of these start-ups, which made coordination highly tacit and specific to the network (ATKearney, 1997; Beam-it, 1999). This resulted in a relatively non-dense network of ties that were strong in terms of frequency and openness but showed less strength in terms of durability and breadth of issues (Dialogic, 1999). The main resources provided by these central actors were business knowledge, capital and market access, whereas the start-up often brought in the idea for a new business model. The learning object of this network was to learn about two issues: a quick understanding of user needs and the subsequent development of a viable business model. An important outcome of this first exploration of business opportunities was the growing insight that to make money out of the Internet, one needs content which captures the attention of consumers or professional users. This was captured by the notion of 'content is king' giving full motivation to and direction for business exploration (directie EDI, 1996; Schaffers et al., 1996; Booz Allen and Hamilton, 1997a). In this search it quickly became clear that, the importance of content notwithstanding, one did not necessarily need to be content-owner but that it was more important to have access to a community of (professional) users who share a common need or interest (Condrinet, 1998). Such a need or interest could range from on-line information on stocks, used cars, cooking recipes, Latin-American novels, French wines to scientific publications and so on. In order to attract such a community, and more important to keep them interested, content should be attractive and needed to be tailored to the particular community. Therefore, 'portals' were created to target such an Internet-community, fuelled by the belief that the establishment of portals to create and maintain attention of the target audience became the key-success factor in the on-line multimedia industry (Booz Allen and Hamilton, 1997; Condrinet, 1998; Dialogic, 1999). This shared belief triggered substantial changes in the multimedia SSI that also affected publishers, being the specialists in creating and managing content in the off-line world.[13] See also Table 7.3.

After ignoring the Internet as a new medium for quite some time, around the mid 1990s publishers started to enter, although mainly from a defensive posture.[14] They feared the Internet as a threat to their existing business. Therefore, what they did was to use the Internet as just another medium to distribute their existing content, but then electronically. So, they made on-line advertisements for new books or magazines just like regular advertisements or commercials (directie EDI, 1996; Condrinet, 1998). In terms of the Cycle of Knowledge, for publishers this process marked the transition from exploitation towards differentiation, namely the exploitation of their existing knowledge base on publishing in a new context provided by the Internet. However, their efforts did not appeal to users and mostly proved unsuccessful, making the limits of their existing knowledge base visible. The potential added-value that the Internet offers to electronic publishing is two-fold. One is the possibility for re-packaging printed matter, with the possibility of adding sound and pictures in an interactive mode. A second possibility is digital archives which offer the possibility to maintain a stock of information around specific topics which appeal to a community of users. These potential benefits were mostly ignored by existing publishers but well understood by various start-ups in their exploration of such new business opportunities. Increasingly, publishers became aware of the need for a more fundamental change in their strategy to make better use of the potential offered by the new medium. These changes marked the transition towards the phase of reciprocation, where novel combinations with outside sources of knowledge were seen to be required. Such outside knowledge sources are formed by start-ups (such as the alliance of publisher VNU with search-engine Ilse) or by individuals with a reputation in the field.[15]

Table 7.3 Analysis multimedia innovation system: learning regime 3

2nd LEVEL INSTITUTIONS

Knowledge Base
Tacitness	High (how to create a successful business model)
Codification	Low
Level of diffusion	Low
Level of systemicness	Low
Rate of change	Medium

Appropriability conditions
Level	Low - medium
Means	Complementary assets
	Brand name

Opportunity conditions
Level	Medium - high
Variety	High
Source	Demand

Competitive Conditions
Intensity	Medium - high
Dimensions	Price
	Flexibility
	Innovation

3rd LEVEL INSTITUTIONS

Network structure
Size	Multilateral
Centrality	High
Density	Low - medium

Structural holes	Medium
Closure	Low - medium
Cognitive distance	Medium
Entry	High

Relational form	
Formality	Medium
Durability	Low - medium
Intensity	Medium - high
Mutual openness	Medium - high
Breadth of covered issues	Low - medium

Governance of relational risk	
Relational Risk	
Strategic need	High
Structure of interests	Converging
Specific investments	High

Governance	
Governance strategy	Mutual self-interest
	Trust-in-competence
	Contracts
Coordinating mechanisms	Direct communication
	Linking pins
	Capital ventures
	Liaison roles

ELEMENTS OF A LEARNING REGIME

Object of learning	User needs and creation of viable business model
Learning process	Searching and learning by doing
Actors	VCs and start-ups Possibly complemented by large established firms with strong brandname
Input	Complementary resources and capabilities (capital, possibly brandname in combination with idea and know-how for new business model, marketing capabilities)
Output	Wide variety of portals

Spillovers	
Outside-in	High (from outside the Netherlands)
Within network	High (tacit knowledge on creation of business Model and supporting organizational processes)
Inside-out	High (to others networks within Dutch SSI as well as outside the Netherlands)
Freeridership	Low
Hold-up	High

The exploration of new business opportunities resulted in a wide variety of business models. The traditional business model in the off-line world is to generate revenues by advertising and subscription. The on-line business model offered mostly free access so that revenues can only be made from web-ads (Booz Allen and Hamilton, 1997). Hence an on-line media business was defined as a website serving as an intermediary between advertisers and possible target audiences whose attention needed to be captured through offering attractive content. Based on this, a variety of models emerged which entailed the offering of intermediary services in the field of either information (infomediaries), on-line marketplaces (for example www.LetsBuyIt.nl, www.chemunity.nl) or e-tailers (for example www.macropolis.nl, www.wehkamp.nl). The assessment of these ideas for business models was done by venture capitalists and/or informal investors, although they were often not really critical (Dialogic, 1999). By allowing for variety and providing abundant capital for exploration, they often accepted half-baked business plans (Steins Bisschop, 2000). Later, this led to a tremendous shake-out of unsuccessful new start-ups, for three reasons. A first reason relates to the easy possibilities for imitation of the various types of business models that lowered entry barriers, eroding initially attractive profit margins (Bughin et al., 2001). A second reason is the unwillingness of website visitors to click through these web-ads. This made 'banner-ads' very ineffective, which lowered interest of advertisers, resulting in insufficient revenues (Bughin et al., 2001). A third reason is that professional users and consumers suffered from a 'liability of newness', with uncertainty and lack of confidence concerning on-line commerce (Booz Allen and Hamilton, 1997a; Condrinet, 1998; Dialogic, 1999). This was not only related to the newness of the medium of the Internet as such but also to the perception that on-line payment is unreliable. The resulting lack of selection by demand spurred new start-ups, convinced of their ability to develop a brandname for a new portal that would bring ultimate success. The near absence of selection forces in this exploration of business models rapidly led to a situation of 'chaos': variety abounded as can be noted from the explosion of portals, while insights into a viable and sustainable business model were still limited (redactie Financiële Telegraaf, 2000). Ultimately, this led to a rapid decrease of confidence in the 'promises' of multimedia and made investors decide to withdraw. With capital funds drying up rapidly then, this finally resulted in a tremendous shake-out of multimedia firms in the early years of the new millennium (Steins Bisschop, 2000).

In terms of our cycle of knowledge, the 'technology side' of the multimedia SSI has consolidated and has subsequently sought applications in all kinds of directions (generalization). In doing so, it provided a new context for various established industries (differentiation) and in this way induced a search process for business opportunities. In our analysis along the cycle of knowledge, we made the conjecture that firms in an exploitation setting actively pursue the transition towards differentiation, for example through exporting or diversification to related markets. The case of publishers shows that application in a novel context can also be forced from outside, from the need not to 'miss the boat'.

SOME REFLECTIONS ON LEARNING REGIMES 1 AND 3

Following our analysis of the different learning regimes in the Dutch multimedia SSI, we can make some reflections on some commonalities and differences between the two exploration oriented learning regimes, namely 1 and 3.

A first observation relates to the potential overlap between the object of learning and learning process in exploration. In learning regime 1 both were mutually entwined making it difficult to distinguish them from one another: the object of learning was the exploration of technological convergence that effectuated a search process characterized by efforts to integrate various technologies. This meant that the search process itself formed part of the object of search and vice versa, which prevented a more structured approach to the search process making it difficult to create a division of labour. On the other hand, in exploration by learning regime 3 there was a clear difference between the object of learning and the learning process: the object was to identify user needs and the development of a viable business model, which was then realised through a clear division of labour between VCs and start-ups. The question now is why this difference in exploration, between learning regime 1 and learning regime 3, with regard to overlap in object of learning and learning process and hence in division of labour?

The reason lies in profound differences in the knowledge bases underlying these learning regimes. The knowledge base in learning regime 1 has become increasingly systemic in the sense of strong mutual dependencies between different technologies. To develop a multimedia-application required the integration of different technologies for which change in one required adaptations in others. This created a complex search-process: when exploring the convergence of different technologies, one needed to consider all relevant technologies simultaneously, making it difficult to take a structured approach

(Smeulders, 1999). This explains the tacitness of knowledge on technological integration and on directions for further exploration so that the search process itself formed part of the object of search and vice versa. In learning regime 3, the knowledge base had a stand-alone nature as a strong integration of different disciplines and competencies was not required. With the right resources available such as capital, experience and eventually a brandname, the knowledge base was basically formed by competencies in the field of marketing (identifying a target group and communicating to them) and organisation such as how to link the front-office, i.e. the portal, with the back-office (Beam-it, 1999; Dialogic, 1999). Although there were interdependencies between parties in terms of complementary assets in learning regime 3, there were no direct interdependencies in terms of knowledge. This could be noted from the fact that start-ups largely explored alone and that they could adapt their strategy and market approach irrespective of the capabilities of their partners. This does not imply that they operated independently from their partners. Given their capital investments, VCs had a clear say in such changes, making start-ups dependent in this respect. So, there was dependency in governance but not in knowledge. This made it possible to take a more structured approach to the search process and hence to create a division of labour between the involved parties.

CONFRONTING HYPOTHESES WITH EMPIRICAL FINDINGS

In this section we discuss whether our hypotheses formulated earlier are supported by our empirical analysis of the multimedia system of innovation. To do so, we discuss learning regime 1, learning regime 2 and learning regime 3. Based on that we draw some conclusions. See Table 7.4 for an overview of our hypotheses.

Learning Regime 1

As analysed in learning regime 1: Exploration of Technology, firms in learning regime 1 needed to cooperate in hard- and software, in joint development, as no single firm possessed the necessary knowledge on all technologies. So, this learning regime developed between small specialized multimedia firms and specialized suppliers of hard- and software. Given the fact that most specialized multimedia firms were start-ups or spin-offs, no prior relations with specialized suppliers of hard- and software existed, making them initially weak ties for one another. This provides support for hypothesis 1 that in a situation of radical change of 2nd level institutions, here originating from change in the knowledge base, weak ties are needed. The outcome of these exploration and search activities was a change of the knowledge base, resulting in an increasingly systemic integration of technologies such as information technology, communication technology, screen display technology and language technology. Competition was hardly an issue yet and demand was highly embryonic and small. In this respect, learning regime 1 emerged largely outside the sight of the established players in the telecommunication, ICT and media industry. Many of these existing firms remained very aloof as they did not recognize the potential impact of the Internet on their business in the early 1990s nor much more later on. This provides support to hypotheses 2a and 2b that exploration takes place in allopatric speciation, outside the existing institutional selection environment, and that feedback by outcomes of a learning regime mainly affect the development of a new knowledge base.

The arrival of the Internet yielded the insight that for its full utilization a more fundamental restructuring was required, in technological convergence. Digitalization provided a technical incentive and opportunity for this integration of technologies. Thus, the Internet, together with perspectives for digitalization provided powerful incentives to actively search for convergence of these technologies, in new applications. This provides support for hypothesis 5a: this new insight into the need for a more fundamental restructuring, marking the phase towards reciprocation, provided the basis for the exploration of a newly emerging knowledge base (2nd level institution) and also meant that a new network was being formed between existing specialized suppliers and new entrants (3rd level institution). The growing number of entrants (see section Learning Regime 1: Exploration of Technology for a rough estimate on numbers) led to an overall loosely coupled network structure. Relations making up this overall network were mainly informal and relatively symmetric to allow for direct communication and quick knowledge diffusion of mainly tacit knowledge, yielding mutual absorptive capacity.

This supports hypotheses 5b and 8a that a new hybrid organizational form emerges (5b), characterized by a dense structure of strong and weak ties (8a). Entrance was governed by professional norms stressing technical novelty and reputation. Furthermore, governance of these fairly symmetric relations was based on trust-in-competence and the assumption of intentional trustworthiness with limited opportunism and freeriding, without extensive formal safeguards, also labelled as coordination by a 'free-souls mentality'. This supports hypothesis 8b that in exploration, relations are coordinated by transfer of reputation, trust-in-competence and mutual self-interest. Based on our analysis of learning 1 in multimedia, hypothesis 9 could not be validated.

As analysed, the search-process was characterized by complexity and variability at the output-side as well as at the input-side, making it difficult to take a structured approach to this search process. To deal with this uncertainty at both the input and output side of the search process required a dense network structure with low centrality and a high number of new entrants. Ties were strong in terms of frequency of interaction that was open on various issues but of fairly short duration. This combination of dimensions of tie strength created the possibility for an easy recombination of ties so that the systemic knowledge base could be explored rapidly. So, the need for diversity in this exploration network was created through novel configurations of members. In this network, it was more rational not to go for full appropriation but rather to stay connected with the exploration activities going on and to 'live and let live' in order to keep up to date with the rapidly changing knowledge base. So, in this respect a 'free-souls mentality' could emerge. This combination of network structure and governance strategy accommodated the highly 'interactive learning' activities that characterized this learning regime.

An important question now is why this complex and rapidly changing network did not fall prey to chaos. This is due to three 'background' selection mechanisms. A first one was technology-related. As argued, the Internet was selected as the worldwide dominant design for on-line communication and in this respect formed a crucial selection mechanism in the search process. Any new technology developed had to fit into this new Internet paradigm. A second selection mechanism was cognition-related. A central binding element was the shared belief of converging multimedia devices. Any exploration activity was basically aimed at creating such devices or enabling their use such as for example speak and language technology, data-transmission technologies. A third selection mechanism was governance-related. Governance was formed by the free-souls mentality that formed an important institution for selecting appropriate behaviour in this learning regime. Deviating from this was prevented by the rapid transfer of reputation. The combination of these three central, 'background' selection mechanisms meant that this network did not fall prey to chaos but was in fact quite effective in its exploration efforts.

In sum, this combination of network structure, relational properties and coordination mechanisms was selected, both from a competence-perspective and from a governance-perspective. It made it possible to cope with uncertainty at both the output-side and input-side as well as with regard to relational risk: staying constantly up-to-date with the rapidly changing knowledge base and with technologies that offered the most promising future prospects as well as with which firms were potentially attractive partners in terms of competence and intentional trustworthiness. So, this resulted in a dense network in which novelty originated from novel configurations of members. These novel configurations of members reflected the constantly changing networks in which firms decided on whom to partner with as well as on the desired output of their local search process. In other words, selection in these local networks took place in relative autonomy, at a decentral level. Some 'background' selection mechanisms prevented this network from falling apart in chaos.

In conclusion, our hypotheses describing the co-evolution of institutional environment and learning regimes are supported as well as our hypotheses describing how this general pattern settles in network structures and governance strategies.

Learning Regime 2

An increasingly codified and more widely diffused knowledge base in combination with a growing, homogeneous mass-market provided the selection environment for learning regime 2. This learning regime was embedded in a rapidly emerging network of new entrants and existing firms. This confirms hypothesis 3a predicting that, towards exploitation, selection by newly forming 2nd level institutions becomes strong (knowledge base and demand) whereas selection by 3rd level institutions is emerging. This emerging selection of 3rd level institutions became manifest by means of a newly arising network form, built up of durable and mostly exclusive relations. This network structure reflected a growing division of labour between the involved firms: communication with customers was done by a 'main-contractor' with a reliable reputation, surrounded by a stable set of firms with competences for solving various technical issues. This confirms hypothesis 3b that towards exploitation a 'dominant design in organization' emerges, a dominant logic of how to organize for the efficient exploitation of the knowledge base. This dominant mode of organizing consisted of a relatively non-dense network of ties as relations mainly existed between the core firm and the various supplying firms. These relations were durable with frequent interaction to accommodate the integration and delivery process and in this respect mainly entailed specific issues that were related to this integration and delivery process. As analysed, these supplying firms only had direct ties among one another when needed in view of the integration process. Hence a network developed that enabled an emerging distribution of labour and the systemic, durable configurations needed for that, which gives a partial confirmation of hypothesis 6a. However, this hypothesis also predicted that relations showed limited strength in terms of frequency whereas we found a relatively high level of frequency ranging from daily to weekly contacts (see also section Learning Regime 2: Technology). Governance was based on mutual dependence and coordination took place by reputation built on past performance and trust-in-intention, this latter explaining why most of the partners came from within a region. Reputation within this local network then acted as an important mechanism to prevent partners from freeriding and poaching. However, these findings that the coordination of relations remained largely informal and relation-based, with contracts playing a limited role, are in contrast with hypothesis 6b.

The explanation for this partial confirmation of hypothesis 6a and rejection of hypothesis 6b is as follows: although various parts of the knowledge base became increasingly codified, they still remained specific to a particular firm with the relevant expertise. The various codified elements of the knowledge base enabled a division of labour but within a stable group of partners as the capability to integrate these various codified parts was still basically tacit, requiring daily or weekly contacts in order to create and maintain a close mutual understanding and trust-in-intention. So, learning regime 2 shows that also in a setting of exploitation governance can still be of a more informal type, if some essential parts of the knowledge base are tacit, such as knowledge on the integration and delivery process.

Hypothesis 7 then predicts that such a dense network becomes vulnerable to lock-in. This could not be confirmed however, at least not throughout the 1990s and the early years of the 21st century. A probable explanation that lock-in did not occur was that firms continuously needed to absorb the new codified knowledge generated by learning regime 1. Due to the presence of competing networks in learning regime 2, in pursuit of the same customers, this state-of-the-art knowledge could not be ignored. This shows the clear connection between learning regime 1 and 2: the continuous influx of spill-overs into learning regime 2 necessitated that firms in this learning regime maintained an open orientation to the exploration activities in learning regime 1. This also explains why hypothesis 4 is partially supported. Although there were various self-reinforcing mechanisms at work in this network fuelled by an increasing selection of the institutional environment, full exploitation could not occur due to the continuous knowledge spillovers from learning regime 1 into 2.

In conclusion, our hypotheses describing the co-evolution of institutional environment and learning regimes are (partially) supported (3a, 3b and 4). Hypothesis 7 could not be validated. Our hypotheses describing how this general pattern then settles in network structures and governance strategies were partially supported. Our empirical findings support the emergence of a dominant organizational form to enable a division of labour (hypothesis 3b), made up of a relatively non-dense network of ties that were relatively strong in durability and frequency (hypothesis 6a). However, in contrast with hypothesis 6b, was the finding that relations remained coordinated by means of mainly informal coordination mechanisms.

Learning Regime 3

As analysed, learning regime 3 developed between small, specialized start-up firms, VCs and existing firms from established industries. The majority of these firms had no prior relations making them initially weak ties for one another, which is in line with hypothesis 1.

The learning object of this learning regime was two-folded: a quick understanding of user needs and the subsequent development of a viable business model. This exploration of new business opportunities resulted in a wide variety of business models and an emerging knowledge base, entailing among others the importance of content, skills on how to capture 'on-line attention' of customers, the role of portals and so on. This confirms hypothesis 2a.

Exploration in learning regime 3 was primarily done by start-ups, backed by VCs. In addition, also established firms from a variety of existing industries engaged in exploration, but in the great majority of cases very aloof from their existing business. This supports hypothesis 2b that exploration takes place in allopatric speciation, although the engagement of also established firms informs us that, apparently, there are different types of allopatric speciation. One type is formed by exploration through new entrants that are complete outsiders with no history in the industry whatsoever. The second type is formed by existing firms that explore at the periphery of their organization.

In terms of our cycle of knowledge, the 'supply side' of the multimedia SSI has consolidated, through learning regime 2, and has subsequently sought applications in all kinds of directions (generalization). In doing so, it provided a new context for various established industries (differentiation) and in this way induced a search process for business opportunities, at the demand side of the multimedia SSI. In our analysis along the cycle of knowledge, we assumed that firms in an exploitation setting actively pursue the transition towards differentiation, for example through exporting or diversification to related markets. The case of publishers shows that application in a novel context can also be forced from outside, from the need not to 'miss the boat'. Still, the case of publishers confirms hypothesis 5a: to be able to make full use of the potential offered by a new context, offered by the Internet, publishers needed to make a fundamental change in strategy, affecting existing 2nd level institutions as outside sources of knowledge were required. In addition, this change in strategy also affected 3rd level institutions as such outside sources of knowledge were formed by start-ups or various individuals with a reputation in the field.

As analysed, towards the end of the 1990s though, the network made up of start-ups and venture capitalists/informal investor, started to dominate. Relations between start-ups and venture capitalists/investors making up these networks were mostly informal and a-symmetric. These VCs/investors had a strong coordinating role by acting as linking pins and taking seats on the board of these start-ups. This supports hypotheses 5b and 8a that a new hybrid organizational form emerged (6b), characterized by a dense structure of strong and weak ties (8a). The central role of these investors, deeply embedded in these networks, made coordination highly tacit and specific to the network. Governance involved a mix of coordinating mechanisms consisting of informal mechanisms such as direct communication and trust-in-competence but also formal mechanisms such as capital ventures, liaison roles and acquisitions. This is in contrast with hypothesis 8b that predicts the use of informal governance mechanisms. An explanation for this is that VCs needed to make substantial investments, not only in terms of committing resources but also in terms of specific, cognitive investments. This combination of economic and cognitive investments created a clear rationale for more substantial governance that entailed a mix of informal and formal coordinating mechanisms, ranging from direct communication to capital ventures and liaison roles. The expansive search of this learning regime fuelled by a lack of selection forces, either by investors or customers, resulted in a wide variety of portals, while insights into viable and sustainable business models were still absent, resulting in chaos. This confirms hypothesis 9.

As argued, knowledge in this learning regime was stand-alone: knowledge and capabilities of the various involved firms needed no integration and a change in search-direction does not imply adaptations in knowledge and capabilities from other partners. This search-process required a combination of distinct and complementary resources ranging from ideas, capital, experience, social networks, reputation, brand names as well as competencies in the field of marketing (identifying and targeting a potential market) and organization (how to link the front-office, i.e. the web-based portal, with the back-office). Given the person-bound nature of most of these resources and the fairly diffuse opportunities, this search process was fairly complex and predominantly tacit. Once these resources were available, uncertainty at the input-side was fairly limited. The diffuse nature of the opportunity conditions created uncertainty at the output-side of the search-process, both in terms of complexity and variability.

To deal with this complexity, firms needed to make substantial investments, not only in terms of committing resources but also in terms of specific, cognitive investments. This combination of economic and cognitive investments created a clear rationale for more substantial governance. As analysed, this governance involved a mix of coordinating mechanisms ranging from direct communication and a combination of capital ventures and liaison roles. This role was often performed by the VC or informal investors and aimed at stimulating and enabling informal networking among start-ups in order to facilitate knowledge sharing. The tacitness of this search process explained why contracts had limited value and why the strength of relations was high in terms of frequency of interaction and mutual openness.[16]

To deal with variability, VCs invested in various start-ups simultaneously, creating a network structure in which they occupied a central position. This combination of a central firm and peripheral start-ups engaging in exploration created a relatively stable configuration of novel combinations of members that cooperated in a division of labour. This division of labour explains why relations showed limited strength in terms of breadth of issues. When opportunities did not prove to be viable, relations were generally terminated which explains why relations showed also limited strength in terms of durability. At the same time, the direct involvement in exploration by the central firm made the network vulnerable: it created an absence of selection inside the network that was not further compensated for by outside-selection forces such as demand.

In sum, the diffuse nature of mostly unrelated opportunities created uncertainty at the output-side of the search process and required that the locus of diversity in this network was at the periphery of the network. However, in this network there was no central selection by the core firm. This core firm itself was actively engaged in exploration and did not select. This created a need for selection from outside such as for example formed by demand. However, as such a selection force was absent this learning regime became prone to chaos.

In conclusion, our hypotheses describing the co-evolution of institutional environment and learning regimes are supported (2a, 2b, 5a). Our hypotheses describing how this general pattern then settles in network structures and governance strategies were partially supported. Our empirical findings confirm that in exploration a new organisational form will emerge (5b), characterized by a loosely coupled structure of strong and weak ties (8a). However, in contrast with hypothesis 8b, was the finding that relations were a-symmetric and based on a combination of informal as well as formal governance mechanisms. Hypothesis 9 was supported.

CONCLUSIONS

The empirical findings on the three learning regimes in the multimedia SSI confirm our hypotheses that describe the general pattern of co-evolution between institutional environment and learning regimes. In other words, our analysis of the co-evolutionary process along the cycle of knowledge holds, both towards exploitation and towards exploration. In addition, we have gained some novel insights into this co-evolutionary process. Such a novel insight is the finding that the concept of allopatric speciation can be further substantiated by differentiating between two types. One is formed by new entrants that explore at the periphery of existing industries, such as in learning regime 1, and one by existing firms that explore at the periphery of their organisation, such as in learning regime 3. Another novel insight from the case study is that differentiation, in an attempt to apply existing competencies in different contexts, is not necessarily driven by voluntary expansion for growth. As the case of publishers has shown, it may also be forced as a defensive strategy of existing firms, to prevent loss of an existing market when confronted with a change in their institutional environment.

Table 7.4 Overview of outcomes from confrontation of hypotheses and empirical findings for multimedia

MULTIMEDIA	Learning regime 1 technological exploration	Learning regime 2 technological exploitation	Learning regime 3 business exploration
Hypothesis 1	+		+
Hypothesis 2a	+		+
Hypothesis 2b	+		0
Hypothesis 3a		+	
Hypothesis 3b		+	
Hypothesis 4		0	
Hypothesis 5a	+		+
Hypothesis 5b	+		+
Hypothesis 6a		+	
Hypothesis 6b		-	
Hypothesis 7		(could not be validated)	
Hypothesis 8a	+		+
Hypothesis 8b	+		-
Hypothesis 9	(could not be validated)		+

Clarification
+ : support
0 : partial support
- : no support

Following Table 7.4, the empirical findings give partial confirmation of our hypotheses that describe how the general pattern of co-evolution settles in network structures, relational properties and coordination mechanisms. We found support for our hypotheses stating that in exploration a new organization form will emerge formed by a loosely coupled structure of strong and weak ties; and that in exploitation a dominant organizational form will be selected in view of an efficient division of labour, formed by a non-dense network of strong ties. But our hypotheses that relate to the properties of these network relations and governance strategies employed were not supported. The explanation for this is that 2nd level institutions do not only differ between different SSIs but also differ between different learning regimes within a SSI. These specific properties of 2nd level institutions make 3rd level institutions, as a lower level of institutions, also specific and therefore not necessarily in line with our general analysis and the hypotheses developed from that.

CONSULTED LITERATURE AND REPORTS ON THE DUTCH MULTIMEDIA SSI

ATKearney (1997), *Bedrijfstaktoets Audiovisuele sector*, rapportage voor het ministerie van Economische Zaken, Den Haag.

Bakker, K. and K. Jonkheer (1999), *Multimedia bedrijven in Nederland*, Zoetermeer, EIM.

Barschot, J. van (2000), VNU wordt met Ilse grootste Internetuitgever, *NRC Handelsblad*, 06-07-2000.

Beam-it (1999), Resultaten On-line Discussie, *Technologieradar Multimedia*, rapportage voor het ministerie van Economische Zaken, Den Haag.

Booz Allen and Hamilton (1997a), *On-line services market benchmarking*, rapportage voor het ministerie van Economische Zaken, Den Haag.

Booz Allen and Hamilton (1997b) *Zukunft multimedia*, Frankfurt am Main.

Bouman, J. and H. Bouwman (2000), De cartografie van de multimedia sector, in: H. Bouwman en W. Hulsink, *Silicon Valley in de polder, ICT-clusters in de Lage Landen*, Lemma, Utrecht.

Bouwman, H. and S. Propper (1994), *Multimedia tussen hope en hype*, Amsterdam, Otto Cramwinckel.

Bouwman, H.and L. van de Wijngaert (1996), *Multimedia en route, tien notities over multimedia en Internet toepassingen*, Amsterdam, Otto Cramwinckel.

Bouwman, H. and R. Jansen (1996), De strategische waarde van multimedia, in: H. Bouwman and L. van de Wijngaert, *Multimedia en route, tien notities over multimedia en Internet toepassingen*, Amsterdam, Otto Cramwinckel.

Bouwman H. and W. Hulsink (2000), *Silicon Valley in de polder, ICT-clusters in de Lage Landen*, Lemma, Utrecht.

Bughin, J.R., S.J. Hasker, E.S.H. Segel and M.P. Zeisser (2001), What went wrong for on-line media, *The McKinsey Quarterly*, 4, web exclusive.

Coerts, G. (1999), ICT-sector concentreert zich in de Randstad, *Financieel Dagblad*.

Condrinet (1998), *Content and commerce driven strategies in global networks*, report prepared for the European Commission, DG 13/Enterprise, Luxemburg.

Couzy, M. (2000), Uitgever blijft bij zijn leest, *FEM/De Week*, 11 november 2000.

Dialogic (1998), *The emerging information and communication cluster in the Netherlands*, report prepared for the OECD Focus Group on Clusters.

Dialogic (1999), *Clustermonitor Multimedia*, rapportage voor het ministerie van Economische Zaken, Den Haag.

Dialogic and Heliview (2000), *Nieuwe-media.com, ICT-strategieën in het nieuwe mediacluster*, rapportage voor het ministerie van Verkeer en Waterstaat, Den Haag.

Dialogic (2000), *Kerngegevens Nederlandse informatie en communicatiecluster*, rapportage voor het ministerie van Economische Zaken, Den Haag.

Directie EDI (1996), *Thema-document Multimedia*, Ministerie van Economische Zaken, Den Haag.

Doorenbosch, T. (2000), KPN koopt inspiratie met risicogeld voor starters, *Volkskrant*, 6-11-2000.

Gelder, H. van (1999), Steviger cluster zijn goed voor de branche, *Adformatie*, 22, 14.

Grinsven, L. van (1999), Kennis kleine bedrijven cruciaal voor groei grote, *Financieel Dagblad*, 19 januari 1999.

Hooff, B. van den and R. Tebbal (1996), Internet in Nederland, in: H. Bouwman, H. en L. van de Wijngaert, *Multimedia en route, tien notities over multimedia en Internet toepassingen*, Amsterdam, Otto Cramwinckel.

Houtsma, M. and J. Schot (1996), Elektronische snelweg: werk in uitvoering, in: H. Bouwman, H. and L. van de Wijngaert, *Multimedia en route, tien notities over multimedia en Internet toepassingen*, Amsterdam, Otto Cramwinckel.

KPMG (2000), ICT in Amsterdam en Haarlemmermeer, hun uitgangspositie vergeleken met New York, Londen, Frankfurt en Stockholm, KPMG-rapport, Amstelveen.

Leisink, P. (1998), Netwerkorganisatie in de multimedia-industrie, *Informatie en Informatiebeleid*, 16(4), 38–43.

Leisink, P., J. Boumans and J. Teunen (1998), *De multimedia sector in beeld, een verkennend onderzoek naar bedrijven en werknemers in de nieuwe media productiesector*, GOC, Veenendaal.

Leisink, P., J. Teunen and J. Boumans (2000), *Multimedia: de pioniersfase voorbij*, Veenendaal, GOC.

McKinsey (1997), *Boosting Dutch Economic Performance*, McKinsey Global Institute, Amsterdam.

Mijland, E. (2001a), Nederland is te klein voor pluriform aanbod webdiensten, *Tijdschrift voor Multimedia*, 13.

Mijland, E. (2001b), Aannemers in multimedia, *Tijdschrift voor Multimedia*, 30–31.

Netherlands Foreign Investment Agency (1997), *Multimedia industries in the Netherlands*, Brochure for foreign investors, Ministry of Economic Affairs, the Hague.

Oerlemans, L.A.G. and M.T.H. Meeus (2000), Clusters en IOP's, *ESB-dossier Clusters in Beeld*, ESB, Rotterdam.

Peelen, E., R.M. Jansen, S.H.A. Kernkamp and J.W.N. van Velzen (1998), *De Amsterdamse multimedia sector en suggesties voor haar groeibeleid*, Universiteit van Amsterdam.

PriceWaterHouseCoopers (1999), Access to capital for content industries, report for the European Commission, DG12, Luxemburg.

PriceWaterHouseCoopers (1999), *Ondernemingsanalyses 1999, Trends in media*, Dordrecht, Elsevier.

Redactie Financiële Telegraaf (2000a), Multimediasector kan eigen groei nauwelijks bijbenen, *Telegraaf*, 26-06-2000.

Redactie Financiële Telegraaf (2000b), Eenderde alle bedrijven heeft eigen website, *Telegraaf*, 9-11-2000.

Roobeek, A. and J. Broeders (1993), Telecommunications: global restructuring at full speed, in: H.W. de Jong (ed.), *The structure of European industry*, Dordrecht, Kluwer, 273–306.

Rooduin, T. (2002), De kater na de branie, *NRC-Handelsblad*, 15-02-2003.

Schaffers, H. (1994), *Perspectieven voor Nederlandse bedrijven in telecommunicatie en multimedia*, Apeldoorn, TNO-STB/94/048.

Schaffers, H., S. Maltha, P. Rutten and A. van Stralen (1996), *Een innovatieperspectief voor de content-keten*, Apeldoorn, TNO-STB/96/025.

Smeulders, A.W.M. (1999a), *Multimedia is beweging*, Universiteit van Amsterdam, rapportage voor het ministerie van Economische Zaken, Den Haag.

Smeulders, A.W.M. (1999b), *Workshop verslag multimedia, 21 mei 1999*, rapportage voor het ministerie van Economische Zaken, Den Haag.

Smilor, R.W., G. Kozmetsky and D.V. Gibson (1988), The technopolis concept, in: F.W. Williams (ed.), *Measuring the information society*, Newbury Park: Sage.

Steins Bisschop, J.S. (2000), Na chaos moet er nu orde komen op internet, *Financieel Dagblad*, 06-11-2000.

Veerman, R. (1999), Amsterdam internet-centrum van Europa, *Financiele Telegraaf* (web-editie), 19-6-1999.

Virtueel Platform (1999), Verslag innovation exchange workshop: hoe kunnen content en technologie elkaar versterken?, Amsterdam.

Wansink, H. (2000), Ondernemende consultants, *Volkskrant*, 16 december 2000.

Wegberg, M. van (1997), Mergers and alliances in the multimedia industry, *MERIT Working Paper*.

NOTES

1. We thank Pim den Hertog and Sven Maltha of Dialogic for their valuable comments on an earlier version of this chapter. Of course, any error remains entirely our responsibility. See for more information on both experts www.dialogic.nl.

2. Based on den Hertog and Maltha (1999), The Emerging Information and Communication Cluster in the Netherlands, Paris, OECD.

3. There is no exact information on the number of new entrants in this period of the early 1990s. Still we can make a rough estimate based on statistics of the Dutch Central Statistical Office (CBS) which would indicate a number of somewhere between 25 and 50 firms between 1993 and 1995. Regarding their size a more accurate number is available indicating that 90 per cent of these firms employed less than 10 people (CBS Statline, Demografie van bedrijven, 1997).

4. An example of this is formed by KPN, the national Dutch telco. At the time, their main focus was on making money out of their existing telecommunication network, i.e. in selling distribution capacity. They were hardly interested in the Internet except for its potential to sell more of their existing capacity without any interest in the content going through their telecommunication networks (source: statement by Wim Dik, former chairmen KPN, during press conference of presentation of 1994 annual report)

5. Again, exact information is not available but a rough estimate based on discussions with multimedia firms in 1998 would indicate an approximate level of duration that varies between 1–2 months and 6–8 months, with 12 months or more being the exception. It was said that the relation had ended when "e-mails were not answered anymore". With regard to frequency a rough estimate would indicate an approximate level between 2–3 contacts a day and 1–2 contacts a week, often by email but also by face-to-face discussions.

6. For a treatise on instruments for governance of collaborative relations, see Nooteboom (1999d).

7. A clear empirical indication for this observed 'free-souls mentality' is for example found in the network of firms that cooperated in the technological exploration of multimedia image processing technology in the period around.

8. Such a free-souls mentality can develop by the condition that one needs each other, and that there are no alternatives. Then one will simply have to make it work, in mutual give and take. Trust is further engendered by mutual respect

among professionals struggling with shared problems. An informal safeguard against free-riding may be that in order to keep up with new knowledge development, all partners have to do their part, in give and take, to keep up with the development of their absorptive capacity, and shared tacit knowledge, to benefit from what partners develop. Due to the high rate of change of the knowledge base, an informal safeguard against hold-up on the basis of specific investments is that no one knows yet which investments will turn out to be generic and which specific, and it is not certain what knowledge could be used as a hostage.

9. Exact data on the market size are not available although there are various indications. The Internet Almanac estimated the total number of users at 1.4 million in 1997 and predicted the number of users to have more than doubled to nearly 3 million users by the year 2000. Booz Allen and Hamilton (1997b) estimated the total market for on-line services through the Internet in the Netherlands at somewhere between euro 410 and 450 million in 1997 with an expected annual growth rate between 1997 and 2001 of around 65 per cent.

10. Clear empirical indications for this dual learning object were that, based on an extensive survey on multimedia firms by Peelen et al. (2000), between 65 and 70 per cent of all multimedia firms especially invested in a better understanding of customers (through improvements in marketing, communication and customer focus) as well as in knowledge on (adjacent) technologies.

11. Exact information is not available but a rough estimate based on discussions with multimedia firms in 1998 would indicate an approximate level of duration that varies between two years or more (often firms did not exist nor were engaged in multimedia longer than two years around 1998). With regard to frequency a rough estimate would indicate an approximate level between daily or weekly contacts, either by email but also by face-to-face discussion.

12. Again exact data are not available but following a study by Leisink et al. (2000), around 85 and 90 per cent of the involved firms indicated that they were positioned in what they regarded as a stable network of on average seven partners and that they considered themselves as well as their partners as independent from one another, indicating symmetry in terms of power. This latter finding was irrespective of the fact whether firms were large or small, indicating that it was knowledge and skills that determined one's position.

13. The expectation was that portal-owners will perform the role which publishers perform in the traditional, off-line world as, in essence, their role is similar: to collect content, to bundle it in an attractive package (portals vis-à-vis books, newspapers, magazines etc) and then distribute it to the respective target markets.

14. Much young talent within publishing companies became increasingly familiar with the possibilities of multimedia-technology and saw digital, interactive publishing as an interesting challenge, complementary to traditional publishing. However, many of their efforts to convince higher echelons of the need to explore the possibilities offered by multimedia technology have failed. An inside source within VNU, a large Dutch publisher, revealed that these higher echelons often had no clue what this new on-line business was about. Why they decided to enter then was not so much from a growing belief in the possible opportunities but because they were increasingly being challenged by stock analysts of Dutch and international banking firms who kept on 'interrogating' them about their Internet-strategy. This external pressure and the fear of losing the favour of investors

formed an important reason to start to explore these possibilities, although it often seemed more acts of window-dressing rather than based on true conviction.

15. An example was WegenerArcade that appointed Maurice de Hondt as head of its New Media division.

16. This empirical finding on dominant governance strategies in business exploration in multimedia is in line with Grandori's framework (1995). She predicts that under conditions of high cognitional complexity, reciprocal interdependence (resources going one way) and diverging interests, a mix of capital ventures and lateral integration roles is selected. Although we need to add one comment, namely that interests among partners in this network do not necessarily diverge as, in general, both start-ups and investors wanted to make an ipo ('initial public offering') as quickly as possible. So, in this case we argue it is more the level of investments made and the fact that most resources are person-bound that explains the substantial involvement of the investor in the search process (Clustermonitor, 1999).

8. The Dutch pharmaceutical biotechnology system of innovation

INTRODUCTION

Biotechnology as such is not an industry *per se* but refers more to a set of technologies that profoundly affect existing industries such as agriculture, food processing and human health. In the agricultural industry firms use modern biotechnology for the improvement of health, nutrition or breeding of agricultural livestock. In the case of plants firms use recombinant DNA techniques for the genetic modification of crops, plants or plants cells in order to enhance their quality or improve their characteristics. In the food industry companies focus on improving the quality of foods and develop new functional foods with added ingredients that supposedly have health-related effects. In the pharmaceutical industry firms develop diagnostic tools for identifying human or animal diseases such as different types of antibodies, genetic diagnostics that use polymerase chain reaction (PCT) technology or other biology techniques. Other companies produce therapeutics, i.e. biotechnology-derived products that are aimed at improving the treatment of human diseases. In addition there are specialized biotechnology firms that develop platform technologies with a potential for a wide variety of applications by making use of various scientific fields such as functional genomics, proteomics, combinatorial chemistry and high throughput screening facilities like DNA array technology. These technologies are essentially research tools and their developers do not aim to become producers but rather providers of tools and service to companies involved in drugs discovery and development.

In this chapter we focus on the impact of the biotechnological revolution on the Dutch pharmaceutical industry.[1] The biotechnological revolution in the pharmaceutical industry has been largely global in nature though (Henderson, 1994). To understand therefore the impact of biotechnology in the Netherlands and the sectoral dynamics that have followed from that, we cannot ignore some of these essential developments that have largely taken place outside the Netherlands. Therefore we start this chapter with an analysis of the profound changes in the pharmaceutical industry caused by the biotechnology revolution. This will be the topic of next section. This then forms the basis for our analysis of the evolution of the pharmaceutical biotechnology system of innovation in the Netherlands over the period from around the mid 1980s towards the beginning of the new century. Finally in last section we confront our earlier formulated hypotheses with our empirical findings, based on which we draw some conclusions.

PHARMACEUTICAL BIOTECHNOLOGY

In this section we analyse the profound changes caused by the biotechnology revolution that have affected the global pharmaceutical industry. To do so, we start with a brief overview of the pharmaceutical industry before the biotechnological revolution arrived. Then we analyse more in-depth the impact made by biotechnology on this industry, based on the cycle of knowledge. Based on this we will then analyse and try to explain the emergence of new organizational forms.

The Pharmaceutical Industry

For a considerable period of time, from around WWII to the early 1990s, the pharmaceutical industry has been remarkably successful. For most of this period, double digit growth rates were the norm for most pharmaceutical companies and the industry as a whole ranked among the most profitable in the world. A number of structural factors supported this high level of innovation and profitable growth.

After WWII, there were many diseases and physical ailments for which no drugs existed. These unmet needs created an enormous amount of R&D opportunities for pharmaceutical companies. In general, there was no in-depth understanding among firms/scientists of the more fundamental biological reasons underlying specific diseases (Pisano, 2002). To exploit this sea of opportunities without detailed knowledge then, pharma companies developed an approach to R&D often labelled as 'random-screening' (McKelvey, 1996). The essence of this approach is that natural and chemically derived compounds are randomly screened for their therapeutic potential. As little of this knowledge was codified, serendipity played a key role and often firms discovered a drug for another disease than they were searching for (Orsenigo et al., 2001). This search process of random screening was based on internal organizational processes and mainly tacit capabilities. Combined with the random character of the screening process, spillovers between different firms were small (Henderson, 1994; McKelvey and Orsenigo, 2001). In addition, patent protection was strong, making it difficult for an imitator to come up with an alternative compound which did not infringe on the patent. Also, consumers have proven to be largely price-inelastic, making demand for pharmaceutical products relatively insensitive to economic downturns. This was also due to the fact that it was often doctors who made the buying decision for which patients (i.e. users) were often compensated for by means of their medical insurance. Another factor here is the regulatory approval process which is time-consuming and costly, making it difficult for imitators to quickly come up with cheaper alternatives (Pisano, 2002).

Taken together, these factors explain both the high and profitable growth of pharmaceutical firms and also why very few new firms entered the industry in this period.

The Advent of Biotechnology

The core knowledge base of the pharmaceutical industry until the early 1980s was formed by organic chemistry. This knowledge base was specialized around an in-depth understanding of the chemical properties of molecules and how they interact with one another. In this respect, organic chemistry did not aim to explain the biological underpinnings of specific diseases. At best, organic chemists could develop a sense of a relation between a chemical compound and its potential therapeutic effect (Pisano, 2002). These chemists therefore tended to focus on the synthesis of chemical compounds which had already been shown to have positive effects. These compounds were then screened for their therapeutic potential. So, the discovery of new drugs was a mainly tacit capability which was mainly dependent on the skills of the individual chemist making it therefore difficult to codify. Still, this search process of random screening worked very well for a large number of years and generated important classes of drugs, making this period after WWII the 'golden age' of the pharmaceutical industry (McKelvey and Orsenigo, 2002; Pisano, 2002). In terms of our Cycle of Knowledge, we can characterize this period as one with a strong focus on incremental innovations and the exploitation of the existing knowledge base of organic chemistry.

From exploitation to differentiation, in the early 1980s some first signs emerged that things were changing. The massive public funding for health related research after WWII began to bear fruits. Substantial progress in scientific areas such as physiology, pharmacology, enzymology and cell biology created a growing understanding of the biochemical and molecular roots of diseases and of the effectiveness of existing drugs in curing these diseases. These new medical insights in diseases offered researchers with opportunities for the development of new drugs. Although the core knowledge base remained firmly rooted in organic chemistry, this new biological knowledge enabled chemists to take a more rational approach to the design of new drugs. It enabled them to define the search space more accurately making it possible to take a more structured approach to the screening process. So, random screening turned in a more guided search process (McKelvey, 1997). In essence, the advent of molecular biology enabled pharmaceutical firms to now fully exploit the possibilities, which the existing knowledge base of organic chemistry provided. Still, the random character of the search process did not disappear as these technological advances were more complementary and did not displace existing competences of the screening process (Santos, 2003). Later on, from the early 1990s onwards, the increasing computational possibilities provided by ICT enabled further improvement in the search process through high throughput screening. Whereas the original process of random screening was fairly labour intensive, this technology of high throughput screening was an automated, robotics-based process that enabled testing of large numbers of chemical compounds, although still in a rather random manner.[2]

Firms did not adopt molecular biology as a goal in itself. As molecular biology is a different technology and complementary to existing organic chemistry, it enabled firms to further exploit the existing knowledge base of organic chemistry. So, the advent of molecular biology provided new inputs to the existing knowledge base of organic chemistry. In terms of the cycle of knowledge: a movement from exploitation to the phase of differentiation which, in this case, is formed by adjusting the R&D process to new inputs provided by molecular biology in order to further exploit the existing knowledge base.

Unlike other industries where technical change involves advancement in product technology or process technology, biotechnology induced changes in the R&D process. It affected methods of R&D and deals with finding new ways to search, synthesize and select chemical compounds for therapeutic applications (Henderson and Cockburn, 1996). R&D in pharmaceuticals is concerned with the discovery of new drugs and involves three, interdependent processes: *search* for therapeutic targets, *synthesis* of potentially therapeutic compounds and the *screening* of those compounds for desired therapeutic activity. The era of random screening was mainly concerned with synthesis and screening. With the development of rational drug design, enabled by molecular biology, a more structured approach to searching developed.

From differentiation to reciprocation, in the late 1980s and early 1990s a second wave in the molecular biological revolution emerged, genetic engineering, which opened up new areas for innovation and altered the drug discovery process in a more fundamental way. Genetic engineering forms an umbrella-name for a newly emerging set of complex and multidisciplinary technologies, formed by among others recombinant DNA (rDNA), monoclonal antibody technology, and eventually combinatorial chemistry and high throughput screening. These new knowledge bases opened up a fundamental new way to define search spaces, identify promising targets and develop potential heuristics. With the advent of this second molecular biological revolution the total drug discovery process has started to change in a profound way.

In terms of our cycle of knowledge, this second wave in the molecular biology revolution marked the transition to the phase of reciprocation. The continued exploitation of the existing knowledge base of organic chemistry made its limitations increasingly visible, first slowly but towards the end of the millennium increasingly more apparent. These limitations became manifest by the increasing number of existing patents by pharma companies which was expiring in combination with a lowering number of potential 'blockbusters' in the pipe-line.

An example is formed by Eli Lilly's patents for its very successful Prozac (against depressions) which expired from the beginning of 2001. The turn-over of 2.3billion US$ in 2001 has halved in a few months and could not be compensated for by increasing sales of other new medicines (FD, January 2002).

According to Jan Leschly, former CEO of SmithKline Beecham, "Big pharma cannot afford to rest on its laurels. If today's successful pharma companies do nothing then their sales will be halved within ten years from now" (Ernst and Young, 2001). Due to this accumulation of failures within a different context, provided by the 1st wave of molecular biology, the importance of this 2nd wave became increasingly apparent. The random nature of the search process did not disappear so that this change was more evolutionary than revolutionary. A more guided search process became possible and as such improved the chance of success for finding effective drugs. The cognitive distance between these new knowledge bases and the existing knowledge base of organic chemistry was fairly large. So, the adoption of this 2nd wave of new or 'foreign' practices marked the transition from differentiation to reciprocation.

As argued by different authors (among others by Gambardella, 1995) the successful adoption of these new technologies has varied substantially among firms. Especially firms that adopted the first molecular techniques in the early 1980s and made the subsequent transition from random to guided drug discovery proved to be successful in managing this change process (Henderson et al., 1999; Pisano, 2002). Firms that had not made this initial transition were often very slow followers and proved unsuccessful in adopting the 2nd wave of new techniques (Henderson, 1994; McKelvey and Orsenigo, 2001). This is in congruence with our analysis along the Cycle of Knowledge, which predicts that it is very difficult to skip one phase and move on directly towards the next. The case of pharmaceutical biotechnology shows that firms which made the transition to the phase of differentiation and then moved to reciprocation had an advantage over firms which tried to move from exploitation directly to reciprocation by skipping differentiation. This especially applied to European firms, which maintained close links to the knowledge base of organic chemistry making them slower in adopting molecular biology when compared with US firms. In Dutch firms organic chemists had occupied powerful positions for a long time and now tried to resist their lose of dominant positions to pharmacologists and biotechnologists, which became an inevitable process through from the end of the 1970s and onwards. Still, the vested interests of existing organic chemists meant that incumbent firms mostly did not jump onto the newly arising technological and commercial opportunities.

New Organizational Forms

In our theoretical analysis in the preceding chapters we have hypothesized that structural changes in the core knowledge base underlying a SSI will create new organizational forms. In general, the advent of molecular biology has created networks of collaboration between different types of firms and also with non-firm actors such universities and (public) research institutes. It is this appearance of new organizational forms, especially in new types of networks, upon which we will now elaborate.

The profound changes in the core knowledge base underlying this SSI required from pharma firms to make fundamental adaptations in their learning and search routines. Therefore most of these firms did not consider it to be a viable option to make such adaptations in-house by re-educating their existing R&D labour force of organic chemists (Degenaars and Janszen, 1996). To exploit the opportunities induced by molecular biology and genetics then required outsiders with expertise in this new technological field. These outsiders were formed by dedicated biotechnology firms (DBFs), universities and (public) research institutes. Collaboration with DBFs and universities allowed large pharmaceutical firms to access new technology and explore new directions, if they had disposed of sufficient absorptive capacity. From a sectoral viewpoint, these DBFs performed a crucial function of transforming fundamental scientific knowledge into technological and commercially valuable knowledge. For these DBFs the rationale to cooperate with large firms was access to finance as well as to complementary assets such as marketing, distribution and the capabilities to deal with regulatory approval procedures. Large firms were faced with an opposite problem. While they needed to explore and develop new knowledge, their monodisciplinary orientation remained largely intact (Allansdottir et al., 2002). Their key-capabilities and structure were mainly in the field of product testing and large scale production and marketing. Confronted with a sharp increase in opportunities and high rate of change of knowledge, these large firms needed to maintain access to a broad knowledge base in order to be able to quickly respond to new developments (Degenaar and Janszen, 1996). Most of them created such access through partnerships with DBFs and/or universities instead of exploring and understanding the new knowledge in-house. So, a network structure developed in which large pharma companies co-existed in a relationship of strong complementarity with small DBFs and/or academia resulting in a clear division of labour: small firms did exploration for which the large firms formed the fundamental source of demand and provided the integrative capabilities that were required to transform the newly explored knowledge into commercial products (Allansdottir et al., 2002). This basically proved to be an effective way of solving the problem of exploration and exploitation by distributing these tasks in a network (Nooteboom, 2000). Still two questions remain open.

A first question is why large pharma firms have made limited use of acquiring DBFs to incorporate the new knowledge bases. Following our analysis as outlined above, an acquisition strategy would have created two distinct disadvantages. One is the difficulty, due to the diffuse opportunity conditions, to identify up-front which search process in a particular technological field is the most likely to yield success, and then, which DBF would be most capable in realizing this potential. A network of various DBFs makes it possible to explore in different directions without the costs of acquisition and the risk of making the 'wrong bet'. A second disadvantage lies in the difficulty of incorporating such a DBF into the mother-firm due to differences in culture and management systems (control, reward, promotion systems and so on). Often this is a time-consuming and costly affair with a limited chance of success and the risk of key-people of the acquired firm leaving.

A second question is why another alternative organizational form has not emerged, namely that of a DBF becoming a pharma firm itself. This would have created two substantial advantages, namely that of direct access to a potentially large, profitable market and the avoidance of being dependent on a large pharma firm, generating relational risk. Although there are a few successful examples such as for example Genentech, Amgen, Chiron, Genzyme and others, in general, this strategy has not been proven to be very viable, for three reasons. A first reason relates to cognition. Most DBFs have a strong monodisciplinary orientation whereas the successful development of a new drug requires a much broader, more general knowledge base, both in technical and in organizational terms (McKelvey and Orsenigo, 2001). A second reason has to do with appropriability conditions. Large pharma firms possess the required complementary assets and tacit capabilities to deal with complex and costly product approval procedures as well as with large scale marketing and distribution. Thirdly, DBFs are in 'desperate need' of cash. In this respect, venture capitalists play a key-role but, in general, they are more prepared to invest when there is support from a large pharma firm. Fourthly, when turning itself into a fully integrated pharmaceutical company, DBFs would lose their advantage of their small size and flexibility for exploration.

In conclusion, networks have emerged as the dominant organizational form opposed to alternatives such as integrated forms or stand-alone forms.

PHARMACEUTICAL BIOTECHNOLOGY IN THE NETHERLANDS[3]

The emergence and growth of biotechnology is shaped to an important extent by the presence and structure of downstream industries that provide demand for biotechnology and its related products. However, large and integrated pharmaceutical firms are absent in the Netherlands. This may explain the relatively moderate position of the Netherlands in the field of pharmaceutical biotechnology. According to recent figures, the Netherlands occupies a 12th position in the overall ranking of nations, based on number of biotechnology companies (Ernst and Young, 2002).[4] Still, three medium-sized multinational firms are clearly involved in pharmaceutical biotechnology, namely AKZO Nobel (Organon, Organon Technika and Intervet), DSM-Gist Brocades (largest global manufacturer of penicillin), Yamenouchi and Solvay Pharmaceuticals. In addition, foreign pharmaceutical firms have clinical research being carried out in the Netherlands and have relations with Dutch DBFs. Moreover, some of these DBFs have relations with firms outside the Netherlands. This indicates that geographical proximity seems of less importance, an issue which we will further address.

From the mid 1980s towards the mid 1990s technologies were primarily based on molecular biology or biology, forming a mainly stand-alone knowledge base. The main focus in this period was on scientific research so that knowledge mainly pertained to universities and research institutes (Ministerie EZ, 1998). There was a low number of entrants of about 1 per annum and most of the DBFs had close relations with academia whereas some of them had relations with pharma firms, either Dutch (mostly AKZO and Solvay) or foreign ones. In general, there was a limited focus on possibilities for a rapid commercialization of this knowledge (Janszen and Degenaars, 1996).

From the early 1990s towards 1998–1999 the number of entrants by DBFs per annum increased from 4 in 1994 to 10 in 1998, making 50 in total (Biopartner, 2001; 2002). Around 50 per cent of these firms in the pharmaceutical industry in the Netherlands were active in the field of pharmaceutical biotechnology. This indicated that a pharmaceutical biotechnology SSI in the Netherlands was emerging in this period. All these young firms saw R&D as their core activity. They were either independently established (60 per cent) or spin-offs from academia or existing firms (40 per cent) with virtually no DBFs created through diversification from existing pharmaceutical firms (Enzing, 2000; Enzing and Kern, 2002). These DBFs had relations with academia as well as with large pharma firms, both inside and outside the Netherlands. Their main sources of income were formed by royalties from licences or by offering a variety of specialized services such as contract research, contract manufacturing and/or custom synthesis (Enzing and Kern, 2002). Examples of such DBFs are among others Pharming (transgenic animals), Crucell (platform technologies, gene therapy), Isotis (human tissue engineering).

The majority of this 'new breed' of Dutch DBFs was engaged, through contract research services, in general platform technologies with a potential for applications in the pharmaceutical industry such as e.g. genomics, combinatorial chemistry, high-throughput screening and bio-informatics (Degenaars and Janszen, 1996; Ernst and Young, 2001b). In these application areas, time-to-market was shorter and there was less risk involved as compared with therapeutics. These latter required lengthy and costly clinical trials and had a higher chance of failure. In our analyses of the Dutch pharmaceutical biotechnology industry we will further focus on firms active in these general platform technologies.

General-purpose, platform technologies: research in these platform technologies could be considered as an important 'engine of knowledge' (Allansdotir et al., 2002). There were many technological spillovers by means of licences to different parts of biotechnology. Especially platform-technologies generate such spillovers by providing platforms also in non-pharma applications such as plant breeding, food processing (for example diagnostic kits), speciality chemicals, bioinformatics and biological catalysis. DBFs that specialized in platform technologies aimed to provide tools and services to pharma firms that were involved in drug discovery and development. The advantage of this strategy was its potential for relative rapid commercialisation with (hopefully) fast cash-flows (Casper, 1999).

So, over the course of the 1990s a 'knowledge exploration value chain' was emerging in the field of general platform technologies, which is schematically depicted in Figure 8.1.

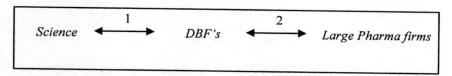

Figure 8.1 Emerging knowledge exploration value chain and learning regimes in the field of general platform technologies

Within this value chain we can discern between two main types of learning regimes, namely:

- Learning regime 1: embedded within a network of DBFs with academia.
- Learning regime 2: embedded within a network of one or more DBFs with a large pharma firm.

As can be understood from Figure 8.1, DBFs performed a key role in commercializing scientific knowledge. They connected a 'basic scientific environment' with its emphasis on the importance of new knowledge with a 'techno-economic environment', which emphasized economic value (McKelvey, 1997). In this respect DBFs were faced with a dual selection environment that stressed economic performance on the one hand and scientific excellence on the other hand. This had implications for the nature of the knowledge base in terms of stand-alone vs. systemic. The knowledge produced by academia was of a mainly stand-alone nature. To turn this knowledge into commercially valuable knowledge, DBFs needed to integrate it with other bodies of knowledge such as adjacent biotechnological disciplines as well as with competences in the field of process technology and ICT. So, when moving from left to right in Figure 8.1, the knowledge base became increasingly systemic (Degenaars and Janszen, 1996; McKelvey and Orsenigo, 2001).

We now further analyse each learning regime more in depth; the next section discusses learning regime 1 whereas the following section discusses learning regime 2.

LEARNING REGIME 1: TECHNOLOGICAL EXPLORATION

Learning regime 1 in the basic-scientific selection environment was embedded in a network that was made up of relations between DBFs and (public) research institutes. In this learning regime the main selection force stemmed from the nature of the knowledge base and its focus was on exploring new knowledge. We distinguish between two periods, one period from the late 1980 towards the late 1990s and a second period from the late 1990s onwards.

From the Late 1980s Towards the Late 1990s

From the 1980s towards the middle of the 1990s the knowledge base on general purpose, platform technologies had a mainly stand-alone nature due to its strong basis in molecular biology or biology. Demand was formed by European and world demand rather than local demand (Ernst and Young, 2001b). Due to some high quality research at Dutch universities there were opportunities for Dutch DBFs, although mainly pertaining to various niches (Janszen and Degenaars, 1996). The fact that there were virtually no DBFs created through diversification from existing pharmaceutical firms provided an indication of the cognitive distance from the existing knowledge base of organic chemistry. Also the unwillingness of the existing labour force of organic chemists to 'give up' their powerful positions to pharmacologists and biotechnologists meant that incumbent firms did not jump onto these new opportunities. The majority of firms cooperated with (public) research institutes, indicating that knowledge was highly science-based (Ministerie EZ, 1998). The learning outcome of this search process was formed by abstract and codified knowledge. The search process of scientific discovery itself was characterized by a lot of trial and error and was highly specific to individual persons and research communities (Enzing, 2000a). This process entailed many elements that were difficult to codify such as test set-up, accurate execution, interpretation of test results and so on. It was characterized by serial, incremental improvements, leading to the accumulation of tacit knowledge within stable research groups of academics and DBFs (Enzing and Kern, 2002). So, a science-based and fast-changing knowledge base developed with cumulative characteristics and high specificity to a network of DBFs and academics (Enzing and Kern, 2002). Relations between these people involved were dense and of fairly high durability (4-5 years or more) with frequent interaction in mutual openness on mainly search-related and technological issues. See also Table 8.1.

In this network a clear spatial concentration could be observed, especially around universities such as those in Amsterdam, Groningen, Leiden, Utrecht, Nijmegen, Wageningen, Maastricht and Delft. The mainly tacit search process meant that personal contacts and frequent interaction were necessary to accommodate an effective transfer of this tacit knowledge (Geenhuizen and van de Knaap, 1997). In addition, physical closeness facilitated easy access to a talent pool of skilled workers, facilitating knowledge spillovers through the mobility of researchers. In addition, opportunities were generally diffuse, requiring regular checks and adaptations of the search process into the most promising search direction (Geenhuizen, 1999). The importance of physical closeness was further indicated by the fact that most patents are assigned to inventors from within the Netherlands (Allansdottir et al., 2002) in this period, making spillovers into this learning regime relatively limited. So, these exploration networks were formed by dense networks of strong ties between universities and DBFs that enabled them to develop an in-depth understanding and critical peer reviews (Enzing et al., 2002).

Table 8.1 Analysis pharmaceutical biotechnology system of innovation: learning regime 1

SECTORAL INSTITUTIONS

	Period late 1980s and late 1990s	Period late 1990s – onwards
Knowledge Base		
tacitness	high (search process)	high (search process)
codification	high (product knowledge)	high (product knowledge)
level of diffusion	high	high
level of systemicness	low	medium - high
		- related biotechnologies
		- initial linkages to ICT
rate of change	high	medium-high

Appropriability conditions

level	high	high
means	publications, patents	publications, patents

Opportunity conditions

level	high	medium - high (niches)
variety	high	medium
source	technology	technology

Competitive Conditions

intensity	low	low
dimensions	innovation	innovation

Type of innovation

knowledge/product/process	new knowledge	new knowledge, initial products

NETWORK INSTITUTIONS

Network structure	1a	1a	1b
- size	multilateral	multilateral	bilateral
- centrality	medium	medium	high
- density	high	high	low
- structural holes	low	low	high
- cognitive distance	low	low	medium
- entry	medium	medium	high

Relational form			
- formality	low - medium	low/medium	high
- durability	medium - high	medium - high	low
- intensity	high	high	low
- breadth of issues	medium	medium	low

Governance of relational risk

Relational Risk	1a	1a	1b
- strategic need	high	high	
- structure of interests	converging	converging	parallel
- specific investments	high	high	low

Governance			
- governance strategy	contracts, mutual self-interest, network position trust-in-intention	contracts, mutual self-interest, network-position, trust-in-intention	contracts (licence)

- coordinating mechanisms	social coordination & control, linking pins, information systems	social coordination linking pins, information systems

ELEMENTS OF A LEARNING REGIME

- object of learning	new scientific knowledge	new scientific knowledge
- learning process	expansive search & exploration	expansive search & exploration
- actors	scientists and DBFs	scientists & DBFs
- input	research skills & scientific knowledge	research skills& scientific knowl.
- output	new scientific knowledge	new scientific knowledge
- spillovers		
- outside-in	low	high
- within network	high (tacit knowledge on search)	high in strong ties low in weak ties
- inside-out	high (codified knowledge)	high
freeridership	low	low
hold-up	high	high (low in weak ties)

LEARNING OUTCOMES

Main outcome	new knowledge on General platform technologies	new knowledge on general platform technologies
level of newness	new to world	new to the world
elements of newness	new scientific insights	new scientific insights

From the Late 1990s and Onwards

Towards the end of the 1990s platform technologies increasingly became more multidisciplinary in nature and entailed varying combinations of disciplines. Examples of such systemic platform technologies are DNA chips, rDNA arrays, proteomic analysis combining electrophoresis and NMR, genomic sequencing (Janszen and Degenaars, 1996; Enzing, 2000). In addition, combinations with software and micro-electronics started to develop that accommodate for miniaturization, automation and data-mining. This was also reflected in a growth of the number of patents with multiple assignees, especially over the 2nd half of the 1990s (Allansdottir et al., 2001). In this respect opportunities increased, which was also reflected by the fact that the number of entrants further accelerated to 22 in 2000 (Biopartner 2001), providing further substance to the Dutch pharmaceutical biotechnology SSI.

Based on a recent survey held in spring of 2003,[5] there were approximately 110 DBFs in the Netherlands that specialized in pharmaceutical biotechnology. Of these 110 firms approx. 38 per cent (42 firms) employ activities that entail both R&D and production whereas approx. 27 per cent (30 firms) also operate, next to their own R&D and production, as subcontractors to others by offering contract research services. Moreover, approx. 21 per cent (23 firms) are fully dedicated to R&D with no other activities (Enzing et al., 2003). Overall, this means that approx. 78 per cent (86 firms) that are active in the field of pharmaceutical biotechnology are active in R&D.

Of these 86 Dutch DBFs that are active in pharmaceutical biotechnological R&D; between 70–80 per cent (60–69 firms) work closely together with a university or a semi-public research institute. Approx. 36 per cent of the mentioned universities and research institutes are based in the Netherlands, with universities in Wageningen, Groningen, Utrecht, Leiden and Nijmegen most frequently mentioned.[6] The focus of this cooperation is on scientific research, developing new research techniques and/or on preclinical trials. Cooperation is mainly formed by means of joint projects to which the involved parties contribute through bringing in (a combination of) finance, specific knowledge or specialized researchers (Enzing et al., 2003).

Due to the mainly monodisciplinary orientation of their academic partners in this learning regime 1, DBFs also actively started to search and access complementary (scientific) knowledge, wherever it was located. As a result these dense networks of strong ties between universities and DBFs were opening up to complementary, outside sources of knowledge. Such outside sources were formed by universities, research institutes and other networks outside the Netherlands, either at various locations in Europe or in the US. Next to Dutch partners also universities and research institutes in the US (18 per cent), the UK (6 per cent) and Germany (4 per cent) are mentioned[7] (Enzing et al., 2003). Because this knowledge at universities and research institutes was codified, it was easily accessible and transferable by means of publications or Internet (Ernst and Young, 2000). In particular the use of the Internet enabled DBFs to share information with anyone around the globe and to access public databases with state-of-the-art (scientific) knowledge. These relations relied much less on geographical proximity and could take place over (very) long distances (van Geenhuizen and van de Knaap, 1997). So, these more virtual linkages with weak ties created a non-dense network that was complementary to these dense research networks. The relations in the former were generally of low strength in terms of duration, frequency and entailed a limited set of specific technological issues (Enzing and Kern, 2002). See also again Table 8.1.

Governance and coordination of these relations took place in various forms such as licences, technology partnerships or by research contracts with scientific organizations. This also explained the large inflows of knowledge from US-based licences into the Netherlands (Janszen and Degenaars, 1996; Enzing et al., 2003).

LEARNING REGIME 2: TECHNOLOGICAL EXPLOITATION AND BUSINESS EXPLORATION

The 'techno-economic face' of the dual selection environment (Figure 8.1) was concerned with the exploration of new products, more than with new knowledge (Janszen and Degenaars, 1996; Ernst and Young, 1999). This meant that learning regime 2 was embedded in a network made up of relations between DBFs and large pharma firms. The rationales underlying this network were as follows. Large pharma firms needed to keep up to date with a rapidly changing knowledge base which was also diverse and systemic as it was built up of various disciplines. At the same time, opportunities pertained to niches and were also diffuse making it difficult to decide for pharma firms in which fields of knowledge to invest and which to ignore (Ernst and Young, 2000; 2001b). Therefore, large pharma firms made use of alliances with various small DBFs which enabled them to explore various opportunities at the same time, without making substantial specific investments. The attractive but diffuse nature of opportunities and the fact that knowledge was highly specific to these DBFs meant that the network structure was made up of mainly bilateral relations between large pharma firms and DBFs. For these DBFs a core performance-yardstick is 'time-to-patent' (Ernst and Young, 1999). Again we distinguish between the two same periods, namely one period from the late 1980 towards the late 1990s and a second period from the late 1990s onwards.

From the Late 1980s Towards the Late 1990s

In contrast with learning regime 1 in this period, selection in this 2nd learning regime stemmed more from the nature of the opportunity conditions, although the knowledge base still played its part. This combination of attractive, diffuse opportunity conditions and a rapidly changing knowledge base required diversity in search spaces. As a result, a network structure emerged that combined a variety of decentralised approaches with the ability to coordinate this diversity in a fairly light way. So, in this learning regime the need for diversity stemmed from a combination of opportunity conditions and knowledge base.

This network structure also explains why in most cases DBFs did not cooperate closely together when they were already cooperating with a large pharma firm. To interact directly with one another would require specific cognitive investments from the involved DBFs. Engaging in such investments was only rational when there were evident opportunities to do so. The stand-alone nature of knowledge in this period did not provide such a rationale as potential linkages between various technological areas were largely absent or difficult to define upfront (Janszen and Degenaars, 1996). As a consequence, spillovers between DBFs were very limited (Ministerie EZ, 1998; Senker, 1998). See also Table 8.2.

An important governance instrument in this network was formed by research contracts, possibly complemented by minority equity arrangements (Ernst and Young, 1999; Enzing, 2000b). These contracts regulated contract research, contract manufacturing, custom synthesis, development, sequencing, testing, software design and so on. These contracts aimed to provide some duration to the relationship and to assure the DBF with sufficient resources (especially money) to do research. In general, these contracts wee being evaluated every two to three years (Ministerie EZ, 1998).

Table 8.2 Analysis pharmaceutical biotechnology system of innovation: learning regime 2

SECTORAL INSTITUTIONS

	Period late 1980s and late 1990s	Period late 1990s – onwards
Knowledge Base		
tacitness	high	high
codification	high	high
level of diffusion	medium	medium - high
level of systemicness	medium	high
- related technologies	- initial linkages to ICT	- clear linkages to ICT
rate of change	medium-high	high
Appropriability conditions		
level	medium	medium
means	patents, compementary assets	patents, complementary assets
Opportunity conditions		
level	medium (niches)	medium (standard platforms) high (advanced platforms)
variety	high	low - medium (standard platforms)

		high (advanced platforms)
source	technology, demand	technology, demand

Competitive Conditions

intensity	low	medium - high
dimensions	innovation	costs, flexibility, innovation

Type of innovation

product/process	products	products

NETWORK INSTITUTIONS

Network structure

- size	bilateral	multilateral
- centrality	high	medium
- density	low	medium
- structural holes	high	medium
- cognitive dist.	high	medium
- entry	medium	medium
Relational form		
- formality	high	medium - high
- durability	medium	medium
- intensity	low	low - medium
- breadth of issues	low	low - medium

Governance of relational risk

- Relational Risk		
strategic need	high	high
structure of interests	diverging	diverging - parallel
specific investments	high from DBF	high from DBF
	low from pharma firm	low - medium
- Governance		
governance strategy	contracts, network-position, trust-in-competence	contracts, network-position trust-in-competence
coordinating mechanisms	licenses, incentive systems, selection systems	licenses, incentive systems, selection systems

ELEMENTS OF A LEARNING REGIME

- object of learning	new technological platforms	new technological platforms & derived products

- learning process	'division of labour'	'division of labour' ; direct interaction between DBFs
- actors	pharma firms and DBFs	pharma firms and DBFs
- input	research skills and knowledge on potential applications	research skills & knowledge on potential applications
- output	new technological platforms	new technological platforms
- spillovers		
- outside-in	high (from academia)	high (from academia)
- within network	low	low
- inside-out	high (through variety of applications)	high (through variety of applications)
freeridership	medium - high (from side of large pharma firm)	medium (from side of large pharma firm)
hold-up	high (from side of DBF)	high (from side of DBF)

LEARNING OUTCOMES

Main outcome	new knowledge on general platform technologies	new general platform technologies
level of newness	new to world	new to the world
elements of newness	new customer function	new customer function

The case of general platform technologies now raises some interesting questions such as: why were contracts such an important coordinating mechanism in a context with a strong focus on exploration? How were these contracts monitored given the high rate of change? And how did the cognitive distance between large pharma firms and DBFs affect the need for specific, cognitive investments?

In essence, the contract regulated a relatively arms-length relationship between two parties. A DBF devoted a lion's share of its resources to explore a specific technological field and to which the large pharma firm contributed by financial resources. From the viewpoint of a large pharma firm, it was basically subcontracting research to a DBF and its interest mainly entailed the codified knowledge as an outcome of this search process, not so much this process itself. This was an important point: although the cognitive distance with its existing knowledge base of organic chemistry was fairly large, a pharma firm did not need to engage in specific, cognitive investments (such as mastering all of these tacit competences and search routines) nor in the build up of trust. This also explained the possibility of cooperating without the need of being physically close. The absence of such social coordination mechanisms then made contracts a rational choice. However, its value was not so much in providing the possibility of recouping specific investments (as these were fairly limited) or in providing a detailed prescription of how things should be done. Its value was mainly in regulating between a large pharma firm contributing to the costs of doing research, manufacturing and so on, in return for the 'first-right-of-refusal'. This entailed the rights to have first, exclusive access to the results upon which to base a decision whether to use these or not. Note that this type of arrangement connected with the network structure that combined a variety of decentralized approaches with fairly light coordination.

The fact that knowledge as an outcome of the search process was highly codified explained why contracts *could* be used in the field of general platform technologies (and in biotechnology in general) as it made it possible to directly assess the amount of progress being made. Still, the high rate of change explained the importance of evaluation on a regular basis. Depending on the outcome of such an evaluation the contractual relation was durable up to the point that opportunities proved to be viable. If not, relations terminated and parties separated. This easy break-up was possible due to the fact that specific, cognitive investments were limited and trust-in-intention was not a key coordinating mechanism. If parties needed to engage in such investments in order to grow closer in terms of cognition and trust-in-intention, this would create an inclination to continue the relationship.

From the Late 1990s and Onwards

At the end of the 1990s, the appropriability conditions were starting to change for DBFs in the field of general platform technologies. Increasingly knowledge on these technologies diffused on a wider scale, such as DNA-cloning or purification techniques (Ministerie EZ, 1998). Compared with therapeutic applications, margins became lower and competition increased (Ernst and Young, 2000). This enabled large pharma firms to command lower prices. To escape from this growing cost pressure DBFs, both existing ones and new start-ups, moved into new and more advanced fields of knowledge such as for example functional genomics that enabled to create more advanced platforms (Senker, 1998). It also forced DBFs to think about alternatives for large pharma firms. One alternative remained to pursue a stand-alone strategy in the market for therapeutics with potentially high margins but with the disadvantage of enormous costs and risks. Therefore, a more viable alternative was emerging that consisted of a hybrid model using elements of both. The general idea was to first develop a strong position around a sophisticated technology platform that generated cash-flow through licensing fees. These initial revenue streams then opened up possibilities to collaborate with other DBFs in order to develop products based on this technology platform and aimed at larger, more profitable markets (Senker and van Zwanenberg, 2001; Enzing and Kern, 2002b). An example were genomics firms that, through contract research, develop genetic libraries based on which they (aspire to) develop potential therapeutics. Some of these products were much more niche-oriented and highly customised to specific diseases, a world-apart from the one-size-fits-all character of most blockbuster drugs of large pharma firms (Pisano, 2002). Such niches generally did not appeal to large pharma firms but were potentially highly attractive to DBFs that could benefit from a more favourable cost structure. So, opportunities seemed to be changing in favour of DBF's. This was also indicated by the fact that some of them had been able to command deals with pharma firms at more favourable terms such as profit-sharing, co-promotion or full commercialization. In addition, to explore this hybrid business model, DBFs increasingly cooperated with other DBFs instead of large pharma firms (PWC, 1999; Enzing et al., 2002). As a result, the proportion of collaborative relationships and alliances between DBFs increased vis-à-vis alliances between DBFs with large pharma firms and made the distinction between platform vs. product-based firms increasingly blurred. This made the network structure in learning regime 2 more multilateral[8] and increased its density (Enzing et al., 2002). See also again Table 8.2. Some reflections on the future: as analysed, until now large pharma firms have adopted the knowledge base on molecular biology in such a way that it enables them to maintain their existing position and business model. This business model can be described as a 'one-size-fits-all model' with a focus on the development of standard drugs that satisfy the average needs of a mass market. In line with this, pharma firms have set-up different kinds of standardized organizational routines, in production (economies of scale) as well as in marketing and sales (large sales forces, standardized distribution channels), all in order to sell high volumes of pills (Pisano, 2002). In essence, the core of this model is to cure (symptoms of) diseases of patients, not to learn more about these patients (McKelvey and Orsenigo, 2001). In this respect, the emerging development of genetic-based products that are more niche-oriented and highly customized to specific diseases and (small) groups of patients is a very interesting one. It opens up opportunities for more specialised DBFs as currently being explored. It reflects a different kind of business model and requires other competences, not only technology-wise but also organization-wise. Clearly this does not fit with the blockbuster-model of large pharma firms and it may turn out to be, and we can only speculate at this point, more competence-destroying for these incumbents than the technological revolution itself. It connects with our analysis along the cycle of knowledge in which we argued that, in order to be able to fully utilise the potential of the novel combinations, this requires a profound change in the total 'script' of the industry (Nooteboom, 2000). From evolutionary theory we know that such 'paradigm-shifts' take time as new technologies do not immediately lead to economic growth, even after they have developed and diffused. As argued along the cycle of knowledge, this requires that the mismatch is overcome between on the one hand the vested interests and the institutional set-up based on the old paradigm and, on the other hand, the unfolding script of the new paradigm. In other words, how the pharmaceutical biotechnology industry will move to consolidation and generalization, in the Netherlands as well as elsewhere, remains an unanswered question at the moment.

CONFRONTING HYPOTHESES WITH EMPERICAL FINDINGS

In this section we discuss whether our formulated hypotheses are supported by our empirical analysis of the Dutch pharmaceutical biotechnology system of innovation. In line with the build-up of this chapter we first discuss the impact by the biotechnological revolution on the global pharmaceutical industry and based on that the emergence of learning regime 1. Next we discuss learning regime 2. Finally, we draw some conclusions. See Table 8.3 for an overview of our hypotheses.

The Biotechnological Revolution

As argued in the first section, the biotechnological revolution has been largely global in nature (Henderson, 1994). Therefore, to understand the impact of biotechnology in the Netherlands and the sectoral dynamics following from that, we have first started with an analysis of the profound changes in the pharmaceutical industry caused by the biotechnology revolution.

Unlike other industries where technical change generally involved advancement in product technology or process technology, the first wave of molecular biology induced changes in the R&D process and affected existing methods of finding, synthesizing and selecting chemical compounds for therapeutic applications (Henderson and Cockburn, 1996). Although in this first wave the core knowledge base remained firmly rooted in organic chemistry, this new knowledge base on biotechnology enabled chemists to take a more rational approach to the design of new drugs. So, the advent of molecular biology enabled pharmaceutical firms to further exploit the possibilities as provided by the existing knowledge base of organic chemistry. In terms of the cycle of knowledge, a movement from exploitation to the phase of differentiation that was formed by adjusting the existing R&D process to new inputs provided by molecular biology. This ongoing exploitation of the existing knowledge base of organic chemistry made its limitations increasingly visible. These limitations became especially manifest by the increasing number of existing patents by pharma companies that was expiring in combination with a lowering number of potential 'blockbusters' in the pipe-line. At the same time, a 2nd biotechnological revolution arrived, genetic engineering, which affected the drug discovery process in more profound ways. In terms of our cycle of knowledge, this second wave in the molecular biology revolution marked the transition from differentiation to the phase of reciprocation, as the cognitive distance with the knowledge base on organic chemistry was larger and provided the basis for a more in-depth understanding of the biological underpinnings of diseases. This opened up the possibility to define search spaces in a more accurate manner. The random character of the search process still remained intact but could now be dealt with a more structured way. So, a new knowledge base developed and new organizational forms started to emerge, such as R&D-alliances between specialized research firms and large pharma firms, replacing the existing model of stand-alone, in-house R&D. This provides support for hypothesis 5a and 5b that from differentiation to reciprocation the insights into the limits of the existing knowledge base strongly affect 3rd level institutions and 2nd level institutions of the institutional environment (hypothesis 5a), and that the dominant organizational form opens up to towards outside sources of knowledge, resulting in a hybrid structure of strong and weak ties (hypothesis 5b).

In the Netherlands these profound, global changes have resulted in the emergence of a pharmaceutical biotechnology system from the mid 1980s and onwards. As analysed, this led to learning regime 1 that was mainly the domain of public research institutes and a few DBFs. In the first period that we analysed, between the mid 1980s and the late 1990s, the main focus of this learning regime was on scientific research. Although codified knowledge through publications by researchers in other countries were used as an input to this search process, explicit relations with such weak ties were mostly absent as can be noted from the fact that most patents were assigned to inventors from within the Netherlands. In addition, there was a very limited focus on possibilities for a rapid commercialization of this knowledge that could be noted from the limited number of relations with pharma firms such as AKZO Nobel, Solvay or foreign firms. This provides support for hypothesis 2a and 2b that feedback by outcomes of an exploration-oriented learning regime mainly affects the development of a new knowledge base, and that this process takes place in allopatric speciation, in a niche outside the existing institutional selection environment. This niche did not only lie outside the selection environment formed by large pharma firms but was also, to some extent, away from other exploration networks in foreign countries as most patents were assigned to Dutch inventors only.

So learning regime 1, as it developed throughout the first period from the mid 1980s towards the mid-late 1990s, focused specifically on the development of an in-depth understanding of stand-alone, science-based knowledge. The output consisted of codified knowledge in terms of publications and patents. This was a well-defined, stable output creating stability on the output-side of this learning regime. As analysed, the search process entailed many elements that were difficult to codify such as test set-up, accurate execution, interpretation of test results, reformulation of hypotheses and so on. Uncertainty did not stem so much from the output-side but from complexity of the search process. This search process was embedded in dense relations of fairly high durability with frequent interaction in mutual openness on mainly search-related and technological issues. In order to deal with this complexity a dense network of strong ties emerged, coordinated by a combination of contracts, mutual self-interest and social mechanisms such as peer control and review. These findings of the first period of learning regime 1 do not provide support for hypothesis 1 and hypothesis 8a that in exploration the institutional environment will select a dense network of strong *and* weak ties. The explanation for this is that in this first period the main focus was on scientific research only. As analysed, the exploration of such a science-based and stand-alone knowledge base created a highly tacit search process that entailed specific knowledge on a limited set of complex issues. The dense structure of strong ties functioned as a repository for this tacit knowledge and enabled critical peer reviews. This connects with findings in the literature that a dense network of strong ties generally facilitates an easy transfer and diffusion of such tacit and specific knowledge in view of developing an in-depth understanding of complex issues (Rowley et al., 2000; Coriat and Weinstein, 2001).[9]

At the end of this first period and especially in the second period from the late 1990s and onwards, the growing need for more systemic knowledge as articulated in learning regime 2 implied a substantial change in the 2nd level of the institutional environment of learning regime 1. This meant that this dense network of strong ties of learning regime 1 opened up to complementary sources of knowledge, held by weak ties at other locations. This does provide support for hypothesis 1 and 8a of an increasing need for weak ties when change becomes more radical (hypothesis 1), resulting in a dense structure of strong and weak ties as the dominant mode of organization in exploration (hypothesis 8a). Access to these weak ties made it possible to create the required diversity at the input-side of this learning regime, i.e. diversity in sources of knowledge. As analysed, these weak ties were coordinated through licences that made it possible to access and use this distant, codified knowledge without the need for the substantial specific cognitive investments and the build-up of trust. This is in contrast with hypothesis 8b predicting that in such exploration-oriented networks coordination takes place through informal mechanisms such as transfer-of-reputation, trust-in-competence and mutual self-interest. The explanation for this is that knowledge held by these weak ties at distant locations is highly codified through publications and patents. Its potential value can therefore readily be assessed given the generally high absorptive capacity present in the dense, local network. The high rate of change of knowledge meant that such distant sources of knowledge succeeded one another on a regular basis, which required constant monitoring for new potential sources. This relatively high turn-over of such weak ties was possible because the knowledge base was mainly stand-alone in nature. Substantial technological interdependencies were absent or weak, so that weak ties could be replaced without the risk of creating bottlenecks in adjacent technological areas. Based on our analysis of learning regime 1 throughout the two periods studied, hypothesis 9 could not be validated.

In sum, a dense network of strong (local) ties to deal with complexity, additional relations with more distant weak ties to deal with variability. The dense, local relations made up the core of a network that provided stability needed to develop an in-depth understanding. This core was then surrounded by a periphery of relations with outside actors with varying levels of entry/exit and durability that were needed in view of the required diversity in inputs (diversity in sources of knowledge). The value of this knowledge that originated from these outside sources was then assessed by the core members in the centre of the network. So, the locus of diversity of knowledge was in the periphery of the network whereas selection took place in the core of the network. This combination of ties and regular change in membership by weak ties created a stable and loosely coupled configuration in which novelty originated from novel combinations of members.

In conclusion, our hypotheses describing the co-evolution of institutional environment and learning regimes are supported (2a, 2b, 5a and 5b). Our hypotheses describing how this general pattern then settled in network structures and governance strategies were partially supported. Our empirical findings support the use of weak ties to deal with radical change (hypothesis 1), creating a dense network of strong and weak ties as the dominant mode of organization in exploration (hypothesis 8a). However, in contrast with hypothesis 8b, was the finding that relations with weak ties were coordinated by means of licences instead of informal mechanisms. Hypothesis 9 could not be validated.

Learning Regime 2

As analysed, learning regime 2 developed between large pharma firms and DBFs. This network emerged due to a strong complementarity between large pharma companies and small specialized DBFs, resulting in a clear division of labour: small firms conducted exploration for which the large firms formed the fundamental source of demand and provided the integrative capabilities that were required to transform the newly explored knowledge into commercial products. As we argued, this basically proved to be an effective way of solving the problem of combining exploration and exploitation by distributing these tasks in a network (Nooteboom, 2000). In other words, from the viewpoint of a DBF this learning regime primarily dealt with exploitation, whereas from the viewpoint of the large pharma firm it primarily dealt with exploration. It is important to keep this duality in mind when interpreting our empirical findings on this learning regime.

For the large pharma firm the combination of attractive but diffuse opportunities and a rapidly changing knowledge base created uncertainty at the output-side of the search process. This uncertainty can be decomposed in complexity and variability. To deal with complexity, a pharmaceutical firm contracted a DBF that explored in his distinct area of expertise in a relatively autonomous way, coordinated through a contract. In essence, the contract regulated a relatively arms-length relationship between both parties: a DBF devoted a lion's share of its resources to explore a specific technological field and to which the large pharma firm mainly contributed financial resources. To deal with variability in opportunities the central pharma firm followed two strategies. A first approach in the bilateral relation with a DBF was to evaluate these contracts on a regular basis. Depending on the outcome of such an evaluation the contractual relation was durable up to the point that opportunities proved to be viable. If not, relations were terminated and the parties separated. A second approach to handle variability was that large pharma firms contracted a number of DBFs to deal with the diffuse opportunities. This resulted in a non-dense network in which the large pharma firm occupied a central position from where it maintained mainly bilateral relations with DBFs, some of which were disposed of after some time and replaced by others.

This network structure enabled a large pharma firm to combine a diversity of decentralized approaches with the ability to coordinate this diversity in a fairly light way. These findings provide support for hypothesis 1 that when change in 2nd level institutions becomes more radical, there is an increasing need for weak ties to deal with this change. The radicalness of this change basically refers to the large cognitive distance between the existing knowledge base on organic chemistry and the new knowledge base on molecular biology and genetic engineering. DBFs formed these weak ties by specializing in research around this new knowledge base. The only way to have these DBFs come up with potentially valuable knowledge then was to let them explore 'far away' from the large in-house laboratories of mainly organic chemists. In this respect, these findings also provide support for hypothesis 2b that for a large pharma firm, novelty from these decentralized search approaches originated in allopatric speciation, outside the existing selection environment formed by traditional R&D-departments.

So, the bilateral relations between the central pharma firm and DBFs created a non-dense network structure made up of relations that were of limited strength and mainly coordinated through contracts (Table 8.2). When taking the exploration-perspective of a large pharma firm, this is in contrast with hypothesis 8a and 8b, predicting that in exploration a dense network of strong and weak ties will be selected as the dominant mode of organization. When taking the exploitation-perspective of a DBF though, these findings provide support for hypothesis 4 that in consolidation the increasing selection by 3rd level institutions becomes manifest by an emerging dominant network form that enables a division of labour. In addition, these findings provide partial support for hypothesis 6a that predicts that in exploitation non-dense networks are selected, made up of relations that are strong in duration and frequency of contacts and show less strength in terms of mutual openness and breadth of issues covered; this is the case in this network except for frequency of contacts that is lower than predicted. In addition, support is also found for hypothesis 6b that in exploitation formal coordination mechanisms are selected such as contracts and formal control mechanisms, eventually complemented by more informal instruments.

In sum, a network composed of a central firm that was surrounded by various weak ties to deal with complexity and variability in the exploration of opportunities. This combination of ties created a non-dense and stable configuration of novel combinations of members that cooperated in a division of labour. The diffuse nature of these mostly unrelated opportunities required that the locus of diversity in terms of exploring opportunities was at the periphery of the network whereas selection took place in the core of the network by the central firm; new knowledge was explored by DBFs, the value of which being assessed by the core firm in the centre of the network.

In conclusion, a key-characteristic of learning regime 2 was the duality of exploration and exploitation. Following our empirical analysis in the section above and the confrontation with our hypotheses, to understand the specificities of this learning regime requires the joint consideration of an exploration-perspective and an exploitation-perspective.

CONCLUSIONS

The analysis of the impact of the biotechnological revolution on the global pharmaceutical industry confirm our hypotheses that describe the general pattern of co-evolution between institutional environment and learning regimes, when moving from exploitation to exploration. In this respect, our analysis along the 'left part' of the cycle of knowledge, towards exploration, holds. As argued, it is too early in the development of this industry to be able to assess in how far the 'right part', towards exploitation, also applies in pharmaceutical biotechnology in the Netherlands or elsewhere. In addition, we found evidence that novelty originates in allopatric speciation, in a niche outside the existing selection environment. In learning regime 1 this niche did not only lie outside the selection environment formed by large pharma firms but was also, to some extent, away from other exploration networks in other countries. In learning regime 2 this niche was created by DBFs exploring without any substantial involvement from large, in-house laboratories of pharma firms. So, in this respect the general pattern of co-evolution between institutional environment and learning regimes could be identified.

Following Table 8.3, our empirical findings give partial confirmation of our hypotheses that describe how this general pattern of co-evolution settled in network structures and coordination mechanisms. We found clear evidence that weak ties as providers of new knowledge are needed when change becomes more radical. The opening up of the dense network of strong ties in learning regime 1 towards distant sources of codified knowledge was needed as a response to the increasing need for systemic solutions as articulated by learning regime 2. This resulted in a dense network of strong (local) ties to deal with complexity and additional relations with more distant weak ties to deal with variability.

Table 8.3 Overview of outcomes from confrontation of hypotheses and empirical findings for pharmaceutical biotechnology

PHARMACEUTICAL BIOTECHNOLOGY	Learning regime 1	Learning regime 2
Hypothesis 1	0 / +	+
Hypothesis 2a	+	+
Hypothesis 2b	+	+
Hypothesis 3a		
Hypothesis 3b		
Hypothesis 4		
Hypothesis 5a	+	
Hypothesis 5b	+	
Hypothesis 6a		0
Hypothesis 6b		+
Hypothesis 7		
Hypothesis 8a	0 / +	-
Hypothesis 8b	-	-
Hypothesis 9	(could not be validated)	(could not be validated)

Clarification
+ : support
0 : partial support
- : no support

This combination of ties and regular change in membership by weak ties created a stable configuration in which novelty originated from novel combinations of members.

The need to deal with radical change for large pharma firms originated from the large cognitive distance with the new knowledge base on biotechnology in learning regime 2. This resulted in a network composed of a central actor that was surrounded by various weak ties, some of which were incidentally disposed of and replaced. This combination of ties created a non-dense and stable configuration in which novelty also originated from novel combinations of members.

Our findings did not provide support for our hypotheses predicting that in exploration a dense network of strong and weak ties was selected and that was predominantly coordinated through informal mechanisms. In learning regime 1 the relations with weak ties at distant locations were mainly coordinated through licences. In learning regime 2 we found a non-dense network of low strength relations with DBFs, mainly coordinated through contracts. The reason for both these contrasting findings lies in the highly codified nature of knowledge, as an outcome of the search process. Codified knowledge, even at distant locations, can indeed be accessed fairly easily and, when of potential value, be absorbed by means of a licence agreement or a contract. In other words, the codified nature of knowledge means that the 'knowledge absorbing party' does not need to be directly involved in the search process but merely needs to engage in a once-off transaction. In this respect, a licence or a contract makes it possible to delegate away the tacit complexities of the exploration and search process. This deviates from our analysis and discussion in Chapter 4, in which we analysed the co-evolutionary process. We argued that in exploration knowledge is primarily tacit with ample uncertainty and informal coordination mechanisms. In exploitation we argued that knowledge is more codified within a context of stability and more formal coordination mechanisms. In this case of exploration however, knowledge as an outcome of a search process is highly codified, meaning that contracts can be used. As analysed, these contracts were needed to provide sufficient duration to the relation with a DBFs. Our counter-argument made in Chapter 3 that contracts are undesirable in exploration, as they would signal distrust when specifying all possible unforeseen contingencies, does not apply in this respect. The division of labour between pharma firms and DBFs and the transaction nature of their relation meant that there was no or only a limited need for specific investments and the build of trust. So, it made sense to coordinate the transactions of codified knowledge in learning regime 1 and learning regime 2 through contracts.

In other words, both learning regimes provide a case that deviates from our theoretical analysis made in earlier chapters. On the one hand, there are characteristics of exploration as there is ample uncertainty on search directions and methods, on the other hand, knowledge is highly codified, which is a key characteristic of exploitation. Clearly, our theory has provided us with archetypes and had not foreseen the possibility of hybrid forms between these archetypes. The case of pharmaceutical biotechnology shows the possibility of such a hybrid structure between exploration and exploitation, a structure that can only be understood by the joint consideration of both perspectives.

CONSULTED LITERATURE AND REPORTS ON THE DUTCH PHARMACEUTICAL BIOTECHNOLOGY SSI

Aitken, M. (2000), A license to cure, *McKinsey Quarterly*, 1, 80–89.
Allansdottir, A., A. Bonnaccorsi, A. Gambardella, M. Mariani, F. Pammolli and M. Riccaboni (2001), *Innovation and competitiveness in biotechnology: a European*

perspective, background report, DG-Enterprise, European Commission, Brussels, 97–133.

Allansdottir, A., A. Bonnaccorsi, A. Gambardella, M. Mariani, F. Pammolli and M. Riccaboni (2002), *Innovation and competitiveness in biotechnology,* Enterprise papers, 7-2002, DG-Enterprise, European Commission, Brussels.

Bachmann, R., R. Berendes and J. Cuntze, *Biotech - why now?,* McKinsey European Chemicals Forum, Frankfurt, 28th September 2001.

Berenschot (2000), *Corporate venturing,* rapportage voor het ministerie van Economische Zaken, Den Haag.

Casper, S. (1999), *High technology governance and institutional adaptiveness: do technology policies usefully promote commercial innovation within the Geman biotechnology industry,* NIAS Working Paper, Wassenaar.

Bhandari, M. (1999), A genetic revolution in health care, *McKinsey Quarterly,* 4, 58–67.

Biopartner (2001), The Netherlands life sciences report 2002, gaining momentum, Biopartner, Leiden.

Biopartner (2002), The emerging Dutch life science sector, Biopartner, Leiden.

Economist (2001), Big is beautiful, biotechnology, *The Economist,* London, 6th November 2001.

Economist (2001), A bio-bubble?, Biotechnology in Europe, *The Economist,* London, 6th November 2001.

Economist (1998), Hardly hybrids, biotechnology, *The Economist,* London, 4th June 1998.

Ernst & Young (1999), *European Life Sciences 1999, sixth annual report,* Ernst & Young Ltd., London.

Ernst & Young (2000), *Evolution, European Life Sciences report 2000,* Ernst & Young Ltd., London.

Ernst & Young (2001a), *Focus on fundamentals, the biotechnology report,* Ernst & Young Ltd., London.

Ernst & Young (2001b), *Integration, European Life Sciences report 2001,* Ernst & Young Ltd., London.

Ernst & Young (2001c), *What's in a name: leveraging a quality brand in the health sciences marketplace,* Ernst & Young Ltd., London.

Ernst & Young (2002), *Beyond borders, the global biotechnology report 2002,* Ernst & Young Ltd., London.

Enzing, C.M. (2000a), *Voorstudie IOP Genomics,* TNO-STB rapport-00-22, TNO-STB, Delft.

Enzing, C.M. (2000b), Bijlage bij de integrale nota biotechnologie, Ministerie van Economische Zaken, *Integrale nota biotechnologie,* Den Haag.

Enzing, C.M. and S. Kern (2002a), Eindrapport Life Sciences Impact, TNO-STB rapport, rapportage voor het ministerie van Economische Zaken, Den Haag.

Enzing, C.M. and S. Kern (2002b), *The Dutch biotechnology innovation system: an inventory and assessment of the major developments since 1994,* TNO-STB report-02-04, TNO-STB, Delft.

Enzing, C.M., S. Kern and A. van de Giessen (2002), De toekomst van de Nederlandse life sciences sector: trends en knelpunten, TNO-STB rapport-02-08, TNO-STB, Delft.

Enzing, C.M., S. Kern and A. v.d. Giessen (2003), *R&D samenwerking door de Nederlanse biotechnologie industrie: uitkomsten van een survey,* TNO-STB rapport 03-22, TNO-STB, Delft.

Gambardella, A. (1995), *Science and innovation in the US pharmaceutical industry*, Cambridge, Cambridge University Press.

Geenhuizen, M. van and B. van der Knaap (1997), R&D and regional networks dynamics in Dutch pharamceutical industry, *Journal of Economic and Social Geography*, **88**, 307–320.

Geenhuizen, M. van (1999), How small biotechnology firms survive in the Dutch pharmaceutical industry: an exploratory analysis, in: R.P. Oakey (ed.), *New Technology-based in the 1990's*, Paul Chapman, London, 200–212.

Heida, H (2002), De bio-economie, *Forum*, Den Haag, 7 februari 2002, 10–15.

Henderson, R. (1994), The evolution of integrative competence, innovation in cardiovascular drug discovery, *Industrial and Corporate Change*, **3**(3), 607–630.

Henderson, R. and I. Cockburn (1996), *Scale, scope and spillovers: the determinants of research productivity in drug discovery*, Rand Journal of Economics, **27**(1), 32–59.

Henderson, R., L. Orsenigo and G. Pisano (1999), The pharmaceutical industry and the revolution in molecular biology: interactions among scientific, institutional and organizational change, in: D.C. Mowery and R.R. Nelson (et al.), *Sources of industrial leadership*, New York, Cambridge University Press.

Janszen, F.H.A. and G.H. Degenaars (1996), *Biotechnologie op weg naar het jaar 2000, Een toekomstperspectief voor de Nederlandse industrie*, Erasmus Universiteit, faculteit Bedrijfskunde, Rotterdam.

McKelvey, M. (1996), *Evolutionary innovation: the business of genetic engineering*, Oxford, Clarendon.

McKelvey, M. (1997), Co-evolution in commercial genetic engineering, *Industrial and Corporate Change*, **6**(3), 503–532.

McKelvey, M. and L. Orsenigo (2001), *Pharmaceuticals as a sectoral innovation system*, ESSY Working Paper, CESPRI, Bocconi University, Milan.

Ministerie van Economische Zaken (1998), Pharmaceuticals, *Technologie-radar*, Den Haag, 65–67.

Ministerie van Economische Zaken (2000), *Integrale nota biotechnologie*, Den Haag.

Nefarma (2002), *Annual report 2001*, Den Haag.

Nelson, RR., D.G. Victor and B. Steil (2002), *Technological Innovation and Economic Performance*, Princeton, Princeton University Press.

NRC-Economie redactie, Nederlandse alliantie in biotechnologie, Crucell krijgt steun DSM, *NRC-Handelsblad*, Rotterdam, 19 december 2002.

Oliver, A.L. Strategic alliances and the learning life-cycle of biotechnology firms, *Organization Studies*, **22**(3) 467–490.

Orsenigo, L., F. Pammolli and M. Riccaboni (2001), Technological change and network dynamics, lessons from the pharmaceutical industry, *Research Policy*, **30**, 485–508.

Pisano, G., (2002), Pharmaceutical biotechnology, in: R.R. Nelson, D.G. Victor and B. Steil (et al.), *Technological Innovation and Economic Performance*, Princeton, Princeton University Press.

Powell, W.W., K.W. Koput and L. Smith Doerr (1996), Interorganizational collaboration and the locus of innovation: networks of learning in biotechnology, *Administrative Science Quarterly*, **41**, 116–145.

PriceWaterHouseCoopers (1999), Key issues facing the pharmaceutical and health care products industry, PriceWaterHouseCoopers Ltd., London.

PriceWaterHouseCoopers (1999), *High-performing strategic alliances in the pharmaceutical, biotechnology and medical device and diagnostic industries*, PriceWaterHouseCoopers Ltd., London.

Rowely, T., D. Behrens and D. Krackhardt (2000), Redundant governance structures: An analysis of structural and relational embeddedness in the steel and semiconductors inductries', *Strategic Management Journal*, **21**, 369–386

Senker, J., (1998), *Biotechnology and competitive advantage, Europe's firms and the US challenge*, Edward Elgar, Cheltenham (UK).

Senker, J. and P. van Zwanenberg (2001), *European biotechnology innovation systems, final report*, TSER-project no. SOE1-CT98-1117, SPRU, Sussex.

Senter (2001), Life sciences: facts, impressions and cases, Senter-beleidsinteractierapport, Den Haag, 19 december 2001.

Trouw-Economie redactie (2002), Magere jaren in de farmacie, *Trouw*, Amsterdam, 28th January 2002.

Zucker L.G. and M.R. Darby (1997), Present at the biotechnological revolution: transformation of technological identity for a large incumbent pharmaceutical firm, *Research Policy*, **26**, 429–446.

NOTES

1. We thank Christien Enzing and Sander Kern of TNO-STB for their valuable comments on an earlier version of this chapter. Of course, any error remains entirely our responsibility. See for more information on both experts www.tno-stb.nl.

2. Random character is still present, even with new drugs that are introduced at today's markets. Pfizer's *Viagra* was initially developed as a treatment for hypertension, which proved to be limitedly successful. However, it has become an enormously successful drug for erectile dysfunctionings.

3. See for the used reports, documents and articles the overview at the end of this chapter.

4. Another reason mentioned is that of the institutional set-up of national healthcare systems. When these favour low priced medicinal products, such as in the Netherlands, this would lead to relatively few biotechnology companies (Senker and Zwanenberg, 2001).

5. Enzing, C.M., S. Kern and A. v.d. Giessen (2003), R&D samenwerking door de Nederlanse biotechnologie industrie: uitkomsten van een survey, *TNO-STB rapport*, Delft, June 2003.

6. The importance of physical closeness in this learning regime is certainly not a particular trait of the Dutch situation, but a common phenomenon in other countries as well. See for example an insightful study of the biotech-regions in Sweden and Ohio (Carlsson, 2002) or for Southern-Germany and Cambridge (UK) (Casper, 1999).

7. The remaining 36 per cent is divided over France (3 per cent), Belgium (3 per cent), rest of Europe (5 per cent), rest of world (2 per cent) and unknown (23 per cent).

8. This is also reflected in patents, which are increasingly assigned to multiple assignees (Allansdotir et al., 2002).

The dynamics of innovation and interfirm networks

9. This also connects with other findings in the literature such as Ouchi and Bolton (1988) and Grandori (1997) that in informational complex activities with a low observability of inputs and outputs and converging interests, firms will see cooperation as integrative without a need for extensive and formal safeguards. The identified combination of network structure and governance strategy accommodated for the expansive and predominantly tacit search and exploration activities that characterized this learning regime.

9. Conclusions

INTRODUCTION

In this chapter we will formulate the main conclusions of our research. To do so, we will first discuss the extent to which our theoretical analysis as made in Chapters 2 to 5 holds after having tested it empirically in Chapters 7 and 8. In other words, what can we say about the tenability of our theoretical framework and hypotheses and are there also some novel insights? This will be the subject of the first section. After that we will discuss the differences that we have observed empirically in network structures and their main forms of coordination between multimedia and pharmaceutical biotechnology. In next section we pick up the issue of external validity as discussed in Chapter 6 on our methodology and reflect on our research by discussing the generalizability of its main outcomes. Finally we discuss the main results and the limits of our research.

TENABILITY OF OUR THEORY AND SOME NOVEL INSIGHTS

In Chapter 2 we introduced a nested view of the institutional environment, consisting of 1st level, 2nd level and 3rd level institutions and a level of institutionalized behaviour, referred to as a learning regime. We have considered 1st level institutions as exogenous and have further focused on the dynamic relation between 2nd level and 3rd level institutions on the one hand and a learning regime on the other hand. To understand this dynamic relation we analyzed in Chapter 4, based on the cycle of knowledge, how these 2nd level and 3rd level institutions co-evolve with the embedded learning regime: how changes in the institutional environment affect a learning regime and how outcomes of a learning regime can also affect the institutional environment. In Chapter 5 we discussed the implications of this co-evolutionary process for firms with regard to the configuration of networks, the properties of interfirm relations and coordination mechanisms.

As discussed in Chapters 7 and 8, our case-studies have indicated that the general pattern of co-evolution, both when technology-oriented and when business-oriented, is adequately captured by the 'dialectic' of the cycle of knowledge. In consolidation, selection by 2nd level institutions such as the knowledge base and demand is strong. Towards generalisation, selection by 3rd level institutions increases and manifests itself by an emerging dominant organizational form that enables a division of labour, whereas in the phase of exploitation there is a strong selection by the existing institutional environment with limited feedback by outcomes of a learning regime. From differentiation to reciprocation, insights into the limits of the existing knowledge base strongly affect the 3rd level and 2nd level of the institutional environment. The dominant organizational form opens up towards outside sources of knowledge, which results into a hybrid structure of strong and weak ties.

From the confrontation between our hypotheses and our empirical findings in Chapters 7 and 8, we can conclude that our case-studies support this general pattern of co-evolution. However, our empirical findings do not fully support our hypotheses on how this co-evolutionary process settles in network structures, relational properties and coordination mechanisms. This is an important conclusion. Our research aim was to determine how the institutional environment of a SSI conditions interfirm learning, how outcomes of interfirm learning may affect the institutional environment, and in how far this varies per type of SSI. As we argued, we are interested in which elements of this co-evolutionary process are more SSI-generic and which elements are more SSI-specific. We can now conclude that a general pattern of co-evolution between 2nd level institutions and learning regimes can be identified. Our empirical findings have indicated that this co-evolutionary process is present in different SSIs and in different parts of a SSI. How this pattern settles in 3rd-level institutions is specific to the institutional set-up within a SIS or within different parts of a SSI. Hence at the sectoral level a general pattern of co-evolution can be identified; how this settles at the network level is specific to the institutional set-up within a SSI. Following this conclusion, it is important to understand in more detail these specificities of 3rd level institutions and the implications for the level of fit of the network structure, relational properties and coordination mechanisms with the 2nd level of the institutional environment. This will be analysed more in-depth in the next section.

Our empirical findings on multimedia and pharmaceutical biotechnology have also generated some novel insights. One such novel insight is formed by the case of publishers in multimedia. As analyzed in Chapter 7, the 'technology side' of the multimedia SSI has consolidated and has subsequently sought applications in all kinds of directions (generalization). In this respect, a new context was provided for various established industries (differentiation) and in this way induced a search process for business opportunities. In our analysis along the cycle of knowledge, we conjectured that firms in an exploitation setting actively and deliberately pursue the transition towards differentiation, for example through exporting or diversification to related markets. The case of publishers has informed us that application in a novel context can also be forced from outside, from a defensive need not to 'miss the boat'.

Another novel insight relates to our notion of allopatric speciation. As discussed in Chapters 7 and 8, exploration in both multimedia and pharmaceutical biotechnology took place in allopatric speciation, in a niche outside the existing selection environment. But we found some clear differences in how this niche was secluded from the existing selection environment. In multimedia we found one type that was formed by exploration through new entrants that were complete outsiders with no relevant antecedents in the industry whatsoever. The other type was formed by existing firms that explored at the periphery of their organization. Although we can classify this second type as a weaker form of the first type, both were secluded cognitively but not geographically. In both cases, firms maintained (some level of) contact and access to knowledge developed outside the Netherlands. In pharmaceutical biotechnology we found that this niche was not only secluded cognitively, by operating outside the selection environment formed by large pharma firms but also, initially, geographically. When learning regime 1 emerged at the end of the 1980s and early 1990s, it was strongly locally embedded, away from other exploration networks in foreign countries, as can be noted from the fact that in this period most patents were assigned to Dutch inventors only.

Another novel insight is the possibility of hybrid structures between exploration and exploitation. Clearly, in our theoretical analysis we have generated two archetypes, one for exploration and one for exploitation. However, our theory has not foreseen the possibility of a hybrid structure between these two archetypes. Learning regime 2 in pharmaceutical biotechnology informs us on the possibility of such a hybrid structure as it shows a non-dense structure with contracts as its main coordination mechanisms as an effective manner for exploration, instead of a dense structure coordinated by mainly informal mechanisms as we expected. This finding again points to the fact that sectoral specificities profoundly affect network structures, relational properties and coordination mechanisms. As said, this will be now dealt with in more detail in the next section.

COMPARING NETWORKS IN MULTIMEDIA AND PHARMACEUTICAL BIOTECHNOLOGY

As concluded in last section, how the general pattern of co-evolution between 2nd level institutions and learning regimes settles in 3rd level institutions is specific to the institutional set-up within a SSI. This is an important conclusion and it connects with our argument advanced in Chapter 5 that optimality of the network structure is liable to be a function of the context in which it is embedded. To differentiate between contexts we made the distinction between exploration and exploitation. Based on our empirical analysis of multimedia and biotechnology we can now conclude that this distinction is too general. Our empirical findings on networks in both SSIs show that there is a strong sectoral effect that determines which specific combination of network structure, relational properties and coordination mechanisms is selected. Even within the same SSI, there can exist substantial differences between networks as could be observed from the various learning regimes being embedded in different institutional environments within the same SSI. Therefore, in this section we will analyse how optimality of the network structure varies with different contexts. To do so, we first introduce a general typology of networks and then relate this to the distinction between organizing for exploration and organizing for exploitation. Based on that we apply this typology and our notions on organising to the various networks in multimedia and biotechnology. Finally we draw some conclusions.

A Typology of Networks

In Chapter 5 (Social Networks: a Typology) we argued that to develop a more in-depth understanding of networks from a learning and innovation perspective, the joint consideration of density of ties and strength of ties is required. Density of ties is relevant as it indicates the potential for cognitive variety, the strength of ties is relevant as it indicates the potential to cross the cognitive distance that is present in this variety. Based on this joint consideration of density and strength of ties we propose differentiating between four archetypes of networks, namely:

Table 9.1 Four different types of networks based on density and strength of ties

	LOW DENSITY	HIGH DENSITY
LOW STRENGTH	1	2
HIGH STRENGTH	3	4

Our key-argument is that the optimality of any of these four archetypes of networks is dependent on the context in which the network is embedded. To further explore this we first turn to some widely accepted ideas on organization.

In their seminal work 'Organisation and Environment', Lawrence and Lorsch (1967) argued that the two key-issues with regard to organization are specialization and integration: specialization refers to differentiation in activities and who performs those activities, integration refers to how those activities are coordinated. These two key-issues have relevance when structuring a division of labour, both within organisations and between organizations, but only in a setting of exploitation. In exploitation the widespread presence of standards, norms, rules and so on mean that activities can be clearly identified, well-structured, divided into sub-parts for specialisation and subsequently be coordinated in view of integration. This distinction between specialization and integration can be clearly identified in learning regime 2 in multimedia with its focus on technological exploitation. Communication with the customer was done by a central firm which integrated the various technical issues that were being taken care of by specialized suppliers. These supplying firms only had direct ties when needed in view of the integration process. As analysed, this 'dominant design' in organization consisted of a relatively non-dense network of ties that were durable with frequent interaction on specific issues in limited mutual openness. Hence this network largely coincides with archetype 3. In addition, this is also in line with hypothesis 7 that in exploitation non-dense networks are selected made up of ties that are strong in durability and frequency of contacts but show lower strength in terms of mutual openness and breadth of issues covered.

However, this distinction between differentiation and integration does not apply in a setting of exploration that is characterized by a shift-away from existing rules and norms and the break-up of old and creation of new routines and activities. One of the central arguments in our research is that such a setting requires variety-in-cognition. This makes the central task in exploration to manage this variety-in-cognition. Managing such variety then consists of two key-aspects, namely how to create variety-in-cognition and next how to coordinate this variety in such a way that new insights are developed without falling prone to chaos. In other words, in exploration the key-question is not where to locate specialization and where integration but where to locate diversity in the network, where to create selection and how to achieve a balance between them.

Exploration Networks in Pharmaceutical Biotechnology and Multimedia

Based on the discussion above, we now further reflect on the exploration networks in multimedia and biotechnology by analysing where in these networks diversity and selection were located and how they were balanced.

Pharmaceutical biotechnology: searching and exploring, in pharmaceutical biotechnology, the focus in learning regime 1 was on technological exploration with the main selection force stemming from the knowledge base. In this network variety-in-cognition was created at the input side of the search process through a non-dense periphery of low strength relations with outside actors with varying levels of entry/exit. This largely coincides with archetype 1. As analysed, the core was made up of a dense structure built up of relations of high strength that enabled to assess the value of this outside knowledge and as such functioned as a selection environment. This coincides with archetype 4. So, overall we observe a network structure that was made up of a combination of two types, namely: type 4 to deal with complexity and type 1 to deal with variability. It is this duality of the network structure that created a stable configuration in which selection and diversity operated in a balanced way and in which novelty originated from novel combinations of members.

Learning regime 2 was characterized by a dual focus on exploration and exploitation. Variety-in-cognition in the network in this learning regime was created through a non-dense network of relations with DBFs that were rather strong in terms of durability but showed low strength in terms of frequency of contacts, mutual openness and breadth of issues covered.[1] This largely coincides with archetype 1. As analysed, the core was made up of a central firm that through its exploitation focus could value the outcomes of these various search processes and as such functioned as a selection environment.[2] This combination of network structure and relational properties created a stable configuration that enabled selection and diversity to operate in a balanced way and in which novelty originated from novel combinations of members.

Multimedia: interactive learning, the focus in learning regime 1 in multimedia was on technological exploration. As analysed, the complex search-process required a dense network structure with low centrality and a high number of new entrants. Ties were strong in terms of frequency of interaction that was fairly open on various issues but of fairly short duration. This combination of dimensions of tie strength led to the creation of variety-in-cognition through an easy recombination of ties. So, in this network novelty originated from novel configurations of members. This network showed characteristics of tie strength of archetype 2 (short duration, fairly open) as well as of archetype 4 (frequent interaction, relative high breadth of issues). The presence of three 'back-ground' selection mechanisms complemented this network structure and prevented it from falling apart into chaos.

In learning regime 3 the focus was on business exploration. As analysed, VCs invested in various start-ups simultaneously, creating a network structure in which they occupied a central position. This combination of a central firm and peripheral start-ups engaging in exploration created a relatively non-dense network of ties that were strong in terms of frequency and openness but showed less strength in terms of durability and breadth of issues. So, a configuration in which novelty originated from novel combinations members. This network largely coincided with archetype 1 and in this respect resembled the network in learning regime 2 in pharmaceutical biotechnology, in which a centrally positioned pharma firm selected among various decentralized exploration efforts by DBFs. Unlike this network in biotechnology however, was the direct involvement in exploration by the centrally positioned VC. This made this network vulnerable as it created an absence of selection inside the network. With an additional lack of other 'background' selection forces or outside selection-forces such as e.g. demand this finally resulted into chaos. Figure 9.1 summarizes our discussion.

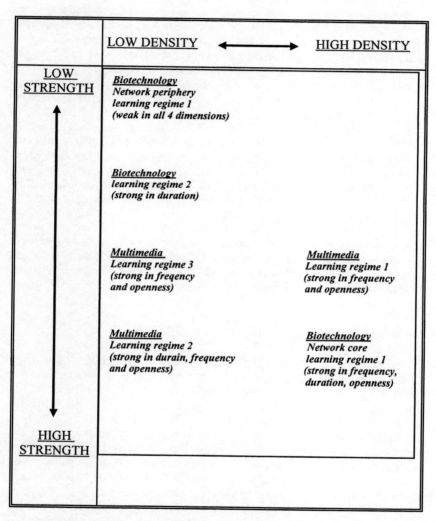

*Figure 9.1 Positioning of networks in multimedia and biotechnology in
        network typology*

In Conclusion

In this section we analysed how the optimality of the network structure varies with different contexts. Based on our empirical analyses of learning regimes in pharmaceutical biotechnology and multimedia we can draw the following conclusions. A network in exploitation generally favours archetype 3, a non-dense structure made up of strong ties. This enables a division of labour for which the key-question is where to locate specialization and where integration. In an exploration network the key-question is where to locate diversity and where selection and how to achieve a balance between them. To further specify this we can differentiate between a context of exploring a systemic knowledge base and exploring a stand-alone knowledge base. A systemic knowledge base selects for a dense, redundant network of relations that are strong in terms of frequency and openness but show low strength in terms of duration. This short duration of relations makes it possible to create diversity through novel configurations of members (hence an intermediate form between archetype 2 and 4). Selection in these continuously changing configurations takes place based on some 'background' selection mechanisms. A stand-alone knowledge base selects for a network structure with diversity at its periphery, through a non-dense structure of low strength relations (archetype 1), and selection in its centre, through a dense structure made up of strong relations or a central firm (archetype 4). When selection mechanisms are absent, such a network becomes prone to chaos.

GENERALIZABILITY OF CONCLUSIONS

One of the key methodological questions in any research is that of external validity, namely the extent to which the outcomes can be generalized to other contexts such as, in our research, to other industries or to other countries. This issue of external validity is the more important given our choice for longitudinal case-studies as our research method of which generalizability is not a particular strength. In this respect, we should differentiate between statistical generalization and analytical generalization. Statistical generalization can be defined as the degree to which the research findings can be considered valid for all the research units in the general population, if only a part of this population is empirically researched. In the case of analytical generalization a previously developed theory is used as a template with which to compare the empirical results of the conducted case studies with the aim to generalize these results to this broader theory (Yin, 1994). Given our methodology as outlined in Chapter 6, in this study we deal with analytical generalization. The question now is how far we can generalize from our case-studies. To address this we follow the distinction made by Groenewegen and Vromen (1996) between the relevance of conditions and relevance of issues. As argued by Groenewegen and Vromen, any theory gives a partial account, as 'no single theory is thought to be able to give a complete account of some set of phenomena of its own' (1996: 371). So, theories have value under certain conditions with regard to specific issues, which makes it important to be aware of those conditions and issues.

Relevance of conditions, in the context of our research, an important condition is the importance of knowledge. With the importance attached to knowledge comes the importance of learning and innovation. We have argued to 'treat' the knowledge base as a central, independent variable that explains the emergence of specific network structures, governance strategies and patterns in learning regimes, forming important dependent variables. This distinction between dependent and independent variables applies when studying the structural conditioning phase of the co-evolutionary process. When studying the structural elaboration phase of the co-evolutionary process, this distinction is reversed: outcomes of a learning regime become independent variables that affect the knowledge base making it a dependent variable. This change in distinction between independent and dependent variables is the methodological consequence that follows from our ontology as advanced in Chapter 1 in which we argued that we adopt an endogenous view on both knowledge and learning. The criterion of internal validity has then led us to select two industries that are indeed highly 'knowledge-intensive', so that assumed causal relations between knowledge and learning behaviour were to be expected. So, when considering the relevance of the outcomes of our research, an important condition is the key-role played by knowledge such as in multimedia and pharmaceutical biotechnology. Our conclusions may not hold when studying non-knowledge based relations in these industries such as for example 'standard transaction' relations with no knowledge exchange whatsoever. Nor may our conclusions hold in industries in which knowledge plays a less prominent role. In such contexts other approaches may have more relevance such as for example a power-based approach or TCE.

Another issue regarding relevance of conditions is that of the national context. The national context is formed by the 1st level in our model of the institutional environment. In our methodological discussion in Chapter 6, we have argued why it is important to keep the national context constant. Our research aim stresses differences among SSIs and our research questions focus on SSI specific institutions, insofar relevant for interfirm learning, and abstract from national institutions. By keeping the national context constant we can focus on differences among sectoral systems of innovation, which enables us to verify the relationships among the relevant variables, enhancing internal validity. Therefore, we have made the choice to select different sectoral systems of innovation within the same national, institutional context. So, our conclusions are applicable to the Netherlands and, strictly speaking, we cannot claim relevance to other countries. However, key sectoral institutions have a structure and life of their own (Mowery and Nelson, 1999), making that the importance of knowledge, given its central role for these industries, may exceed the role of some national institutions. This may be more so because both industries have been characterized, and still are to the present day, by substantial knowledge inflows from outside the national territory, a phenomenon shared by these two industries in other countries as well. So, although we cannot make any claims based on our research, we expect at least some resemblance with regard to the co-evolutionary processes in the multimedia and pharmaceutical biotechnology in other countries.

Relevance of issues, an important issue is the relevance of our level of analysis. The central model in our research is formed by the Cycle of Knowledge. Nooteboom (2000) claims that this heuristic tool applies to different levels of analysis, ranging from people, firms, industries and economies. Based on our research we cannot confirm nor reject this claim as the focus of our study has been on learning and innovation process in the context of a SSI, which is largely comparable with the industry-level. Given this restriction, we have concluded in the first section of this chapter that on an industry-level the general pattern as set out in Chapter 4 was largely confirmed: the four sub-phases that connect exploration with exploitation and *vice versa* could be identified, mostly also in the sequential manner as conjectured. However, our case-studies have not confirmed our hypotheses with regard to network structures and governance strategies. So, our case-studies have indicated that the 'general pattern' of learning, both when technology-oriented and business-oriented, is adequately captured by our 'dialectic' of exploration and exploitation. How this pattern then settles in network structures, governance strategies and learning regimes routines is specific to the institutional set-up within a SSI.

Another issue that relates to the external validity of our conclusions is the relevance of the cycle of knowledge in describing patterns of change, either technological or non-technological. In our case-studies we have studied patterns of (technological) change that, although characterized by substantial dynamism and in some cases abrupt change, all had a substantial level of cumulativeness in them. Let us further clarify this.

The multimedia innovation system is characterized by a duality in types of firms: new entrants with no relevant antecedents in this industry whatsoever as well as firms that have been around for a long(-er) period of time such as specialized suppliers of hard- and software, audio-visual firms, printing firms, publishers and telcos. This duality in types of firms reflects the dual face of multimedia: on the one hand the newness of multimedia technology and the new economic activities generated by it, on the other hand the convergence process of previously distinct industries that were increasingly affected by these new technological and economic developments. In pharmaceutical biotechnology we also see this duality in types of firms: small DBFs that explore in cooperation with large pharma firms that maintain a strong exploitation focus. The fact that appropriability takes place by complementary assets makes that this duality is maintained, at least for the time being. So, in both SSIs we see radical technological change and new entrants going together with the persistence of existing firms. The latter were needed as the continuity of innovative activities strongly depended on (some of) their capabilities and resources, indicating that for innovation in multimedia and pharmaceutical biotechnology there certainly is clearly also cumulativeness of knowledge and capabilities, next to substantial change. This connects with the social constructivist ontology underlying the cycle of knowledge. Perception, interpretation and evaluation are contingent upon the institutional environment and people are influenced in their thinking by prevailing cognitive institutions and other institutions that enable and constrain their actions. So, different people see the world differently to the extent that they have developed in different social and physical surroundings and have not interacted with each other. In other words, environment and past experience determine absorptive capacity (Nooteboom and Gilsing, 2003). This explains why the cycle of knowledge is indeed capable of describing the processes of cumulative (technological) change in these two SSIs.

RESULTS AND LIMITATIONS OF OUR RESEARCH

An important assumption in our research is that we see industry evolution as a dynamic disequilibrium and evolutionary process of constant adaptation and renewal of network structures, coordination mechanisms and learning regimes. To be able to explain why a specific combination of these three elements has emerged, we need to understand the co-evolutionary process that has generated it. Rather than providing a detailed account of the structure of the system at a certain moment in time, we have concentrated on trying to develop an understanding of how the system has evolved over time as a result of endogenous change within the system itself. So, we have focused on the dynamics within a SIS. The potential danger of such a dynamic analysis is that it may quickly lead to a high level of complexity and the risk of getting lost. To prevent us from falling into this trap we have set a number of limits to our research.

Limits, one limit is in time. We have not focused on the entire history of both SSIs but have limited our analysis to the past 10–15 years. Both the multimedia and pharmaceutical biotechnology SSIs have been characterized by a high rate of change in this period with abundant dynamic processes that we have analysed in terms of the co-evolution of institutional environment and learning regimes.

A second limit is in level of analysis. Our focus has been on the changing nature of networks and the changing properties of the relations making up these networks. In doing so, we have ignored acts of individual firms. This choice reflects the notion that relations form the core of a SSI and form an integral element of these learning and innovation processes within a SSI (Malerba, 2002).

A third limit is set by our choice of keeping the national level, the 1st level in our model of the institutional environment, constant. In our methodological discussion in Chapter 6, we have argued the importance of keeping the national context constant. By keeping the national context constant we can focus on differences among sectoral systems of innovation which enables us to verify the relationships among the relevant variables, enhancing internal validity. Therefore, we decided to select different sectoral systems of innovation within the same national, institutional context.

A fourth limit is set by our focus on knowledge-based relations. Obviously, firms may have different relations with different firms. The engagement in frequent economic transactions does not need to imply that these transactions are knowledge intensive. Transactions can entail mainly the exchange of standard products or services without any knowledge exchange whatsoever. Given our research aim, we have ignored such relations and we only studied those relations in which various sorts of knowledge are exchanged, in varying intensity.

A fifth limit is that we have not systematically compared the performance of different combinations of network structure, relational properties and coordination mechanisms.[3] This followed from our research aim and questions, based on which we developed our research design. Our choice then for longitudinal case-studies and for data-collection based on archival records made it possible to analyse those combinations of network structures, relational properties and coordination mechanisms of which ex-post could be determined that this combination proved to be successful. As a consequence, we have not been able to compare these forms with alternative forms of organization and their specific performance characteristics.

Results our research aim was to study the co-evolution between institutional environment and learning regimes. Based on the cycle of knowledge we have been able to systematically describe and analyse this co-evolutionary process in multimedia and pharmaceutical biotechnology. This analysis has brought us three important results.

One is that we have been able to explain why a specific combination of network structure, relational properties and coordination mechanisms was selected. In other words, our research has led us to understand and explain the 'inside-causations' of this co-evolutionary process, and how it settled in these 3rd level institutions.

A second result, which builds on the first, is that we have been able to develop some more insights into how optimality of the combination of network structure, relational properties and coordination mechanisms varies with the context. As we have shown, context-specificities profoundly affect the optimality of networks, which is a far cry from the universalistic tone of social network theory. In this respect, our study informs us on two issues with regard to the use of social network theory. A first issue is that social network theory has proven to be useful in systematically describing the structure and functioning of networks. The insights offered by social network theory on the distinction between on the one hand properties of the network structure such as density and on the other hand properties of relational ties making up this structure such as strength of ties, have proven to be useful in understanding social networks and differentiating between them. A second issue is that social network theory has not been useful in its normative implications with their strong universalistic tone. As argued, our study has clearly indicated that optimality of the combination of network structure, relational properties and coordination mechanism is subject to 2nd level institutions of a SSI. Hence the universalistic tone of social network theorists is not appropriate when studying networks from a perspective of learning and innovation. A third result is that our findings shed some more light on how a network-perspective, as taken in our research, can complement a firm-perspective. The increasing importance of networks, especially in knowledge-intensive industries, makes that both perspectives become increasingly interwoven. Our findings indicate that a network-perspective brings in a new view with implications when taking a firm-perspective. This especially applies to exploration networks as we predominantly found in multimedia and pharmaceutical biotechnology. In this respect, we concluded that in networks the key-question with regard to organizing for exploration is not 'how to combine specialization and integration' but 'how to combine diversity and selection'. This has implications for firms when developing a strategy on how to structure their network, where to position in such a network and which role to play. As said, such considerations were beyond the scope of our research but certainly justify further exploration in future research.

NOTES

1. One could now argue that there is specialization in this network (in terms of Lawrence and Lorsch) as DBFs are specializing through these decentralised exploration efforts. We argue though that this is not the case. As analysed, there is no need for these firms to have substantial interaction as they explore different and often unrelated opportunities. So, from a cognitive point of view there is no systematic coherence among these exploration activities and therefore no specialization in terms of Lawrence and Lorsch's argument; these authors focus on specialization of related and interdependent activities because only then there is a need for integration. A second counter-argument is that the central firm does not integrate these decentralized activities but only selects them in view of exploitation. Were these decentralized exploration efforts cognitively interdependent, chances for overload at the core firm would increase as he would need to integrate them. That would require more substantial coordination from his side. However, as he 'only' selects, this coordination is fairly light as can be noted from the fact that direct, operational involvement from his side is limited.
2. Although a firm is clearly not a network, we could interpret a firm in terms of our typology as an example of a very dense network of relations of very high strength,

which resembles in a way the dense network of strong relations of learning regime 1 in biotechnology
3. Obviously, there are different ways to see performance such as learning performance, economic performance or whether it relates to firm performance or network performance.

References

Abernathy, W.J. and J.M. Utterback (1978), Patterns of industrial innovation, *Technology Review*, **81**, 41–47.

Ahuja,, G. (2000), Collaboration networks, structural holes and innovation: a longitudinal study, *Administrative Science Quarterly*, **45**, 425–455.

Aldrich, H.E. and M.C. Fiol (1994), *Fools rush in? The institutional context of industry creation*, The Academy of Management Review, US, **19**(4), 645–671.

Archer, M. (1995), *Realist social theory: the morphogenetic approach*, Cambridge, Cambridge University Press.

Argyris, C. and D.A. Schon (1978), *Organizational learning*, Reading, MA.: Addison-Wesley.

Argyris, C. and D.A. Schon (1996), *Organizational learning II, theory, method and practice*, New York, Addison-Wesley.

Arthur, B. (1988), Competing technologies: an overview, in: G. Dosi e.a. (eds.), *Technical change and economic theory*, London, Pinter Publishers.

Arthur, B. (1989), Competing technologies, increasing returns, and lock-in by historical events, *Economic Journal*, **99**, 116–131.

Baden-Fuller, C. and G. Lorenzoni (1995), Creating a strategic center to manage a web of partners, *California Management Review*, **37**(3).

Baker, W.E. and Obstfeld, D (1999), Social capital by design: structures, strategies and institutional context, in: R.Th.J. Leenders and S.M. Gabbay (et al.), *Corporate social capital and liability*, Kluwer Academic Publishers, Dordrecht.

Baum, J.A.C. and J.V. Singh (1994), *Evolutionary dynamics of organizations*, New York, Oxford University Press.

Bettis, R.A. and C.K. Prahalad (1995), The dominant logic: retrospective and extension, *Strategic Management Journal*, **16**(1), 5–14.

Berger, P. and T. Luckmann (1966), *The social construction of reality*, New York, Doubleday.

Bolwijn, P.T. and T. Kumpe (1989), What comes after flexibility?, *M&O*, **2**, 91–104.

Burt, R.S. (1992), *Structural holes, the social structure of competition*, Harvard University Press, Cambridge (MA).

Burt, R.S. (1998), *The network structure of social capital*, paper presented at the Social Network and Social Capital Conference, Duke University, Durham, NC.

Buchko, A.A. (1994), Barriers to strategic transformation : interorganizational networks and institutional forces, *Advances in Strategic Management*, **10**(B), 81–106.

Carlsson, B.(ed.) (1995), *Technological systems and economic performance: the case of factory automation*, Dordrecht, Kluwer Academic Publishers.

Carlsson, B.(ed.) (1997), *Technological Systems and Industrial Dynamics*, Boston and Dordrecht, Kluwer Academic Publishers.

Carlsson, B. and S. Jacobsson (1997), Diversity creation and technological systems: a technology policy perspective, in: C. Edquist (ed.), *Systems of innovation, technologies, institutions and organizations,* London, Pinter.

Carlsson, B. (ed.) (2002), *Technological Systems in the Bio Industries, An International Study,* Boston and Dordrecht, Kluwer Academic Publishers.

Carlsson, B. and G. Eliasson (2003), *Industrial Dynamics and Endogenous Growth,* working paper, Case Western Reserve University, Cleveland, Ohio.

Chen, S. (1997), A new paradigm for knowledge-based competition: building an industry through knowledge sharing, *Technology Analysis & Strategic Management,* **9**,(4), 437– 452.

Cohen, W.M. and D.A. Levinthal (1990), Absorptive capacity: a new perspective on learning and innovation, *Administrative Science Quarterly,* **35**, 128– 152.

Coleman, J.S. (1988), Social capital in the creation of human capital, *American Journal of Economic Sociology,* **94** – supplement, 95– 119.

Coleman, J.S. (1994), A rational choice perspective on economic sociology, in: N. Smelser and R. Swedberg, *The handbook of economic sociology,* Princeton, Princeton University Press, 166– 180.

Dahl, M.S. and C.O.R. Pedersen (2003), Knowledge flows through informal contacts in industrial clusters: myths or realities?, *DRUID-Working Paper 03-01,* Aalborg University.

Dansereau, F., F.J. Yammarino and J.C. Kohles (1999), Multiple levels of analysis from a longitudinal perspective: some implications for theory building, *Academy of Management Review,* **24**(2), 346– 357.

DiMaggio, P.J. and W.W. Powell (1983), The iron cage revisited: institutional isomorphism and collective rationality in organizational fields, *American Sociological Review,* **48**, 147– 160.

Dosi, G. (1982), Technological paradigms and technological trajectories, a suggested interpretation of the determinants and directions of technical change, *Research Policy,* **11**, 147– 162.

Dosi, G., C. Freeman, R.R. Nelson, G. Silverberg and L. Soete (1988), *Technical change and economic theory,* London, Pinter Publishers.

Dosi, G. (1997), Industrial structures and dynamics: evidence, interpretations and puzzles, *Industrial and Corporate Change,* 6(1), 3– 24.

Dosi, G. and L. Marengo (2000), On the tangled intercourses between transaction cost economics and competence-based views of the firm: a comment, in: N. Foss and V. Mahnke (eds.), *Competence, governance and entrepreneurship,* Oxford, Oxford University Press.

Douglas, M. (1986), *How institutions think,* New York, Syracuse University Press.

Doz, Y. (1992), Strategy process: managing corporate self-renewal, Strategic Management Journal ; 13.

Drew, C.J. (1980), *Introduction to designing and conducting research,* C.V. Mosby, St. Louis.

Duysters, G. (1995), *The evolution of complex industrial systems, The dynamics of major IT sectors,* Doctoral Dissertation, Maastricht, MERIT.

Edquist, C. (1997), *Systems of innovation, technologies, institutions and organizations,* London, Pinter.

Edquist, C. and B. Johnson (1997), Institutions and organizations in systems of innovation, in : Edquist, C.(ed.), *Systems of innovation, technologies, institutions and organizations,* London, Pinter.

Eisenhardt, K.M. (1989), Building theories from case-study research, *Academy of Management Review*, **14**,(4), 532– 550.

Eldredge, N. and S.J. Gould (1972), Punctuated equilibria: an alternative to phyletic gradualism, in: T.J.M. Schopf (ed.), *Models in paleobiology*, San Francisco, Freeman, Cooper & Co, pp. 82–115.

Freeman, C. and C. Perez (1989), Structural crises of adjustment : business cycles and investment behaviour, in: G. Dosi e.a. (eds.), *Technical change and economic theory*, London, Pinter Publishers.

Fukuyama, F. (1995), *Trust, the social virtues and the creation of prosperity*, New York, Free Press.

Gargiulo, M. and M. Benassi (1999), The dark side of social capital in: R.Th.A.J. Leenders and S.M. Gabbay (eds.), *Corporate social capital and liability*, Dordrecht, Kluwer Academic Publishers.

Georghiou, L., J.S. Metcalfe, M. Gibbons, M. Ray and J. Evans (1986), *Post-innovation performance: technological development and competition*, London, MacMillan.

Gomes-Casseres, B. (1994), Group vs. group: how alliance networks compete, *Harvard Business Review*, July-August, 145–153.

Grabher, G. (1993), *The embedded firm - on the socio-economics of industrial networks*, London, Routledge.

Grandori, A. and G. Soda (1995), Interfirm networks : antecedents, mechanisms and forms, *Organization Studies*, **16**(2), 183–214.

Grandori, A. (1997), An organizational assessment of interfirm coordination modes, *Organization Studies*, **18**(6), 987–925.

Grandori, A. (1999), *Interfirm networks, organization and industrial competitiveness*, London, Routledge.

Grandstrand, O., P. Patel and K. Pavitt, Multi-technology corporations: why they have distributed rather than distinctive core competencies, *California Management Review*, **39**(4), 8–25.

Granovetter, M. (1973), The strength of weak ties, *American Journal of Sociology*, **78**, 1360–1389.

Granovetter, M. (1985), Economic action and social structure; the problem of embeddedness, *American Journal of Sociology*, **91**(3), 481–510.

Groenewegen, J., F. Kersholt and A. Nagelkerke (1995), On integrating new and old institutionalism: Douglas North building bridges, *Journal of Economic Issues*, XXIX, **2**.

Groenewegen J. and J.J. Vromen (1996), A case for theoretical pluralism, in: J. Groenewegen (ed.), *TCE and beyond*, Dordrecht, Kluwer, 365–380.

Gulati, R. (1998), Alliances and Networks, *Strategic Management Journal*, **19**, 293–317.

Hagedoorn, J. (1993), Understanding the rationale of strategic technology partnering: interorganizational modes of cooperation and sectoral differences, *Strategic Management Journal*, **14**(5), 371–386.

Hagedoorn, J. and J. Schakenraad, (1994), The effect of strategic technology alliances on company performance, *Strategic Management Journal*, **15** (4), 291–310.

Hagedoorn, J. and G. Duysters, *External appropriation of innovative capabilities: the preference for strategic alliances or M&A's*, MERIT Working Paper, May 1999.

Hagedoorn, J. (2002), Interfirm R&D partnerships: an overview of major trends and patterns since 1960, *Research Policy*, **31**, 477–492.

Hakansson, H. and J. Johansson (1993), The network as governance structure - interfirm cooperation beyond markets and hierarchies, in: G. Grabher (ed.), *The embedded firm - on the socio-economics of industrial networks*, London, Routledge.

Hamel, G. and Prahalad, C.K. (1990), The core competence of the corporaration, *Harvard Business Review*, May-June, 79–91.

Hannan, M.T. and J. Freeman (1984), Structural inertia and organizational change, *American Sociological Review*, **49**, 149–164.

Jarillo, C., (1988), On strategic networks, *Strategic Management Journal*, **9**, 31–41.

Johnson, B. (1992), Institutional learning, in: Lundvall, B. (ed.), *National systems of innovation*, London, Pinter.

Klein, K.J., H. Tosi and A.A. Cannella (1999), Multilevel theory building: benefits, barriers, and new developments, *Academy of Management Review*, **24**(2), 243–248.

Knoke, D. and J.H. Kuklinski (1982), *Network analysis*, Beverly Hills, Sage Publications.

Knoke, D. (1999), Organizational networks and corporate social capital in: R.Th. Leenders R.Th.A.J. and S.M. Gabbay (eds.) (1999), *Corporate social capital and liability*, Dordrecht, Kluwer Academic Publishers.

Kuhn, T. (1962), *The structure of scientific revolutions*, Chicago University Press, Chicago.

Lakatos, I. (1978), *The methodology of scientific research programmes: philosophical papers vols. 1 and 2*, by J. Worrall and G. Curry (eds.), Cambridge, Cambridge University Press.

Lawrence, P.R. and J.W. Lorsch (1967), *Organization and environment*, Boston, Harvard Business School Press.

Lawson, T. (1997), *Economics and reality*, London, Routledge.

Lazonick, W. (1994), *Business organization and the myth of the market economy*, Cambridge (UK), Cambridge University Press.

Leenders R.Th.A.J. and S.M. Gabbay (1999), *Corporate social capital and liability*, Dordrecht, Kluwer Academic Publishers.

Lesser, E.L. (2000), *Knowledge and social capital : foundations and applications*, Butterworth – Heinemann.

Lorenzoni, G. and A. Lipparini (1999), The leveraging of interfirm relationships, as a distinctive organizational capability: a longitudinal study, *Strategic Management Journal*, **20**, 317–338.

Lundvall, B-A (1988), Innovation as an interactive process, from user-producer interaction to the national system of innovation, in: G. Dosi e.a. (eds.), *Technical change and economic theory*, London, Pinter Publishers.

Lundvall, B.A. (1992), *National systems of innovation*, London, Pinter.

Lundvall, B-A. (1993), Explaining interfirm cooperation and innovation: limits of the transaction-cost approach, in: G. Grabher (ed.), *The embedded firm*, London, Routledge.

Lundvall, B-A. and S. Borras (1997), *The globalising learning economy: Implications for innovation policy*, draft report based on the preliminary conclusions from several projects under the STER Programme, DG XII, Commission for the European Union.

Malerba, F. and L. Orsenigo (1996), The dynamics and evolution of industries, *Industrial and Corporate Change*, **5**(1), 51–87.

Malerba, F. and S. Breschi (1997), Sectoral innovation systems: technological regimes, Schumpetarian dynamics and spatial boundaries, in: C. Edquist (ed.), *Systems of innovation, technologies, institutions and organizations,* London, Pinter.

Malerba, F. (2002), Sectoral systems of innovation and production, *Research Policy,* **31**(2), 247–264.

March, J. (1991), Exploration and exploitation in organisational learning, *Organisation Science,* **2**(1), 71–87.

Marsili, O. (2001), The anatomy and evolution of industries, technological change and industrial dynamics, Cheltenham, Edward Elgar.

McClave, K. (2000), New challenges in smart markets, *Commercial Lending Review,* New York, **15**(3), 61–67

McEvily, B. and A. Zaheer (1999), Bridging ties: a source of firm heterogeneity in competitive capabilities, *Strategic Management Journal,* **20**, 1133–1156.

McKelvey, M. (1996), Evolutionary innovation: the business of genetic engineering, Oxford, Clarendon.

McKelvey, M. (1997), Using evolutionary theory to define systems of innovation, in: Edquist, C. (ed.), *Systems of innovation, technologies, institutions and organizations* London, Pinter.

Ministry of Economic Affairs (1999), *Clustermonitor,* The Hague.

Mowery, D.C. and R.R. Nelson (eds.) (1999), *Sources of industrial leadership,* New York, Cambridge University Press.

Murdick, R.G. and D.R. Cooper (1982), *Business research, concepts and guides,* Grid, Ohio.

Nahapiet, J. and S. Ghoshal (1998), Social capital, intellectual capital and the organizational advantage, *Academy of Management Review,* **23**, 242–266.

Narula R. and J. Hagedoorn (1999), Innovating through strategic alliances : moving towards international partnerships and contractual agreements, *Technovation,* **19**, 283– 294.

Nelson, R.R. and S.G. Winter, (1977), In search of a useful theory of innovation, *Research Policy,* **6**, 36–76.

Nelson, R. R. and S.G. Winter (1982), *An evolutionary theory of economic change,* Harvard University Press, New York.

Nelson, R. (1987), *Understanding technical change as an evolutionary process,* Amsterdam, Elsevier.

Nelson, R. R.(ed.) (1993), *National systems of innovation,* Oxford, Oxford University Press.

Nelson, R.R. (1994), The co-evolution of technology, industrial structure, and supporting institutions, *Industrial and Corporate Change,* **3**, 47–63.

Nelson, R.R. and B.N. Sampat (2001), Making sense of institutions as a factor shaping economic performance, *Journal of Economic Behavior & Organization,* **44**(1), 31–54.

Nelson. R.R., B. Steil, B., D.G. Victor (2002), *Technological Innovation and Economic Performance,* Princeton University Press, Princeton.

Nooteboom, B. (1999a), *Interfirm alliances, analysis and design,* London, Routledge.

Nooteboom, B. (1999b), Learning, innovation and industrial organisation, *Cambridge Journal of Economics,* **23**, 127–150.

Nooteboom, B. (1999c), The dynamic efficiency of networks, in: Grandori, A. (ed.), *Interfirm networks: organizational and industrial competitiveness*, London, Routledge.

Nooteboom, B. (1999d), Innovation and interfirm linkages : new implications for public policy, *Research policy*, **28**, 793–805.

Nooteboom, B. (2000), *Learning and innovation in organizations and economies*, Oxford, Oxford University Press.

Nooteboom, B. and V.A. Gilsing, Co-evolution of routines: exploration and exploitation in the multimedia industry, submitted to Industrial and Corporate Change and presented at the Conference 'Empirical Research on Routines in Business and Economics', 3-4 November 2002, Odensee, Denmark.

Oerlemans, L.A.G. (1996), The embedded firm, innovating in industrial networks, Tilburg, Tilburg University Press.

Ouchi, W.G. (1980), Markets, bureaucracies and clans, Administrative Science Quarterly, **25**, 129–141.

Ouchi, W.G. and M.K. Bolton (1988), The logic of joint research and development, *California Management Review*, **30**(3), 9–33.

Pavitt, K. (1984), Sectoral patterns of innovation, *Research Policy* **13**, 343–373.

Pavitt, K. (2002), Knowledge about Knowledge since Nelson & Winter: a mixed record, SPRU, http://ww.sussex.ac.uk/spru/publications.

Pianka, E. (1978), *Evolutionary Ecology*, Harper & Row, New York.

Pisano, G., Pharmaceutical Biotechnology in: B. Steil, B., D.G. Victor & R.R. Nelson (2002), *Technological Innovation and Economic Performance*, Princeton University Press, Princeton.

Polanyi, M. (1966), *The tacit dimension*, London, Routledge.

Porter, M.E. (1990), *The competitive advantage of nations*, London, Macmillan Press.

Porter, M.E. (1991), Towards a dynamic theory of strategy, *Strategic Management Journal*, **12**, 95–117.

Porter, M.E. (1998), *On competition*, New York, Free Press.

Powell, W. (1990), Neither market nor hierarchy: network forms of organization, in L.L. Cummings and B. Staw, (eds.), *Research in organization behaviour*, Greenwich, CT: JAI Press, 295–336b.

Powell, W.W. and K.W. Koputt and L. Smith-Doerr (1996), Interorganizational collaboration and the locus of innovation: networks of learning in biotechnology, *Administrative Science Quarterly*, **41**, 116–145.

Prahalad, C.K. amd G. Hamel (1994), Strategy as field of study: why search for a new paradigm, *Strategic Management Journal*, Summer Special Issue, **15**, 5–16.

Rindova, V.P. and C. J. Fombrun (1999), Constructing competitive advantage : the role of firm-consituent interactions, *Strategic Management Journal*, **20**, 691–710.

Rosenkopf, L. and M.L. Tushman (1994), The co-evolution of technology and organization in: J.A.C. Baum and J.V. Singh (eds.), *Evolutionary dynamics of organizations*, New York, Oxford University Press.

Rowley, T., D. Behrens and D. Krackhardt (2000), Redundant governance structures: an analysis of structural and relational embeddedness in the steel and semiconductor industries, *Strategic Management Journal*, **21**, 369–386.

Rumelt, P., D.E. Schendel, D.J. Teece and L. Fleming, Fundamental issues in strategy: a research agenda, *Administrative Science Quarterly*, **41**(1), 196–198.

Sandefur, R.L. and E.O. Laumann (1998), A paradigm for social capital, *Rationality and Society*, **10**(4), 481–502.

Scott, W.R. (1995), *Institutions and organizations*, Thousand Oaks, Sage Publications.

Shannon, C.E. (1957), A mathematical theory of communication, *Bell System Technical Journal*, **27**, 379–423.

Smith Ring, P. and A. van de Ven (1994), Developmental processes of cooperative interorganisational relationships, *Academy of Management review*, **19**(1), 90–118.

Spekman, R.E., Th.M. Forbes III, L.A. Isabella and T.C. Macavoy (1995), Alliance Management: a view from the past and a look to the future, Journal of Management Studies, **35**(6), 747–772.

Spender, J.C. (1989), *Industry recipes*, Oxford, Basil Blackwell.

Stankiewicz, R. (1990), Basic technologies and the innovation process, in: J. Sigurdson (ed.), *Measuring the dynamics of technological change*, London, Pinter.

Stankiewicz, R. (2002), The Cognitive Dynamics of Biotechnology and the Evolution of its Technological Systems, in: Carlsson, B. (ed.) , 2002, *Technological Systems in the Bio Industries, An International Study*, Boston and Dordrecht, Kluwer Academic Publishers.

Stinchcombe, A.L. (1965), Social structure and organizations, in: J.G. March, (ed.), *Handbook of organizations*, Chicago, RandMcNally College Publishing Company.

Suarez, F.F. and J.M. Utterback (1993), Innovation, competition and industry structure, *Research Policy*, **22**, 1–21.

Suarez, F.F. and J.M. Utterback (1995), Dominant designs and the survival of firms, *Strategic Management Journal*, **16**, 415–430.

Swanborn, P.G. (1987), *Methoden van sociaal-wetenschappelijk onderzoek*, Amsterdam, Boom.

Teece, D. (1986), Profiting from technological innovation: implications for integration, collaboration, licensing and public policy, *Research Policy*, **15**, 285–305.

Uzzi, B. (1996), The sources and consequences of embeddedness, for the economic performance of organizations: the network effects, *American Sociological Review*, **61**, 674–698.

Uzzi, B, (1997), Social structure and competition in interfirm networks : the paradox of embeddedness, *Administrative Science Quarterly*, **42**, 35–67.

Uzzi, B. and J.J. Gillespie (1999), Corporate social capital and the cost of financial capital : an embeddedness approach in R.Th.A.J. Leenders and S.M. Gabbay, *Corporate social capital and liability*, Dordrecht, Kluwer Academic Publishers.

Veblen, T. (1898), Why is economics not an evolutionary Science?, *Quarterly Journal of Economics*, **12**, 373–397.

Von Hippel, E. (1988), *The sources of Innovation*, Oxford, Oxford University Press.

Wasserman, S. and K. Faust (1994), *Social network analysis: methods and applications*, Cambridge (UK), Cambridge University Press.

Whitley, R. (1994), European business systems, *Organization Studies*, **15**(2).

Whitley, R. (1999), Business systems, firm types and patterns of Innovation, *NIAS Working paper*.

Wijvekate, M.L. (1991), *Onderzoekmethoden*, Het Spectrum, Utrecht.

Williamson, O.E. (1975), Markets and hierarchies, analysis and anti-trust implications, New York, Free Press.

Williamson, O.E. (1985), *The economic institutions of capitalism; firms, markets and relational contracting*, New York, Free Press.

Williamson, O.E. (1996), The mechanisms of governance, Oxford, Oxford University Press.

Williamson, O.E. (1999), Strategy research: governance and competence perspectives, *Strategic Management Journal*, **20**, 1087–1108.

Yin, R.K. (1994), *Case study research, design and methods*, Thousand Oaks, Sage.

Zwaan, A.H., van der, *Organisatie-onderzoek*, van Gorcum, Assen.

Index